The

ART

of

HER DEAL

The Untold Story of Melania Trump

MARY JORDAN

SIMON & SCHUSTER

New York   London   Toronto   Sydney   New Delhi

Simon & Schuster
1230 Avenue of the Americas
New York, NY 10020

First Simon & Schuster hardcover edition June 2020

SIMON & SCHUSTER and colophon are registered
trademarks of Simon & Schuster, Inc.

For information about special discounts for bulk purchases,
please contact Simon & Schuster Special Sales at
1-866-506-1949 or business@simonandschuster.com.

The Simon & Schuster Speakers Bureau can bring authors to your live event.
For more information or to book an event, contact the
Simon & Schuster Speakers Bureau at 1-866-248-3049 or
visit our website at www.simonspeakers.com.

Manufactured in the United States of America

1   3   5   7   9   10   8   6   4   2

Library of Congress Cataloging-in-Publication Data is available on file.

ISBN 978-1-9821-1340-7
ISBN 978-1-9821-1342-1 (ebook)

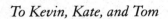

To Kevin, Kate, and Tom

Contents

PROLOGUE

"I have an opinion"

DONALD TRUMP and his top advisors were gathered around campaign spokeswoman Hope Hicks as she clicked PLAY to start a video on her laptop. It was late afternoon on Friday, October 7, 2016. In one month, voters would choose between Trump and his Democratic presidential rival, Hillary Clinton. Trump and his aides had been strategizing before a crucial Sunday night debate in a conference room on the twenty-fifth floor of Trump Tower. But now they shifted into crisis mode and all eyes were riveted on the video.

It showed Trump and *Access Hollywood* host Billy Bush, nephew of the forty-first president, engaged in a lewd exchange on an NBC Studios lot. Nothing about the tape was flattering. After a voice offscreen said, "She's still very beautiful," Trump was heard boasting, "I moved on her, actually. You know, she was down on Palm Beach. I moved on her, and I failed. I'll admit it."

After someone off camera says, "Whoa," Trump replied, "I did try and fuck her. She was married."

"That's huge news," came the reply. Then Trump again, "I moved on her very heavily. In fact, I took her out furniture shopping. She wanted to get some furniture. I said, 'I'll show you where they have some nice furniture.' I took her out furniture—I moved on her like a bitch. But I couldn't get there. And she was married. Then all of a sudden I see her, she's now got the big phony tits and everything. She's totally changed her look."

There was some back-and-forth with Billy Bush, including Bush saying, "Yes! The Donald has scored. Whoa, my man!" Then Trump said, "Yeah, that's her. With the gold. I better use some Tic Tacs just in case I start kissing her. You know, I'm automatically attracted to beautiful—I just start kissing them. It's like a magnet. Just kiss. I don't even wait. And when you're a star, they let you do it. You can do anything." Bush replied, "Whatever you want," to which Trump spoke the now infamous line, "Grab 'em by the pussy. You can do anything."

The room was stunned into silence.

New Jersey governor Chris Christie zeroed in on the video's date stamp: September 2005. Eleven years ago. That meant that Trump was not some young, single guy when he said these words. He was fifty-nine years old and had recently married his third wife, Melania, then nearly three months pregnant with their son, Barron.

Trump was quiet. Christie knew what Trump was dreading:

facing Melania. "She was the elephant *not* in the room," Christie said. Trump was so embarrassed that, as one person in the room recalled, "He turned red; red was coming up his neck to his ears. I think he understood early on that it was going to create ramifications for him at home, too."

The video went viral, breaking online viewership records at the *Washington Post*. But Team Trump was focused on one person sitting more than thirty floors above them in the penthouse. They could spin and divert attention—strategist Steve Bannon, Trump son-in-law Jared Kushner, and others were already formulating ideas for how to do that—but if Melania walked out, the campaign was all but over. If she said she couldn't tolerate her husband's behavior, why should female voters?

"Everybody was saying, 'You should go upstairs and see Melania. Why don't you go upstairs now and see Melania?' And he was not rushing to go up there," Christie remembered. "I said to him, 'It ain't going to get any easier. The longer you wait, it's not going to get any easier.'" Another person in the room said, "That night he seemed frightened to go face his wife." It took Trump two hours to finally step into the elevator.

Melania does not yell or throw lamps. She shows her fury quietly and deliberately. "Now you could lose," she said to him, according to someone who heard the account of what she told Trump. "You could have blown this for us." Melania had been one of the few around Trump who had been telling him he would win. Others thought he would lose but believed the campaign would be a win for the Trump brand: maybe a new Trump

TV network, probably more Trump hotels, and certainly more Trump merchandise. But Melania was a believer. Now she told him his mouth had jeopardized their chance at the White House. Trump apologized. He said he didn't mean any of that; it was just his shtick. She left him to stew and retreated to her own bedroom.

Several of Trump's aides said that Melania needed to be seen in public with him immediately. They wanted a joint TV appearance, where she would sit beside him and say that the words on the tape in no way reflected the man she admired. Some said that Ivanka, Trump's elder daughter, should join them, too, and that both women should look into the camera and say how much Trump respects women. Trump aides played the tape of Hillary Clinton joining her husband on a *60 Minutes* interview when allegations of his infidelity arose during the 1992 campaign. They watched to see how close Hillary sat to her husband, what phrases she used to stand by her man. When Melania eventually joined the strategy session, she had a one-word reply: "No." She said she would decide on her own what to do. And right now she was *not* going on television with her husband.

As Melania watched the nonstop TV coverage, she was particularly upset by how she was characterized. People said that they felt sorry for her. Poor Melania. That irked her. She was not fragile. She was strong and in control. "I am putting out a statement," she said, according to Christie. "I am not going to sit here and pretend that I don't have an opinion. I have an opinion and people need to know my opinion." The next day, October 8, Melania, campaign manager Kellyanne Conway, and others gathered in the penthouse kitchen, where Melania told them what she wanted to say.

Trump didn't try to stop her. He just asked to read her statement before it went out. "He understood that his conduct had put her in an embarrassing position and that this was not a woman who was just going to sit there and take it," Christie said.

Shortly before 3:00 p.m. that Saturday, Trump read Melania's response. "The words my husband used are unacceptable and offensive to me. This does not represent the man that I know. He has the heart and mind of a leader. I hope people will accept his apology, as I have, and focus on the important issues facing our nation and the world." Trump, sitting in the living room with his advisers, read it quietly and passed it back to an aide, who returned to Melania in the kitchen.

"This could have been a lot worse," Trump said, relieved.

Soon he was back, tweeting: "I WILL NEVER DROP OUT OF THE RACE."

Melania's handling of the *Access Hollywood* tape was telling. She may not like what is said about her or her husband, but she has an exceptional capacity to shrug it off, or at least press her lips together and say nothing. She never feels the need to explain herself, her marriage, or even what drove her to wear a jacket with "I REALLY DON'T CARE. DO U?" scrawled on its back. Her press office doesn't answer questions about where she is on many days. She has always been independent, highly focused, and acutely aware of her own power and when to deploy it. Among her small staff, she inspires loyalty and an instinct to protect her.

Only she and those close to the president truly know the strength of her influence behind the scenes, but it has been felt in her long-standing support for his political ambitions, how he campaigned in 2016, his choice of a running mate, and in many personnel and policy decisions in the White House. Those who dismiss her as nothing more than an elegant accessory do not understand her or her influence. She works at remaining mysterious. In her own way, she is as complex and complicated as her husband. She is also much more like him than it appears.

"This is not some wallflower; this is somebody who is so self-confident and so self-assured," Christie said. He added that people who speculate that Melania doesn't love Trump are "misreading the signs" and simply seeing what they want to see. She has not liked everything her husband has said, and definitely has not liked everything he has done, but she has always been fully behind him. "She understands that she's married to a very big personality, and someone who is impulsive at times—in his personal life as well as in his policies, and she gets that," said someone who has known the couple for years. She is willing to overlook a lot because though she craves a quiet life at times, the girl from a small central European town, who couldn't wait to get to New York City, also delights in being where the action is. "Melania is so underestimated."

Trump struggled with his own response to the tape, and around midnight Friday, he issued a videotaped apology. "I said it, I was wrong, and I apologize." But after those rare words of contrition, he pivoted back to his more familiar attack mode: "I've said some foolish things. But there's a big difference between the words and actions of other people. Bill Clinton has actually abused women, and Hillary has bullied, attacked, shamed, and intimidated his victims."

Sunday night at the debate, he said that he had apologized to his family for what he called "locker-room talk." Melania shook Bill Clinton's hand before the debate. Then she took her seat. Also seated in the audience were guests Trump had invited to divert attention from his history with women: three women who had previously accused Bill Clinton of sexual misconduct, and a fourth whose alleged rapist Hillary had been assigned to defend as a young attorney in the 1970s. Trump attacked Hillary all night, while Melania said nothing, but made headlines with an $1,100 fuchsia blouse with a bow tied at her neck, a style called a "pussy bow." "Have we underestimated the wit of this former nude *GQ* cover star?" *The Telegraph* of London asked, referring to one of her most famous modeling shoots.

"She makes good choices," said Marina Masowietsky, a modeling agent who first met Melania when she was twenty-two. "She is quiet and looks around. Then she makes a move." Masowietsky said that Melania has not shied from risk: first leaving a prestigious architecture program to try modeling, and then leaving the comfort of Europe for the promise of the United States: "She took a chance. She got on the plane and went to New York."

After the *Access Hollywood* video broke, every TV host in America wanted to interview Melania. It was one month to the election. Polls were showing that women who had been on the fence about Trump were moving toward Clinton. Melania knew she had more to gain by standing by her husband than walking away. Several people in her orbit said she was aware of her power in that moment and planned her next move carefully. "She's very deliberative," agreed Corey Lewandowski, Trump's first campaign manager. "When she goes and does something, it is well executed, it is well thought-out."

For her first interview, Melania chose Anderson Cooper, son of the famous socialite and designer Gloria Vanderbilt, also no stranger to family drama, and the franchise face of CNN. He offered a lengthy sit-down to hear Melania's side of the story. What she could not have known is that Cooper would drop his usual more hard-hitting style. He treated Melania gently. "This has obviously been a difficult time," Cooper said, opening the interview in Melania's opulent gilded sanctuary in the Trump Tower penthouse. "How are you holding up? How are you doing?"

Sitting very straight, wearing a white dress with a high collar, her hands folded on her lap, Melania looked directly at him. "I'm great. I'm very strong. I'm very confident. And I live my life." She would not describe the conversation with her husband, saying, "When we talk in private, I will keep it private." She said that her husband had apologized to her—and that it should be good enough for everybody else. "I accept his apology. I hope the American people will accept it [as] well."

She added, "My husband is real. He's raw. He tells it as it is. He's kind. He's a gentleman." At another point, she added, "People think and talk about me, the—like, 'Oh, Melania, oh, poor Melania.' Don't feel sorry for me. Don't feel sorry for me. I can handle everything." She said that she had seen people on television who "think they are celebrities" criticizing her and suggesting others should feel sorry for her. "I would suggest to them to look themselves in the mirror and to look at their actions and to take care of their own families," she said, adding she had a "great marriage and a strong relationship." She said of her husband, "He said many times . . . that I'm rock for whole family." (The Slovenian language does not use articles such as "a" and "the," and Melania and others who learn English as a second language sometimes drop those words.)

But she also emphasized that she was not Donald Trump, and that she made her own decisions. "We are—we are two independent people, thinking on their own, and have a very open conversation . . . I don't listen [to] anybody about what to do, what to say, when to say it, when to do interviews," she said.

Her choice in that moment was to back up her husband.

She painted Trump as the victim of a conspiracy of "left-wing media" and attacks "organized from the opposition," including the Clintons. She dismissed his statements as "boy talk" and said he had been "egged on" by Billy Bush to "say dirty and bad stuff." She echoed what the Trump campaign was stressing: Donald Trump is a great promoter of women. "He supports everybody. He supports women. He encourages them to go to the highest level, to achieve their dreams, to—employs many, many women."

Then she tried to lighten the conversation by saying, "I have two boys at home. I have my young son and I have my husband." Cooper also asked about women who have come forward and made allegations of sexual misconduct against Trump. "Some of them go back more than thirty years. He's said they're lying. Do you believe him?" Cooper asked.

Melania replied, "I believe my husband. I believe my husband. This was all organized from the opposition and with the details that they go—did they ever—did they ever check the background of these women? They don't have any facts."

Not only was she defending her husband, but she was attacking the credibility of the women who had accused him. And then she surprised many by saying she had seen women pursue her husband. "I see many, many women coming to him and giving phone numbers and, you know, want to work for him or inappropriate stuff from women. And they know he's married."

"You've seen that?" Cooper said.

"Oh, yes, of course. It was in front of me."

"In front of you?"

"In front of me. And I said, like, why you need to give your number to my husband?"

She had clearly followed the news coverage of the tape. "It was hour after hour. I watched TV, was hour after hour bashing him because they want to influence the American people how to vote. And they're influencing in the wrong way."

Melania's interview with Cooper was a powerful display of loyalty but she ended with a declaration of independence: "He will do what he wants to do on the end, as I will do what I want to do." As Melania was defending her husband, Trump's personal attorney, Michael Cohen, was preparing to pay $130,000 to

Stephanie Clifford, an adult-film star whose professional name is Stormy Daniels, to not go public with her story about the night she claimed to have had sex with Trump. In sworn testimony before Congress in February 2019, Cohen said Trump "asked me to pay off an adult-film star with whom he had an affair, and to lie to his wife about it, which I did. Lying to the First Lady is one of my biggest regrets. She is a kind, good person. I respect her greatly—and she did not deserve that."

Five days before the election, Melania made a rare solo campaign appearance in the swing state of Pennsylvania. Standing in the audience, I watched as she spoke to a packed auditorium outside of Philadelphia. Melania promised the crowd, particularly the women, that her husband cared about them, and "respects women and provides them with equal opportunities." She said, "He will make a fantastic president."

I spoke to the Republican women who stood beside me in the audience. Not all were completely persuaded, but many said Melania offered a convincing case for her husband. "This beautiful woman could have a lot of rich guys—he can't be that bad," one attendee said.

On election night, Trump won Pennsylvania by less than 1 percent, ensuring that he and Melania would be moving to the White House, not Hillary and Bill Clinton.

The Trumps greet the Obamas on Inauguration Day 2017

CHAPTER 1

Olive Branch?

IT WAS the walk of Melania Trump's life, and she began it alone.

The massive SUV caravan with red and blue flashing lights had snaked its way from St. John's Episcopal Church, where U.S. presidents-elect since Franklin Roosevelt have attended services before taking the oath of office. It slowly drove the short way along H Street, and down the normally barricaded Jackson Place to Pennsylvania Avenue, where it made a wide, sweeping turn onto the grounds of the White House. TV viewers caught a brief glimpse of the soon-to-be first lady waving through the tinted windows, only her hand visible, covered by a pale blue glove. Vehicle after vehicle passed the North Portico until, deep in the middle of the pack, a custom-built Suburban rolled to a stop; its blast-proof doors required the strength of two U.S. Secret Service agents to open. Near the portico's white columns, photographers were jockeying for the best positions.

The clicking of their camera shutters nearly drowned out the greetings.

President-elect Donald Trump hopped out and strode up the stairs to greet President Barack Obama and First Lady Michelle Obama, who were standing at the door on the chilly, gray January morning on which Trump would become president. Eight years earlier, the Obamas had arrived to meet George W. and Laura Bush for coffee before the ride to the Capitol for the swearing-in, and now it was Donald and Melania Trump's turn to be welcomed. Trump did not wait for his wife or glance at her. Seconds later, Melania exited from the black Suburban on the far side, walked around the hulking vehicle, and ascended the stairs solo. Barack Obama was the one to take her hand, guide her up the last step, and kiss both her cheeks. If Melania was the least bit disappointed that her husband didn't wait for her, her face betrayed nothing. "That's Donald," she would say later.

"Horrible," commented one woman who had worked in the White House for several administrations and was watching that morning. But what she and millions of television viewers did not know was that the greater Trump family inaugural drama had already happened, out of public view. Since Jimmy Carter became president in the 1970s, it has been tradition for incoming presidents to stay at Blair House for anywhere from a couple of days to nearly two weeks. A complex of four town houses that were merged together, Blair House is described as "the world's most exclusive hotel" and is located diagonally across from the White House. Donald Trump, a man who likes his own bed and his own homes, wanted none of it. He had sent Keith Schiller, his long-time personal bodyguard and one of his most trusted aides, to visit Blair House in advance. Schiller knew what Trump liked, and he told his boss, "It's small." That was enough for the president-elect. Trump repeated, "It's very small." He is so particular about where he sleeps that during the campaign, his schedule was often dictated by whether or not he could sleep in his own bed at one of his own properties.

Trump indicated that he planned to stay a mile away, at the Trump International Hotel. Its luxurious Trump Townhouse billed itself as the largest hotel suite in Washington, at 6,300 square feet, with two stories and two spacious bedrooms, designer bed linens, a spa bathroom, fitness room, upper- and lower-level living rooms, a dining room able to seat sixteen—and a 55-inch HDTV. (After his 2005 wedding to Melania, Trump said that they would be honeymooning at Mar-a-Lago, because it was hard to find anyplace better.) Trump was used to having things exactly as he wanted, especially his television and remote controls. He was not a fan of Blair House's much more modest TV setup. In keeping with the historic feel of the house, some of them were small and set on dressers—not the latest or biggest flat-screens that Trump preferred. Once in the White House, Trump quickly arranged for a large multiscreen digital setup so he could watch different feeds simultaneously.

"Up until the last minute, he was not staying there," said a person closely involved with the inauguration. But Trump's team pushed back, as did the Secret Service, which was not keen to protect the incoming president inside a public hotel swarming with guests. Trump finally relented, agreeing to stay for one night only and to have his children and grandchildren join him. Ivanka brought sheets from the Trump International Hotel to Blair House for the overnight stay, to "feel more at home."

The Trump family works together and sometimes vacations together, but they are used to having their own space and a lot of it. Ivanka, her husband, Jared, and their three children have their own separate mansion at Bedminster, Trump's private golf club on over five hundred acres in New Jersey. Donald and Melania aren't known for inviting their grandkids to cuddle with them in bed in the morning, as George H. W. Bush and his wife, Barbara, famously used to do with their grandchildren. In fact, no matter which of his properties he is visiting, Trump sleeps in a separate bedroom that has been decorated to his taste—he favors darker colored walls and rugs, while Melania likes whites and light colors. Trump typically wakes around 5:00 a.m., well before Melania, and turns on his televisions.

But that night at Blair House, there were eight grandchildren, including Ivanka's ten-month-old son, Theodore, as well as nannies and in-laws. And despite the fourteen bedrooms, it seemed to some of the Trumps that they were in close quarters in a tight space. Before arriving at Blair House, the family had been briefed on all the famous people who had slept at Blair, from Abraham Lincoln to Winston Churchill, and had been given the schedule for their minute-by-minute movements the next day. The excitement was palpable. Some of the Trumps barely slept, and others rose before dawn. Trump himself started the day in a foul mood, "really out of sorts," as one of his group described it. Another said he felt "trapped," cooped up with too many family members "all under the same roof." He was antsy and wanted to go out, but the Secret Service insisted that he stay put.

Even worse, the morning of the inaugural, the Secret Service security procedures delayed the arrival of a whole group of personal stylists and assistants hired by the Trumps to fix their makeup and hair. Once they finally entered, there was a mad rush to get camera ready and out the door in time for the service at St. John's. By the time the family departed, some seemed to agree with the soon-to-be-president's hesitation about the accommodations. "It wasn't what we were expecting," Melania was heard to say that morning. But she was also used to dealing with her husband's moods and, as she has so often, simply focused on what came next.

She had been married to him for twelve years and knew his habits. Their White House arrival, where he left Melania trailing behind him, was in many ways typical Trump. (He would cause a stir the next year by walking in front of Queen Elizabeth at Windsor Castle.) Melania Trump smiled for the cameras, politely greeted the Obamas, and then stood beside her husband.

Standing outside on the North Portico, the men were predictably dressed: dark suits, white shirts, Obama in a blue tie, Trump in a red one. The ties were seen as a fashion nod to the TV news networks' blue and red electoral maps. The "money shot" for photographers was what Mrs. Trump and Mrs. Obama were wearing.

Michelle, in her understated red and black tweed jacquard dress, stood beside Melania in a powder blue cashmere dress with a matching bolero jacket. Her blue outfit had been designed by Ralph Lauren—who had also designed the white pantsuit worn that day by Hillary Clinton. (There are many unexpected connections between the Trumps and the Clintons, who were among the guests at Donald and Melania's wedding.) While many others would bundle up in full-length coats, Melania did not. Her choice was "classic and sophisticated," according to Robin Givhan, the fashion critic for the *Washington Post*, who noted that others had compared her silhouette to that of the first lady Jackie Kennedy.

For years, Melania Trump had set her sights on walking the fashion runways of Milan, Paris, and New York. As a model, she had spent years studying how to walk, how to stand, how to tilt her head for a better camera angle. Her preparation for political life was different from that of any president's spouse before her. In slightly more than two hours, her husband would be sworn in as president of the United States, and she would become its first lady. Her image would be broadcast around the world. She would hold two Bibles for the swearing-in, smile through a bill signing and lunch, wave to the crowds during the parade up Pennsylvania Avenue, and awkwardly dance with her husband at three inaugural balls. (Donald Trump is not known as a dancer. Even when he used to frequent the New York nightclub Studio 54, no one remembered ever seeing him on the dance floor.)

Her husband delivered a dark "America First" inaugural address, in which he vowed to "protect our borders from the ravages of other countries." Melania made no public comments but posted a photo to Instagram of herself holding the Bibles as her husband took the oath of office. With little but her appearance to go on, thousands of words of commentary would be written and spoken by journalists, fashion writers, and others, dissecting every Melania facial expression and wardrobe choice. Givhan would note that selecting the French-born designer Hervé Pierre for her off-the-shoulder white crepe inaugural ball gown "seemed like a bit of an olive branch after so much talk of closed borders and nationalism."

Every public movement for an inauguration is choreographed, from where to stand to how fast to walk, with some of the more interesting moments taking place behind the scenes, inside the fleet of presidential cars and Capitol building "holding rooms." Melania's gesture of bringing a gift to Michelle Obama turned into an awkward incident because it had not been scripted and there was nowhere to set the box during the group photo. Other encounters that day were more challenging because of the highly divisive campaign. Although it appeared that there was no one else except the incoming and outgoing first ladies riding in the limo to the Capitol, in fact, there was. Waiting inside a limousine with blackened windows was Abigail Blunt, wife of Missouri Republican senator Roy Blunt. As chairman of the Senate Rules Committee, Blunt was responsible for overseeing the presidential inauguration. He was already seated inside the presidential limo to accompany Barack Obama and Donald Trump, presumably also to help ensure a more cordial ride to the Capitol.

For prior inaugurals, sometimes a third official rode with the two presidents, but the tradition was not to have Senate spouses ride in the car with the two first ladies. But this was no ordinary inauguration. Abby Blunt's presence was meant to smooth over what had the potential to be an exceptionally awkward trip. During the ten minutes together, the conversation stayed on the weather and children.

For all the pomp and circumstance of a presidential inauguration, the arrival at the Capitol is remarkably ordinary. The outgoing and incoming presidents and their spouses enter through a side door into a narrow gray hallway. From there, they are led to a windowless interior room to wait for the precise moment to begin their walk out to the inauguration platform. Trump's five children—Donald Jr., Ivanka, Eric, Tiffany, and Barron—would go first. Three prior presidents and their wives would be next, each stepping into the light drizzle as television cameras zoomed in. Only toward the end would Melania walk through the Capitol's dark underground stone crypt, up a flight of stairs, and through the bright, soaring Rotunda. She entered through the heavy, red velvet curtains, escorted by a marine in full-dress uniform, who would lead her to the specially constructed platform where the swearing-in would occur.

The stage was another minefield of protocol. Those seated closest to the podium had comfortable, high-back cushioned chairs. But after the first two rows, guests, including Ivanka, Don Jr., and Eric, sat on ordinary black folding chairs. Trained on the key dignitaries, the high-definition television cameras missed nothing. Clips showing Melania alternately smiling at her husband and then appearing to scowl when he turned around flooded the internet, with the hashtag #FreeMelania, while other images captured Michelle Obama looking skeptically at the newly inaugurated president.

Purposefully out of the spotlight but in the crowd were Donald Trump's two ex-wives, Ivana Trump and Marla Maples. Trump had instructed his aides to make sure that they were never in the same photo as Melania, telling them it was "her day." Ivana, mother of Don Jr., Ivanka, and Eric, was seen wading through the thousands along the parade route pushing her ninety-year-old mother in a wheelchair. Marla posted an Instagram picture of herself wearing a New York Yankees cap to keep dry in the drizzle. Even though her daughter, Tiffany, was in the parade, she was not in the covered seating offered to donors and close friends.

Guests on the podium noted that Melania "understood the gravity of the moment." She had grown up under a Communist dictator in Yugoslavia, and now at age forty-six, her husband was being sworn in as president and she was becoming the first lady of the United States, her Slovenian parents and her American son beside her.

"PEOPLE SAY, 'Oh, she's a model, therefore she must be dumb.' There's nothing dumb about her," Trump campaign adviser Roger Stone, who was later convicted for lying and witness tampering, told me in 2016, before his legal troubles began. Stone had known Melania since the late 1990s, when she started dating

Trump. "She's a balancing influence on him, a very positive influence," he said. According to Stone, Melania encouraged Trump to run. "She's the one who ultimately said, 'You know, Donald, stop talking about running for president and do it. If you're going to do it, do it. But if you're not going to do it, stop talking about it because it's getting old. And if you run, you're going to win.'" During the campaign, Trump would describe Melania as "my best pollster." It was Melania who told Trump that his poll numbers would shoot up once he officially announced. "There's a lot of people inclined to you," she told her husband, "but they won't vote for you in the poll because they don't think you're running."

The night before the inauguration, Melania and Trump hosted a private candlelight dinner for hundreds of guests inside the atrium at Union Station, the Beaux Arts–style train station dating from 1907. The dinner for friends and supporters was an event that Melania had helped plan, down to the slender gold candlesticks, the centerpieces of white roses flanked by bunches of green grapes, and the coordinating gold flatware on the tables. She wore a sleek, custom-made gold Reem Acra gown. Trump's list of personal guests included more than one hundred fifty people, among them a big group of pilots who flew "Trump Force One," his personal Boeing 757. Don Jr. invited nearly as many people. Ivanka and Eric had long lists of attendees, too.

But Melania had fewer than forty people on her personal invitation list, including a number who had recently helped her or worked for her, such as lawyer Charles Harder, decorator Tham Kannalikham, and makeup artist Nicole Bryl. Melania also invited a doctor who had reportedly cared for her mother—a signal to some guests that one of the reasons Melania had been so invisible during the campaign was that she was helping her mother through an illness. There were no childhood friends; even her sister, Ines, was absent.

The Trump inaugural was held on a Friday, and the next day a massive Women's March of Trump protesters, some carrying #FreeMelania placards, would fill the same Washington streets. By Sunday, Melania Trump would be gone. She had flown back to New York with Barron. The ten-year-old had school that week, and Melania had already declared that he would be finishing the term before moving to Washington. That Sunday, January 22, also happened to be the Trumps' twelfth wedding anniversary. Trump tweeted about the Women's March, protesters, his standing ovations at the CIA, and his television ratings, but there was nothing public from either spouse to mark their wedding day.

The Trumps in the Oval Office

CHAPTER 2

Chasing Melania

"SHE IS like a ghost," said Jarl Alé de Basseville, who photographed Melania in New York when she first arrived in the United States in 1996. "Everyone knows her, but no one does."

Melania's life unfolds like the acts of a play. Act One: the little girl who grew up in socialist Yugoslavia, a country that valued conformity and sameness, where the birthday celebration for the country's dictator was a national holiday. Act Two: The young woman who, as her nation broke apart, chased success in the competitive modeling world in Europe. Act Three: the immigrant who arrived in New York and caught the eye of a well-known real estate mogul and became his wife. Melania's Act Four is still being written. Strikingly, when the curtain falls on one period of her life, it is almost as if it never happened. The characters, the staging, everything changes. Many of the people who knew her as a girl or working model have little or no role to play in her current world. To an exceptional degree, she no longer stays in touch. Her immediate family members are among the rare few who have known her throughout her whole life.

Classmates and neighbors of Melania's in Slovenia never heard from her after she moved to Milan to model full-time. Almost no one from her pre-Trump modeling career was invited to her wedding. People who socialized with Donald Trump said that, apart from her parents and sister and the modeling agent who brought her to America, they never met anyone who knew her before she started dating "The Donald," as his first wife called him. One man who hung out with Trump at the time said: "Melania just appeared one day," adding, "She looked the part—another young model—but she was different. She didn't bring friends. She didn't talk about what she had been doing. She just appeared, this woman with no history."

Differences in age and demeanor mask how alike Melania and Donald Trump are. Both are avid creators of their own history. With the help of others, Trump wrote seventeen books about himself. He burnished his larger-than-life image by starring in fourteen seasons of the NBC reality television shows *The Apprentice* and *The Celebrity Apprentice*, and by constantly angling to be mentioned in newspapers and magazines. Melania, too, has engineered her own persona, but she has done so in the exact opposite way. She watched Trump build his brand through relentless media exposure and built hers by strategic reveal and scarcity: her remarks are always brief, the tidbits she shares are often little more than crumbs, and she is skilled at ducking questions and disappearing. Her playbook is very much the Ralph Lauren one. The celebrated designer—born Ralph Lifshitz in the Bronx, son of a Russian immigrant house painter—learned early on that it pays to wrap yourself in mystery.

But the hologram that she has created leaves so much unknown that people view her in vastly different ways. She is seen as the good-hearted princess who needs to be saved from her rapacious and bullying husband, the vulnerable immigrant swept up in his presidential ambitions who cried the night he was elected, the vapid and shallow model with nothing much to say about the world, the lucky beauty who just happened to be in the right place at the right time. Yet she is none of those things.

Finding out more about Melania—her past, her motivations, her daily life—has been an unprecedented challenge. In three decades as a correspondent working all over the world, I have often written about the reluctant and the reclusive, including the head of a Mexican drug cartel and a Japanese princess, but nothing compared to trying to understand Melania. Most people I spoke to would not speak on the record. Many in the Trump world are governed by NDAs (nondisclosure agreements). Some had been warned by lawyers, family members, and others close to Melania not to speak publicly about her, and many would talk only on the same encrypted phone apps used by spies and others in the intelligence community. Old photos that were once an easy Google search away no longer pop up online. I first began making calls about Melania in 2015 when Trump announced his candidacy for president. Who was this woman, so unknown and yet one of the most recognized faces in the world? After interviews with more than one hundred twenty people in five countries, a fuller, richer portrait emerged.

As I reconstructed her journey, I learned that Melania has strengths that her husband lacks, but she also shares many of the qualities that landed him in the Oval Office. In that sense, Melania *is* like her husband. They are both independent, ambitious, image-conscious, unsentimental, and wary of those outside their inner circle. They are both fighters and survivors and prize loyalty over almost all else. Even their signatures are strikingly similar: sharp-angled up-and-down streaks.

It's true that their differences tend to be more obvious: she is as quiet as he is loud, as mannered as he is crude, and as cautious as he is impulsive. But in crucial ways, they mirror each other. Neither the very public Trump nor the very private Melania has many close friends. Their loner instincts filter into their own marriage. To a remarkable degree for a couple, Melania and Donald Trump have always lived quite separately; they are often in the same building but rarely in the same room. That, however, is part of their deal, and it suits both of them.

Asked years ago if she would be with her husband if he were not rich, she shot back, "If I weren't beautiful, do you think he'd be with me?" More than once, she has pushed back on the notion that she is somehow the lucky one in their marriage. She sees it as a partnership. When she met Trump in the late 1990s, he was younger, charming, and fun. Other women were also interested, but Melania landed him. She understood what he wanted from a third wife: an eye-turning beauty who kept the focus on him. From the start, she was aware of the complications included in a Trumpian life—including those involving his former wives and four children. She knew what Trump said about the things that wrecked his first marriage (Ivana was too involved in business) and his second (Marla tried to change his habits and brought too many family members around). Melania did neither. As Melania often says, in direct contrast to Marla, "I don't try to change him."

She has survived by focusing more on the upside of life with Trump than on his behavior. From the start of their relationship, she saw how complicated his world was. When they began dating, Marla and Tiffany, Trump's second daughter, were still living on the top floor of the family triplex at Trump Tower, which presented an unusual arrangement for any new girlfriend. Workers built a door in the staircase between the penthouse's second and third floor. For months until they moved out, young Tiffany would walk down the stairs and open the door to see her father and sometimes Melania would be there, too.

An advantage to dating someone who has written so much about himself is that you get to learn what he doesn't like in a woman. When Melania dated Trump, he had recently written *The Art of the Comeback*, in which he shared what had gone wrong in his past relationships. Melania figured out early it was best never to discuss past boyfriends—Trump didn't like the idea she had even fleetingly belonged to someone else. She also knew how much he liked praise, and she bathed him in it. She proved to him that she possessed his (and her) favorite trait: loyalty. When he broke up with her around the very end of 1999, she stayed home and avoided becoming involved with anyone else. Her patience paid off. Within a few months, they were a couple again.

"Melania is very smart and understands him," said Anthony Scaramucci, who briefly served as Trump's White House communications director. "With Trump, there are no costars—one spotlight on the stage." Just before they married, Trump was asked about Melania's "ambitions." He said: "At this moment, she's really only interested in what's good for me. And I say that with the greatest respect. She's really far more interested in me than she is in herself."

But on January 22, 2017, Melania was most interested in a plane back to New York, and she left her husband in the White House. There are many reasons why Melania left, but her absence had a clear effect on Trump, and the longer it persisted, the more many people around the new president wanted her back.

In Melania's absence, Ivanka was often called the de facto first lady. The duties of public office would be yet another thing to compete over. Eleven and a half years apart in age, both women had started companies selling jewelry. Both Melania and her stepdaughter were former models, although their modeling careers could not have started out more differently. When Melania was well into her twenties, she was still hoping for her career-making break. Ivanka was featured, at age fourteen, in a six-page *Elle* magazine spread. At fifteen, she was on the cover of *Seventeen* magazine and modeling for Sasson Jeans and Tommy

Hilfiger. Fourteen-year-old Ivanka was quoted as saying to the *Sunday Telegraph* in Australia: "I've wanted to be a model since I was very young—ten or eleven or so. I'd be like, 'There's Cindy [Crawford]! There's Claudia [Schiffer]!' and I guess I always wanted people to say that about me."

Ivanka and Melania insist they have a good relationship, and they continue to attend many of the same events. When Trump and Melania traveled to India on a presidential trip in late February 2020, Ivanka and Jared joined them. But the campaign, the planning for the inauguration, the move to Washington, and the early months of the administration, had intensified the friction between the two women.

It had been easier for them to keep a comfortable distance before Ivanka began introducing her father at public rallies and assuming many of the duties of a political spouse while Melania stayed home with Barron. Ivanka is a polished public speaker and has wowed audiences. Before her father's swearing-in, she studied photos of past ceremonies, including Obama's, and circled the prime seating spots. According to others who saw the photos, she wanted to be placed in the best position to be seen in the historic images. Ivanka also looked carefully at the parade route. An avid Instagram user, she posted many inaugural shots, including those of her and her young children heading to the parade on Pennsylvania Avenue. In many photos, Ivanka is usually the child closest to her father.

But Ivanka's jockeying for position raised eyebrows among those who were partial to Melania and were looking out for her interests. In the end, Ivanka sat directly behind Melania at the swearing-in ceremony. Barron sat beside his mother. Although Ivanka still had a choice aisle seat and was in plenty of photos, she was not visible in some tight camera shots. But she made her status in the family clear that night, the family's first in the White House, when she claimed the Lincoln bedroom for herself and Jared. Ivanka knows how to look out for herself—as does Melania. Melania has been heard calling Ivanka "The Princess" out of earshot. When she was younger, Ivanka privately called Melania "The Portrait," telling classmates that her father's girlfriend spoke as much as a painting on the wall.

Early on, Ivanka made it clear that she planned to remain in the limelight after Inauguration Day. Already, there had been press leaks about Ivanka and Jared's search for a D.C. home in pricey Kalorama, the neighborhood where Amazon billionaire Jeff Bezos and the Obamas have grand residences. Bill and Hillary Clinton also have a place nearby. After Ivanka and Jared rented a $5.5 million home, paparazzi waited outside their door, plastering photos in the *Daily Mail* and other tabloids of the designer-dressed daughter headed to work as a special adviser in the West Wing. Ivanka had easy and frequent access to the Oval Office, and was setting up her own office and initiatives.

While Ivanka dove right into White House life, Melania did not even like to be called by her new title at first. "She said, 'Stop calling me first lady,'" recalled one of the people who worked with Melania after the election. The New York City mother known for sending emoji-filled texts was now being invited to give speeches around the country. For years, she and her husband had a bodyguard, but now she was being protected twenty-four hours a day by Secret Service agents. There was always someone standing guard outside her door, and the animosity directed at her husband worried her. "At the core, I think she's a private person who's spent a lot of time adjusting to public life," said one person who worked with Trump on the campaign and has remained close to the family.

Other first ladies have found the sudden adjustment difficult as well, and Melania, a careful planner, likes to take her time doing things. No matter how intense the pressure during the campaign, she refused to be hurried. The election night win came as a surprise even to Trump, according to many on his campaign, and little preparation had been done for what came next. Trump had even talked about going to one of his golf courses in Scotland immediately after the election so he didn't have to watch Hillary Clinton bask in her success. One campaign aide recalled that candidate Trump had "told the pilot [of his private jet], 'Fuel up the plane.'" He didn't receive as many votes as Hillary, but he won key states and the electoral college tally that made him president. Trump and his team scrambled to write an acceptance speech and begin a White House transition. Melania wasn't prepared to move to Washington, either.

It did not help that the campaign revelations of Trump's alleged serial infidelities still stung. She learned many of the reported details along with the entire nation. While she very much wanted Barron to finish his academic year in New York and not be yanked from his friends, staying in New York also bought time to prepare for her new role as first lady. She needed her own staff. Trump's staff had already pushed back on her desire to focus on online bullying, and there was huge interest in what she might do. And, according to several people close to the Trumps, she was in the midst of negotiations to amend her financial arrangement with Trump—what Melania referred to as "taking care of Barron."

Prenuptial and postnuptial agreements are as standard as wedding rings in Trump's marriages. His first wife, Ivana, re-negotiated hers three times; Marla Maples, who separated from Trump after four years of marriage, walked away with such a relatively small sum that even a Trump lawyer said he felt she should have gotten more. Trump wrote about prenups and boasted about them and said any rich man who didn't have one was "a loser." During the presidential campaign, Melania felt that a lot had changed since she signed her prenup. She had been with him a long time—longer than any other woman. She believed she made crucial contributions to his success. There was talk that Trump likely wouldn't return to overseeing the Trump Organization after running the country, and Melania wanted to ensure that Barron got his rightful share of inheritance, particularly if Ivanka took the reins of the family business.

While she sorted out her plans as first lady and a new school for her son, she also worked on getting her husband to sign a more generous financial deal for her and Barron. It was smart timing. "The best thing you can do is to deal from strength, and leverage is the biggest strength you can have," Trump wrote in *The Art of the Deal*. "Leverage is having something the other guy wants. Or better yet, needs. Or best of all, simply can't do without." While in New York, Melania had new leverage. The vacant first lady's office annoyed him. He wanted her with him.

A few of Trump's pals were upset with Melania, not only because her decision to remain in Trump Tower fanned rumors they were not getting along. They also wanted her in the White House because when she was around, Trump was calmer. They believed that if she were with him, he would not have been tweeting as often and acting as impulsively. The opening weeks of his administration were marked by personnel clashes, embarrassing leaks, and a controversial travel ban that caused major protests at airports. Trump held a seventy-five-minute press conference on February 16, repeatedly denying any chaos and saying, "this administration is running like a fine-tuned machine," and adding, "I'm not ranting and raving."

"That woman! She will be the end of him," Thomas Barrack, Trump's friend who chaired his inaugural, was overheard saying at a meeting, as he talked about Melania remaining in New York. "She is stubborn. She should be with her husband. He *is* the president of the United States." As the weeks passed, more people around Trump began to appreciate Melania for what she brought to their relationship. At least one of Trump's older children even called her, urging her to spend more time with their dad, telling her that he needed her balance. Melania knew that some people in

New York dismissed her as a gold digger, but now, finally, others were starting to realize her worth.

But staying in New York carried a high price. Melania hadn't realized the overwhelming cost and inconvenience caused by the security measures needed for Barron and her in a large urban area—it was costing millions of dollars a month. The Secret Service sought more funding. The New York Police Department said a conservative estimate for its costs alone was $125,000 a day. Simply getting Barron to his classes unleashed massive traffic problems around his school, Columbia Grammar and Preparatory School on Manhattan's Upper West Side. Many of the other parents were busy, wealthy people, and some began to seethe over the disruption and inconvenience, including delayed drop-offs and pickups and being told to "hold" for Melania and Barron. Parents also worried about the safety of their own kids, even with the constant presence of the Secret Service. Not to mention that many of them were progressive New York Democrats who had voted for Hillary Clinton and couldn't stand Trump.

Melania knew protesters stood in front of Trump Tower every day holding signs and shouting that her husband hated immigrants and women. Hundreds of thousands of people signed an online petition demanding that the Trumps pay the "exorbitant" costs of her choosing to remain in New York. And the longer she stayed, the greater the speculation that her decision to remain in New York meant that their marriage was on the rocks. On Valentine's Day, Melania did not return to Washington. Stephanie

Winston Wolkoff, the senior adviser helping her set up her White House office, had just told CNN that Melania was "committed" to preserving Michelle Obama's First Lady's Kitchen Garden. Her husband was in the White House, tweeting about "illegal leaks."

Melania did not like what was being written about her. For years her experience with the media was fielding softball questions from fashion magazines; now, instead of receiving questions about her beauty regime or fashion choices, she was being asked what, as an immigrant, she thought of her husband's tough border policy. She had little control over the script or photos being published. She told people that no matter what she did, she would be criticized, and that she would do what she wanted. Melania had said that she would stay in New York until the school year ended, and she stood her ground.

That didn't sit well with everyone around Trump. Barrack, who was in close touch with Trump, began asking Melania's friends to get involved in "domestic issues," which to them was interpreted as urging her to "lay off the prenup renegotiations" or, as another put it, "get down to Washington." Barrack was seen as closer to Ivanka than to Melania. While Melania stayed in New York, Ivanka continued to establish herself in the West Wing, notorious for its cramped and limited working spaces. According to several people, she was eyeing real estate in the East Wing as well, the domain of the first lady. Among other proposals, Ivanka suggested renaming the "First Lady's Office" the "First Family Office." Melania did not allow that to happen. It was tradition, and she was not going to let her stepdaughter change it. Ivanka's office remained in the West Wing.

Melania's delay in moving from New York initially put her at a disadvantage. Even some of the staff positions and budgets that would have been available to support the first lady's office were gone, diverted to support those in the West Wing, including Ivanka. Especially in the first two years of the administration, some in the White House felt that the West Wing was actively putting up roadblocks and purposely not lending support to the first lady's office. But others believed that it was just an oversight in the chaos.

Ivanka is both especially close to her father and spent far more time around him than his other children. Not only did father and daughter work closely at the Trump Organization but she also had played a key role in his campaign, and now was the child with the most active role inside the White House. With Melania away, Ivanka used the private theater, with its plush red seats, and enjoyed other White House perks. Some said she treated the private residence as if it were her own home. Melania did not like it. When she and Barron finally moved in, she put an end to the "revolving door" by enforcing firm boundaries.

In those early months, Ivanka seemed to get involved in every major issue. In May, the *New York Times* wrote an article headlined "Ivanka Trump Has the President's Ear: Here's Her Agenda," in which the reporters described the first daughter as being determined to act as "a moderating force in an administration swept into office by nationalist sentiment." The article stated that Ivanka planned to review executive orders before they were signed, and that, according to officials, she had already weighed in on "climate, deportation, education, and refugee policy." In an interview, she told the *Times*, "I'm still at the early stages of learning how everything works, but I know enough now to be a much more proactive voice inside the White House." That would turn out to also include weighing in on details such as the décor of the Oval Office.

Ivanka had enlisted a decorator from the Trump Organization, and a gold shimmery silk fabric wallpaper was selected for the office walls. Stephanie Winston Wolkoff, Melania's adviser in the first lady's office, knew Melania would want to decorate the Oval Office. She also thought that the type of fabric would not look good on TV and told Trump so. Soon Winston Wolkoff and Melania, with Trump's blessing, were making their own plans for the office. In the end, Trump avoided any showdown between his daughter and wife by putting off a costly overhaul. On his own, he chose a combination of furnishings used by previous presidents: Bill Clinton's gold curtains, a rug designed by Nancy Reagan, and George W. Bush's pale sofas. Winston Wolkoff said it still felt like a clear win for Melania.

All the while, Melania stayed out of the news, away from the microphones, while others were busy promoting themselves. Melania didn't need to trumpet that she had the president's ear, because she already did. In fact, when Trump heard a TV commentator talk about the outsize influence of his children, he laughed and said, "Do you think I became successful by listening to my kids? They listen to me." People working in the West Wing say they have heard Trump criticize Don Jr. and Eric and even Ivanka for doing or saying something that the president thought was not helpful, but none could recall hearing him say anything negative about Melania. He appreciated that she didn't need publicity, and that she didn't boast about her influence, saying little more in interviews than, "sometimes" he listens and sometimes he doesn't.

At the White House, Trump felt he was surrounded by people who were constantly jockeying for position and focused on their own self-interest, and he valued Melania's loyalty and insights more than before he entered politics. Sean Spicer, the president's first communications director, explained the dynamic this way: "Melania is very behind-the-scenes but unbelievably influential. She is not one to go in and say, 'Hire this person, fire this person.' But she lets the president know what she thinks, and he takes her views very seriously." Rather than tell Trump what to do or not do, Melania's style is to give her opinion, and in the end, "he tends to agree with her," Spicer said. Often, if Melania was present for a discussion and spoke up, "The president would say, 'She is right,' and that was the end of the discussion."

Spicer recounted having dinner with the president and first lady and seeing how Trump constantly solicited his wife's opinion. He found their banter fascinating, a seamless back-and-forth, with one speaking and the other interjecting. "It's almost like watching color commentating on a game. They are a team," Spicer said. More than a dozen past or current White House officials interviewed attributed Melania's influence to the fact that Trump believed that just about everyone else had an agenda, except Melania. He believed she had no ulterior motive and just wanted him to succeed. Trump's wariness of others has grown during his presidency, as people he hired for high-profile jobs have left his administration and then criticized him publicly.

Melania tells him what she believes is resonating with voters and what is not. According to Spicer, the first lady is a "voracious consumer of news and information" and has "her finger on the pulse of not just what is going on issue-wise, but what is in her husband's best interest." She focuses less on policy than on positioning him in front of an audience. Spicer explained her style as being dramatically different from others' in and out of the West Wing. "There are people who go to the president and say, 'Here is what we should be doing.' 'Here is what the country should be doing.' 'Here is what the party should be doing.'" That is not Melania. "She knows exactly who he is as a person, what he believes and what his brand is about. She really understands positioning him. She says, 'This is who you are. You don't need to do that.'"

Others' agreement with Melania has become something of a loyalty test for Trump. In conversations, he will sometimes ask,

"This is what Melania thinks. What do you think?" Spicer recalled a phone conversation he had with Trump after leaving the White House. Spicer made a comment, and Trump replied, "You know what? Melania says the same thing. You are right."

The depth of Melania's influence, as well as her operating style, can be seen in one of the key decisions from Trump's campaign: his July 2016 vice presidential pick. Over the July 4 weekend, Trump summoned Indiana governor Mike Pence and his wife, Karen, to the Trump National Golf Club in Bedminster, New Jersey, a property set amid rolling hills about an hour outside of New York City. Melania and Barron—and often Melania's parents—have spent large parts of each summer there.

Longtime Republican operative Paul Manafort was leading the vice presidential search, but it was Melania whom Trump assigned to spend time with the Pences. Trump was also considering, as running mates, then–New Jersey governor Chris Christie and former House Speaker Newt Gingrich. Melania knew Christie well and had met Gingrich. Pence was very conservative, deeply religious, and from the Midwest—all of which stood to help Trump with conservatives still wary of a New Yorker who was once a registered Democrat. Trump also recognized that he needed someone who could help him navigate Capitol Hill, which touched off speculation among pundits that Gingrich had the edge. But Trump arranged the entire weekend so that Melania could get acquainted with the Pences.

Melania and the Pences ate meals together, and she spoke

at length with both of them. Afterward, she gave Trump her assessment, telling him that they were good people, and that Mike Pence had a big advantage over Gingrich and Christie: he was not too ambitious. She believed that he would be content in a number-two spot and not gun for the top job, which was something she could not say about the other two. "She played a big role. It was beyond consulting," said one person with direct knowledge of the selection. "She thought he would be a loyal adviser, not an alpha."

Another telling moment for Melania came when Trump asked Pence to give his opinion of the other contenders. Pence highlighted their strengths. When Trump asked Gingrich and Christie the same question, "they were total assassins," a former administration official recounted. Melania took note of their ability to unload on a rival and urged her husband to pick Pence. She thought that he was the most likely to stay in his lane, step aside, and let Trump be Trump.

Ivanka, Don Jr., and Eric also met with Pence, a social values conservative who had signed restrictive abortion laws and opposed both same-sex marriage and the right of gay people to serve in the military—both of which worried some in the Trump campaign. But whatever other advisers thought in the end, Melania had made the case for the Indiana governor in a way that appealed to Trump.

This was the pattern that would repeat itself inside the White House. Melania would not weigh in on many issues, but when she did speak up, her words mattered. Christie told me, "The idea that she is *not* a big influence in the administration is just dead wrong. She picks her spots when she wants to speak assertively, but when she does, the president listens." It became clear to those working in the West Wing that Trump placed significant value on those Melania liked (such as counselor Kellyanne Conway) and those she didn't (including chiefs of staff Reince Priebus and, eventually, John Kelly). "He absolutely consults her on personnel matters," Christie explained, noting that Melania "doesn't waste a lot of words." It also became clear that one of the most lethal places to find oneself was in Melania's crosshairs. As one former White House official said: "People cross Melania at their own risk—and that risk is, 'off with your head.' I'm not kidding . . . You are gone if she doesn't like you."

Melania moved into the White House on June 11, 2017, with almost no fanfare. She is not nearly as active on social media as her husband. But on moving day she posted a picture out a White House window with a view of the Washington Monument. She had just replaced the White House chief usher, who had worked for the Obamas, overseeing a residence staff of nearly a hundred people and everything from family dinner menus to the residence's budget. Instead, she selected Timothy Harleth, who had been the director of rooms at the Trump International Hotel in Washington. Donald J. Trump might not be able to live at his local Trump property, but that did not mean that the Trump property could not, in many ways, be brought to him. And his wife, the newly arrived first lady, would be the one to do it.

In the end, her arrival was not much of a story. Melania was now in the White House, quietly beginning the latest remarkable chapter in her highly improbable life.

Melanija Knavs, second from the right, on the runway at age seven

Melania at age twenty-one

CHAPTER 3

Face of the Year

"I GREW up in a small town in Slovenia near a beautiful river and forest. Slovenia is a small country that, back then, was under Communist rule. It was a beautiful childhood." That is how Melania Trump described her youth at a Pennsylvania campaign stop in 2016.

But it only hinted at the most unconventional path to the White House in history. Born on April 26, 1970, in Novo Mesto, Melanija (the original spelling of her first name) is the second daughter of Viktor and Amalija Knavs, both of whom had been directly affected by World War II. Viktor was born in a territory that was under German occupation. His parents, in a move that made their son's life easier and safer, registered his name as the more German-sounding "Waldemar." Amalija, known to some friends as Malci (pronounced "Malchee"), was born in Austria, where her family had fled to avoid forced labor camps, returning home after the war.

Many people in the town of Sevnica (pronounced "SEH-oo-nee-tsa"), where Melanija grew up, knew and remembered Viktor and Malci because they stood out. Viktor's friends there today describe him as a big guy with a big personality. Not everyone was a fan, but many found him a charming rascal who made people laugh. Growing up, he loved to play soccer and was good at it. "He was a really handsome guy and he always dressed nice; if you met him thirty years ago, you'd fall in love with him for yourself," said one old friend of Viktor's, sitting in a Sevnica café in the summer of 2018. Of his appeal, the friend added, "He never had a problem with women." Many in Slovenia and the United States have compared Viktor to his son-in-law. They are less than five years apart in age and bear a physical resemblance to each other.

In the Socialist Federal Republic of Yugoslavia, uniformity was prized. The government promoted equality; families of the same size typically lived in apartments of the same size. Every building seemed to be painted the color of a storm cloud. Workers went to the same factories, shopped in the same stores, and took the bus or walked. Viktor drove. He had trained as a mechanic and developed a passion for cars, especially the top-of-the-line German-engineered Mercedes.

Well dressed, tall, and the owner of a car, Viktor won over Amalija, a talented seamstress, who loved fine clothes and worked at a local factory called Jutranka, which manufactured high-end children's wear. "She had the skill to make things beautiful, to draw, to design, and to sew. She is really an artist," recalled Estera Savić, a designer who worked with her. Because she lacked a degree, she was employed as a "konstruktor," a patternmaker. Designers would sketch a dress or a blouse, and then she would turn that design into a pattern for mass production. She worked among hundreds of others in Jutranka's huge open factory floor in a building that had once been a monastery.

Viktor and Amalija married in 1967, daring to have a quiet Catholic ceremony at a time when Yugoslavia's Communist leader had clamped down on celebrating religious holidays and had nationalized land that had belonged to the Church. They would also baptize their daughters in the Catholic Church. Viktor set himself apart from other workers in town by joining the Communist Party, according to records in the National Archives. Igor Omerza, a former member of parliament who has written two books on Melania and her family, says Viktor likely joined the party to increase his chances of securing a more desirable and higher-paying job, not because he believed in Marxist philosophy: "I think it was opportunism." Viktor, who had driven a bus and repaired cars, did, in fact, become the chauffeur for both a nearby local mayor and the Jutranka factory director.

Car parts were often hard to come by, but Viktor always seemed to have what he needed, and several people I interviewed said they suspected that he snuck the car parts over the border to avoid the exorbitant duty fees. Italy and Austria were only a couple of hours' drive away. "Everybody smuggled," said Urska Faller, a Slovenian anthropologist who has researched Melania's family. Yugoslavia lacked many items, especially luxury goods. Travel was not restricted, and Slovenians would cross into Italy and wear five pairs of jeans in different sizes, layered on top of one another, on their return. Everyone seemed to know an unlikely smuggler—the priest who carried a hidden desk lamp, an old lady with chocolate and coffee balanced under her hat.

Of the many distinctive things about the Knavs family, neighbors especially recall their brightly painted apartment, an unusual splash of color in an otherwise monochrome world. "There were different colors in different rooms. I can't tell you how unusual that was," explained a family friend. "Everybody else had white, maybe beige, walls. When you walked in their apartment, one wall was green! Green!" After Slovenian independence in 1991, many people started painting their homes bright colors. But the Knavses' cheery rooms were an early statement and maybe a little sign of independence.

Melanija and her whole family also avoided the "village radio," the small-town gossips. In the intense and divided political environment under Tito, people tended to keep their thoughts and feelings to themselves. Even those who thought they knew the Knavs family well were surprised to learn in 2016 that Viktor had a son in a nearby town. Journalist Julia Ioffe found Melania's half-brother, Denis Cigelnjak, during research for a 2016 *GQ* article. Cigelnjak had not met the first lady or her older sister, Ines.

Melanija was not a common name, and from the beginning, her parents believed that their little girl with the startling blue eyes was someone special. Her mother, in particular, was determined that Melanija's clothing should be as exceptional as she believed her daughter was. "Melanija has elegance in the blood," said Meri Kelemina, a manager of Lisca, another local factory. Ana, a close friend of Amalija's since elementary school, said, "At every moment, even inside her home, Amalija dressed better than everybody else. I wore high heels for special occasions. She wore them all the time! We called her Jackie Kennedy." A man who has known her for fifty years said, "Never, never, would she be seen in a sweat suit in a shop. She always looked like she belonged in a big city."

Amalija even wore heels for her shifts on the factory floor, where work typically started at 6:00 or 7:00 a.m. and ended sharply at 2:00 or 3:00 p.m., to give mothers time with their children. She bought her shoes in the Italian border city of Trieste and wore them as exclamation points to the dresses and coats she created. Her bosses sometimes invited her to travel with them to Florence and other European cities to scout fashion trends. She returned with ideas and fabric—and fashion magazines for Melanija and Ines. "The light in Amalija's window did not go off until late at night—the mother was making clothes for her two daughters," said Faller, the researcher.

"Why do you think she ended up a model?" a family friend said to me. "Her mother had been dressing her up since birth. When Ines and Melanija would walk by, people would say, 'Beautiful! Beautiful!'" Slovenians often talk about the vital role mothers play, quoting some variation on this phrase: "A mother holds up three of the four pillars of a home." With her husband frequently traveling for work, Melanija's mother often seemed to hold up all four pillars. Every morning before going to the factory, Amalija made her daughters breakfast, coffee or tea and toast with butter and honey, Ines would recall years later.

Amalija instilled in her younger daughter confidence and a belief that others were no better, and passed along her love of fashion and style. By age seven, Melanija was already learning exactly how to walk the runway. With the adorable grin of a little girl missing a front tooth, she was a model for children's clothes at her mother's factory. (Because towns then often produced one product for the whole country, such as glass or washing machines, Slovenians joke that if Melanija had not grown up in a town producing high-quality clothes, her passion might have been for farming tools instead of fashion.) In one photo, young Melanija wears a checkered scarf, a white blouse with fashionably large buttons, a skirt flared at the knee, and little white ankle socks. Her hair was cut in a brown bob with bangs. The fashion shows at Jutranka gave children a chance to shine. With her mother's encouragement, Melanija learned to float down a catwalk with poise, shoulders back, head held high. She quickly became so comfortable that a friend remembers a time when another girl cried as she faced the crowd, and little Melanija took her hand and helped her down the runway.

"It was just something fun to do," said Nena Bedek, a childhood friend of Melanija's, about their modeling days for Jutranka. Bedek lived on the second floor of the apartment building next to the Knavses' building. For fun, she and Melanija would pass messages to each other from one building to the next using a loop of yarn that they tossed and tied between their balconies. They would fasten notes or little bags with cookies with a clothespin and pull them back and forth to each other. "It was technology before smartphones," Bedek said.

Teachers would excuse Nena, Melanija, and other children from school for photo shoots for the Jutranka catalog or fashion shows. Bedek recalled taking the train to the capital, Belgrade, three hundred miles away, for a fashion show. She and her mother made the trip with Melanija, Ines, and their mother. "I remember bouncing up and down on the beds in the hotel where we stayed overnight," said Bedek. Belgrade had so many things that Sevnica did not, from hotels to a grand palace. It was a city of a million people, a faster world. The Sava River, which flows slowly through Melanija's little town, runs all the way to Belgrade, where it joins the Danube and then keeps on going out into the world. Soon, Melanija would do the same.

Melanija didn't stand perfectly tall just on the runway. Her classmates remembered practicing with her for the day when they would pledge allegiance to Yugoslavia and its dictator, Comrade Josip Broz Tito, wearing identical uniforms: a cap with a red star, a red scarf tied around her neck, and a white shirt. "For the homeland and with Tito we go forward! That I shall love my country, self-managing socialist Yugoslavia, and all of its brotherly peoples, and build a new life full of joy and happiness," they said, reciting the words all children said on the day they were inducted into Tito's Union of Pioneers of Yugoslavia.

The students promised to study hard, respect their parents, uphold socialist ideals, and spread "the principles for which

Comrade Tito fought." Becoming a pioneer was a Yugoslavian rite of passage, sometimes compared to First Communion in the Catholic Church. By the time Melanija was seven, Tito had been running the country for more than three decades.

Melanija was a good student and so responsible that she was selected to be a school treasurer. Nationally, there was a Tito-driven emphasis to save, and Yugoslavian youngsters in the 1970s collected coins the way American kids were collecting Barbies and baseball cards. So many youngsters had piggy banks that the National Museum of Contemporary History even recently displayed some from this era. Melanija's job was to collect money from her classmates for school trips, keep track of it, and pay bills. "It was an honor; the teacher trusted us," said Vladimira Tomšič, who was picked at the same time Melania was for school banking duty and who now runs the Sevnica health center. The banking job at such a young age, Tomšič said, "was quite challenging work for us at the time. But we learned how to manage money."

On May 4, 1980, one week after Melanija turned ten, Yugoslavia came to a standstill. Four code words, "The match is canceled," passed from one high-ranking official to the next, a way of announcing that Tito, president of the League of Communists of Yugoslavia and supreme commander of the military of the Socialist Federal Republic of Yugoslavia, had passed away days before his eighty-eighth birthday. State-run television reported: "Comrade Tito has died. His great heart stopped beating at 15:05."

Tito had led the country since World War II. Many rushed home to watch the tributes to him. Flags flew at half-staff for seven days. Newspapers were printed with black borders. His body was loaded on a train that chugged through the country. When it passed through Sevnica, some recall seeing Melanija's family pay their respects. Many wept and threw flowers. Tito's funeral was the most extensive state mourning in the country since the 1963 assassination of John F. Kennedy. That killing shocked Yugoslavia; only one month before, Kennedy had welcomed Tito to the White House. With Tito at his side, Kennedy proclaimed: "This is a difficult and dangerous world in which we live. I think it's most important that we have—across the distance of water and across perhaps a difference in political philosophy—that we have an understanding . . . so that danger may be lessened." When Yugoslavians watched the images of Comrade Tito with the young American president, Melanija's mother was eighteen and her father, twenty-two. Against mind-boggling odds, they, thanks to their daughter, would one day have their own bedroom in the White House and sit in the Rose Garden designed by Jackie Kennedy.

Melanija was born when Richard Nixon was in office, but it was another American president who made an impression when she was young. Six months after Tito's death, Democrat Jimmy Carter was defeated by a Republican named Ronald Reagan. "President Reagan's Morning in America was not just something in the United States. It began to feel like morning around the world, even in my small country," she said during the 2016 campaign. "It was a true inspiration to me."

The first stop after she left her hometown was Ljubljana, a

city of around 250,000, about fifty miles from the Italian border. She enrolled at the Secondary School for Design and Photography, housed in a former monastery downtown. The specialized high school offered courses in design, visual art, and photography. Ines attended the same school and, as the older sister, went ahead to the city. In one of her periodic social media postings about her upbringing, Ines tweeted about her high school years: "When I was 14–15, 16, I lived alone in Ljubljana . . . life was great." She described a busy life of "lots of homework," jazz ballet, evening swims with friends, and skating in Tivoli Park. Her father often had work in the city and her parents owned an apartment in Ljubljana where she stayed. When Melanija was old enough to start high school, she joined Ines and they roomed together. Their mother kept her job in Sevnica, a ninety-minute train ride away, but she also visited and sent homemade food.

Ines and Melanija's apartment was in a cluster of nearly identical high-rises. Railroad tracks ran close by. Many residents grew their own tomatoes, carrots, potatoes, and lettuce in communal garden plots. When I visited twenty-five years later, people were drying clothes on lines strung across tiny balconies.

School records show that teachers praised Melanija for her discipline, and one wrote at the time that she would soon be creating her own designs. Classmates remembered Melanija for being seen more than heard. They saw her in their classes, but she did not spend a lot of time outside of school with other students. "She was a very quiet girl and very, very beautiful," recalled Tomi Lombar, another student.

Now in the big city, Melanija began losing touch with her hometown. Friends she had once seen every day no longer heard from her. She had moved on. Around her fourteenth birthday, her parents drove her and Ines to the far bigger Yugoslavian city of Zagreb to hear Elton John, who was on a European tour. The British rocker, dressed up as a cowboy in a metallic jacket amid a dazzling light show, sang "Rocket Man" and "Candle in the Wind." The next year, 1985, CNN International began broadcasting around the world. It was a powerful force in Eastern and Central Europe, including Yugoslavia, which had state-run TV. The twenty-four-hour American network brought images of John Travolta waltzing Princess Diana around the dance floor at the Reagan White House into Yugoslavian homes. CNN even helped make Trump famous in other parts of the globe. Melania's sister said the first time she ever saw Donald Trump was in 1990, when she was twenty-two and he was being interviewed by talk show host Larry King on CNN. In 2018, after a report that Trump was not happy that she had tuned her TV on Air Force One to CNN, Melania's spokeswoman said in a statement that the first lady watches "any channel she wants."

ON A dreary, chilly evening in January 1987, Melanija was leaning against a pillar outside a large festival hall in Ljubljana, illuminated by an overhead light bulb. Her coat was short and her boots high and she caught Stane Jerko's eye. An experienced photographer, Jerko knew that the camera made a person appear heavier and noticed how very slim this girl was. Her legs were so long that he remembered thinking, "They were endless." He stopped, later recalling, "If her coat had been longer, I might not have noticed her and just kept walking."

Jerko explained that he scouted and photographed models. "Are you interested in modeling?" he asked. She looked surprised. Or was she skeptical that he really was a photographer? Jerko wasn't sure. As he opened his bag to show her his Canon EOS and photos, Melanija's friend arrived. The three kept talking. Jerko was a pioneer in fashion photography in Yugoslavia. As socialism faltered, there was a budding industry in fashion, magazines, and commercial advertising, and all of these outlets needed models. "If you want, you can come to my studio sometime," he offered. "I can take some photos of you."

She told him she had a lot of schoolwork.

"How old are you?"

"Sixteen and a half."

He handed her his number, and days later she called.

Melanija arrived at Jerko's studio, a converted bakery with high ceilings and good light, alone and early. She wore jeans and brought a bag of clothes. He logged her information in his ledger. Over tea in his apartment in 2018, Jerko showed me his old records. In careful penmanship, he had written her details, alongside those of many others:

"Melanija Knavs"
176.5 cm [5 feet 9½ inches]
55 kg [121 pounds]

85 prsa [33.5-inch bust]

65 pas [25-inch waist]

93 boki [36-inch hips]

Melanija posed for a couple of hours, fixing her makeup and hair herself. She asked how the lighting would affect her look and which angles were most flattering to her. He was struck by how analytical she was for a sixteen-year-old. As Jerko clicked, Melanija let her hair down, then swept it up into a wild ponytail at the top of her head. She posed with her hands on her hips, behind her head, at her side. In the photos, she is pensive and playful. In some, she looks like so many girls did in their high school yearbooks in the 1980s.

But one photo knocked Jerko out. In it, Melanija is beaming, with an open smile framing perfect white teeth, her hair down and slightly mussed, her eyes twinkling. Her face is tilted slightly upward, catching the light on her cheeks. "In that photo, I saw that she could make it as a model."

He asked her to return for another shoot, and to wear more fashionable clothes so she looked more like a working model. She told him she was studying visual arts and design, and he thought that helped her envision the photos: "She followed the camera naturally." Jerko circulated his pictures of her among those looking for models. "She made the most of the opportunity," he said. "When she was here, it was like she was in a cocoon. Then slowly, slowly, slowly she became a beautiful butterfly."

Five months later, when editors at two fashion magazines

hired Jerko for shoots, he called Melanija to offer her the work. But she told him: "Oh, I'm sorry. I don't have time now. I cannot come." He never heard from her again. "I don't know why," he said. The photographer said he never got as much as a "thank-you" back then, or when he sent photos that he took of her at age sixteen to Trump Tower in 2016. "I find it strange."

This would become a pattern in her life. Melanija would seize an opportunity and put great effort into it. Then she would move on and never look back. People she met found it hard to square her in-the-moment kindness with her ability to later cut loose those who had helped her along the way. But it also meant that she was never dependent upon or indebted to any one person. She was the one driving her life.

Although neither of Melanija's parents attended college, they made sure both their daughters had the chance. Melanija applied to the competitive architecture program at the University of Ljubljana. Three out of four applicants were rejected, but Melanija was accepted. She started classes in the fall of 1989. That November, the Berlin Wall fell in Germany, sending shock waves through Yugoslavia. Less than two years later, Slovenia had declared its independence and made Ljubljana its capital. But the economy was unraveling. Melanija had grown up saving Yugoslavian dinars, and then the currency changed to Slovenian tolars and hyperinflation cut their worth, leaving many families unable to afford the basics.

One of her university professors, Blaž Matija Vogelnik, said that Melanija earned good grades when she did the work, but then she just stopped. His records show that she did not fulfill the requirements to sit for his exam at the end of the year. "I think she realized there was another path for her," Vogelnik said. He believes she calculated that only half the students finished the rigorous course and that, with limited jobs available, very few would get the chance to be "true architects." The professor recalled one hardworking graduate who moved to Germany and designed only windows. Melanija, he said, "was very well aware that she could do something more with her beauty than stay where she was." Others were telling her that she had the looks, height, and poise to be a famous model. So Melanija, with her parents' blessing, left the university at age nineteen.

As she explored how far her looks could take her, an early stop was a competition at a movie studio five hundred miles away, in Rome. Melanija arrived with her mother at Europe's biggest film studio, Cinecittà, or Cinema City, to enter a competition. Cinecittà, often called "Hollywood on the Tiber," had advertised a contest for a fresh face. The winner would receive a movie role. Melanija loved movies—there were not many entertainment options in her town, but *Ben Hur*, *Cleopatra*, and other classics shot at the Italian studio were shown. She had a special admiration for Sophia Loren, the feline-eyed Italian beauty who rocketed from poverty to global fame. Loren had started her movie career at Cinecittà. Many people told Melanija that she resembled a young Sophia.

Amalija believed that her daughter could win the contest; Melanija believed in and admired her mother. She thought that if

Amalija had had the opportunities she deserved, she would have had other options than working in a factory for three decades. One day, Melanija told a friend, she would show her mother new places.

The Cinecittà contestants were judged in three categories: a photo shoot, how they wore different outfits, and their movement in front of the camera. Riccardo Colao, a judge in the contest and the editor of the Cinecittà magazine *Hollywood*, remembers that there were twenty-five to thirty people competing and that Melanija stood above all others: "Seeing her and falling in love with her was automatic."

Melanija won and was featured in the December 1989 issue of *Hollywood*. The text read, in part: "Melania Knaus . . . has not turned twenty yet . . . The jury praised her truly remarkable measurements: approximately 1.77 meters high [nearly 5 feet 10 inches], 55 kilos in weight [121 pounds], 85 cm (breasts) [33.5 inches], 65 cm (waist) [25 inches], 93 cm (hips) [36 inches], she is a size 38–40—what a girl needs to become a real top model. Her mother, who was with her, described herself as a dress-maker and told us that Melania's father is in charge of buying and selling cars. Melania passed the photogenic test, but how could that be otherwise since she said she has been working as a model since age 16." The article continued, "She speaks several languages perfectly, among them Slovenian, Serbian, German, English and French. She would like to move to Italy, so she is looking for a teacher who can teach her our language. Quite a few people have offered to help. Melania is certainly destined to become a queen on the world runways because she has determination and desire for success."

Accompanying the article were the photos shot by Stane Jerko.

Melania never claimed her prize and did not appear in a movie. In these days, long before the #MeToo movement and greater public awareness of how powerful men demanded sexual favors from young women, Colao recalled that some men in the film industry were trying to get aspiring actresses "into their bed." He said one approached Melania. "She told the producer to buzz off, that she isn't game, that he could not get her to have sex with him," Colao said. "Melania was accompanied by her mother, who protected her from this," and the two of them just walked out. She did shoot a shampoo commercial, Colao said.

She left Rome with a new spelling of her name: the more westernized Melania Knaus. As she began modeling in other European cities, she settled on the spelling Knauss.

In a near repeat of Stane Jerko's encounter, another photographer, Nino Mihalek, saw Melania at age twenty-one walking down a street in Ljubljana. She was so striking that Mihalek hit the brakes and got out of his car to introduce himself. He told her that he was looking for a model for a milk commercial. She agreed to pose for a shoot, but in the end, she was considered too thin, and a young woman with larger breasts was selected. But Mihalek thought that she was beautiful, and, with her encouragement, he sent her photos to a highly regarded modeling agency in Milan headed by Riccardo Gay (pronounced "guy"). Then he never heard from her. A couple of years later, Mihalek ran into Melania and asked why she'd never returned his favor with a call to tell him what happened, especially because he heard that she had gone to Milan. He said that her reaction was as memorable as her looks: flat and indifferent. He felt that she was so ambitious, so determined to be a success, that she had no time for stepping-stones like him.

Melania's first big modeling break came in 1992. Life was changing drastically all around her: the Soviet Union had collapsed, and the two million people of Slovenia declared their independence from Yugoslavia. In a decision that would greatly affect Melania, a thirty-two-year-old screenwriter she did not know, Marina Masowietsky, decided to create Slovenia's first modeling contest. The 1980s and early 1990s were the age of the supermodel: Linda Evangelista, Cindy Crawford, Stephanie Seymour, Naomi Campbell, Paulina Porizkova, and Claudia Schiffer. Their faces were splashed on the covers of glossy magazines, their lives tabloid fodder. As much as Hollywood actresses, supermodels were glamorous, famous, and rich. A single ad campaign could earn them $1 million or more; Linda Evangelista was famously quoted as saying about supermodels, "We don't wake up for less than $10,000 a day."

Masowietsky had a history of finding photogenic women for television programs and commercials. Capitalism was seductive, and she saw herself as an entrepreneur who could make a living out of her scouting talent and launch lucrative careers. For years, she had been approaching women on the street or anywhere she saw them, asking if they had ever thought about modeling or being on TV. "Some of these girls I stopped looked at me like I was from Mars," she said, as we talked in a restaurant near Rodeo Drive in Los Angeles, where she now works as a talent agent.

She was determined to find a Slovenian version of Claudia Schiffer, who had been spotted by the head of Paris's Metropolitan Model Agency at age seventeen in a Düsseldorf nightclub. Now, five years later, the German woman was among the most recognized models in the world. Masowietsky flew to Paris and went directly to see the famed Michel Levaton, who ran MMA. She didn't have an appointment, but she had a book of photos of Slovenian women and she was persuasive. She left with a letter promising the winner a contract at Metropolitan.

She called her modeling competition Face of the Year and enlisted as a sponsor the popular Slovenian women's magazine *Jana*. Melania was reading that magazine when she saw the picture of Schiffer alongside the headlines, "Young Beauties Marching on Europe!" and "Do you want to be on the catwalk with the best models in the world?"

Schiffer was twenty-one, Melania's age. She'd had a four-year head start, but Melania told friends that she thought modeling could be her ticket out of Slovenia. She read the details: the competition would be held in June in the seaside resort town of Portorož, and the winners would get contracts with major European modeling agencies. It sought "charming, long-legged, and appropriately thin Slovenian girls to make their mark on Europe as elite models." Melania clipped out the entry form and mailed it in. Two hundred other women between the ages of fifteen and twenty-three who were, as required, at least five-foot-eight also applied.

As Masowietsky sifted through the mountain of entry forms, rejecting most of them, she stopped at Melania's Stane Jerko photos and thought, "Yes, she could be a model. There is something there." She called Melania and arranged to meet at an outdoor café, well aware that many young women do not live up to the promise of their photos. Melania did. Masowietsky remembered thinking, "She could be in the top three for sure." In fact, Melania was better looking in person. "I liked her a lot. She was a bit serious. She's not the joking type. But she wanted to model, she wanted to travel. She was very professional and not chatty and talkative like the others."

Melania told Masowietsky that she had left her architecture studies to pursue modeling but might one day return to college. The fact that she had been admitted to such a difficult university program impressed Masowietsky. Melania and eleven others were ultimately selected as finalists. A winner would be chosen at a televised event held in Portorož. "She had the eyes of a tigress," recalled *Jana* editor Bernarda Jeklin, one of the judges. When the young contestants arrived, many joined the party scene, but not Melania, who faded into the background amid the effervescent personalities. "She was really quite anonymous," recalled Jeklin. "She was very, very introverted. She didn't talk to other competitors. She preferred to be in her own world."

The finale was held on a steamy Saturday in front of a few

hundred people. A stage was set up with a view of the Adriatic. Channel 1, Slovenian state TV, broadcast the show live. The *Jana* editor spotted Melania backstage and watched her studiously practice her walk alone. Melania had more experience on the catwalk than the other contestants, yet she was the only one practicing right up until the last minute. She looked twenty-two but acted older.

Onstage, the twelve finalists had been told not to make a sound, only to convey an impression, as they walked and turned in front of the judges. There was no onstage interview as there are in beauty pageants, but stage presence was only one factor for the judges, who also viewed contestants' photos. The photographs were a reality check. A model had to be photogenic, and the lens was kinder to some than others.

Petar Radović, the director of the event, said that Melania had a "very special face," but one that was so expressionless that it was impossible to know what she was thinking. He noted that her aqua eyes were memorable: "The color, the shape—those eyes!" Despite the impression she left, Melania did not win. First place and the Paris contract went to an eighteen-year old, and Melania tied for second place. When she was handed a bouquet, she did not smile. She did nothing. Masowietsky believes she expected to win. Others said she was disappointed when her name was called out as a runner-up, which meant that she was not the one heading to Paris. Instead, Melania received a contract with the RVR Reclame agency in Milan. It wasn't as prestigious as Metropolitan in Paris, but it was her next stop. She packed her bags and left for Italy a few days later. She was twenty-two in an industry that demanded youth. The clock was ticking.

MILAN WAS one of Europe's richest cities and the headquarters of Italy's fashion industry. The designers Giorgio Armani and Gianni Versace were rivals lifting Italian style and setting global fashion trends. Money washed through the city like spring rain running off the nearby Alps. In 1992, the annual per capita income in Yugoslavia was $4,200, while a supermodel could charge $20,000 for a fifteen-minute catwalk in Milan.

Melania arrived in the heat of the summer with a suitcase filled with clothes she and her mother had designed. Her first stop was the modest office of RVR. It had been founded by Vesna Zarkov, a striking blonde from the former Yugoslavia who came to Milan as a model and then started her own management firm. She had married a wealthy Italian and was pregnant, and RVR was now largely run by Dejan Markovic, a powerful personality from Serbia, one of the last remaining parts of Yugoslavia. Zarkov, the former model, thought that Melania was beautiful but needed training to make it in the high-fashion world. "Dejan was key," Zarkov said to me over dinner in Milan, at a hotel that she and her husband own. "Dejan saw her raw potential and helped prepare her for the runways."

But when I tracked down Markovic, who has become a significant player in the global modeling world, he told me that Melania the model was "created" in New York. Milan was crucial, perhaps even the most important step in her career, he said, but when he worked with her she was just beginning. Everything was new for her, and she only stayed at RVR for two or three months. Markovic would go on to start and run major modeling agencies and work in Milan and New York. I asked him about something that Italian photographers who'd attended the Slovenian Face of the Year contest had said to me: that it was not just Melania but many of the young women who did not smile or show emotion. "There were issues of that kind. We told them to be more open. They were very closed," he said. But Markovic insisted that Melania was not like others. She was "at a different level." He called her "the girl who never made mistakes—never." She went to the gym, dressed well, and never stayed out too late. She was educated, sophisticated. He never saw her with a boyfriend, which was unusual for a model, but believes her mother came to Milan. He added, "There is something about her that you cannot explain."

Markovic could not recall the details of Melania's modeling jobs. But others in Milan said that in this era, before online shopping, there were many photo shoots for catalogs. Models showed up for castings and then waited to hear if they were picked to model jeans or lingerie or some other item. Dashing from one casting call to another and competing against dozens, sometimes hundreds, of other women for a single job could be exhausting. Many models found it was hard not to take it personally when the phone didn't ring. "Fashion is a business of glamour, but it is also hard work," Melania said during the 2016 presidential campaign.

"There are ups and downs, high highs, and ridicule and rejection, too." To survive, models needed to believe they could make it and develop a thick skin. Melania's mother frequently called her daughter, bucking her up, assuring her success would come. But when *Jana* magazine asked Amalija how Melania's modeling career was progressing one month after she arrived in Milan, she was hardly effusive. "The girls have to stand for a long time in front of the cameras and all of that is very difficult work, but Melania does not complain."

It wasn't easy to make a living as a new model in town. "She was just one of the thousands of models around Milano in that period," said Sergio Salerni, a well-known figure in the Milan fashion industry. With the collapse of Communism, beautiful young women from Russia, Lithuania, Hungary, Czechoslovakia, and other countries were flooding into Milan. There seemed to be an endless supply of fresh faces. Even when a model got the job, agents often took up to 50 percent of her fee. Back in Slovenia, although she was landing modeling jobs, family friends heard that Melania felt "that her check was being stolen."

In Yugoslavia, everyone with the same job earned pretty much the same money, but in Milan there were huge disparities in the modeling industry. Unknown models earned a tiny fraction of what famous models were paid to headline the same fifteen-minute runway show. Big names appeared on one catwalk after another and earned as much as $300,000 in a single week, in cash. "Nobody asked about tax or anything. It was one of the most profitable things in the world," said Čedo Komljenović, a photographer and businessman born in Yugoslavia. He threw famous parties in Milan that Naomi Campbell, Linda Evangelista, and other celebrities attended. He said he knew Melania, too, and that at the time, the domination of the big stars was so strong that it left many other models in the shadows. Melania didn't break into the big leagues, but he described her as "very different, clear-eyed."

Lauren Gott, an American model who worked in Milan when Melania was there, explained the atmosphere: "If you had your wits about you, you could have a great time." But models burned out. To keep the pace even as they stayed razor-thin, many injected vitamins—under their toenails, to hide the needle marks. Some shot more than vitamins. During Fashion Week in Milan—and in London and New York—it was a common joke that all the river fish were high from all the drug residue in the urine that was being flushed into the wastewater system. "It was very decadent and very unapologetic in being decadent," said Anna Momigliano, an Italian journalist who has written extensively about those years. Models typically stayed together in dorm-like apartments because they came and went so frequently, often staying just a few months in one place. PierCarlo Borgogelli, who worked at RVR and was a judge in the Slovenian contest in which Melania was a runner-up, recalls, "Many of these girls destroyed these places. You wouldn't believe it. They were young, there were drugs, they had orgies."

The residences—including one famously known as Clitoride, Italian for "clitoris"—were magnets for a certain kind of man. Men known as "PRs," who worked in public relations to advertise nightclubs, often stood outside the apartments, offering free rides to casting calls and free drinks and food to models who came to their clubs. Borgogelli recalled that the city was full of wealthy playboys, and that it was not uncommon for a model to meet a man at a disco who would say, "How about going on a yacht with me to Monte Carlo?" Then they would be gone.

Borgogelli said maybe only 10 percent of the aspiring models in Milan were really serious about their careers. Many had come from small towns in poorer countries, and their goal was "to find a rich guy to marry." Whatever Melania wanted in a husband, she also was seeking a successful career of her own. "She told me something about her mother being very, very ambitious for the daughters. Sort of groomed her to do something special . . . to become rich," said a person who has known Melania for many years. She stayed away from the drugs and hard party scene and kept herself so apart that she often did not even chat with other models at auditions. Her closest friends were her mother and her sister, now a designer and artist. Melania was constantly in touch with both of them, and Slovenian neighbors said her sister lived with her for a time in Milan.

Slovenia was an easy trip from Italy, and after a short stint at RVR in Milan, Melania returned home. As models often do, she began traveling to wherever she found work—and a photographer remembered that she even spent a few days at sea modeling for a company that sold boats. In 1993, she shot a short video that aired on Slovenian TV, playing the role of the first female president of the United States. "It's the most extraordinary historical coincidence" that Melania ended up in the White House, said Jožica Brodarič, a well-known fashion journalist who wrote the script. In the video, Melania wore clothes, shoes, and accessories made by Slovenian brands. Andrej Košak, the director, said that the idea was that in their newly independent country, more women were in the market for stylish clothes to wear to the office. He thought that the Oval Office idea was clever, and Melania was cast to play the female president. Košak even inserted archival footage from John F. Kennedy's 1960 presidential campaign. A Swissair jet was used as Air Force One, and a maroon Chevy Caprice Classic was the presidential limo. The Slovenian Ministry of the Interior lent police cars and a couple of officers to film the motorcade.

In the video, Melania steps out of a plane, wearing a tan women's business suit and a trench coat with padded shoulders. She waves to the crowd, descends the steps as two uniformed military officers salute her, and makes a brief statement to reporters. "The shoot was very relaxed and fun," recalled Brodarič. As refined and elegant as Melania was, Brodarič said, no one could have guessed how closely her life would imitate the role she played in the video. At the time, Melania was aiming to find work as a model in the United States and was inching closer by way of other cities in Europe.

THE MARQUEE modeling firm in Milan at the time was Riccardo Gay, the agency to which photographer Nino Mihalek had sent photographs of Melania. She used her connections and determination to move to Gay's agency, which handled some of the biggest models in the world, including Naomi Campbell and Linda Evangelista. "At Riccardo Gay, it was sink or swim," said a woman who knew Melania. "It's a business. The client calls and says he wants brunettes and the booker tells all her brunettes—maybe all the brunettes with blue eyes—to show up at five o'clock. Then brunettes from other agencies go, too, and they all might stand in line for two hours, three hours. And then you get the book—or not."

Gay told me in 2018 that he represented Melania for maybe a year and a half. "She was a beautiful, professional lady." He doesn't remember the first time he met her but called her a "commercial model." In fashion-speak, commercial models typically did catalog work and wore or posed alongside something a client was selling in a TV, billboard, or print advertisement. They were distinct from "high-fashion" models, who did more sought-after work, including designer fashion shows and prestigious magazine covers.

Sergio Salerni, who has the largest video archives of Milan runway shows, said he does not believe Melania appeared in any of the major ones. As many as one hundred fashion shows were held during Fashion Week, when the world's most famous models and photographers descended on the city. The buzzy shows by Valentino, Gucci, or Dolce & Gabbana, or those that featured famous models, got the attention. "Melania to me is—a nice, beautiful lady," said Salerni, "but if you ask me, 'Do you remember her in one show?' I say, 'No, I don't remember her.'"

A woman who knew her at the time recalled, "She would shoot in Milan and then Paris, then Vienna. It was all a circle. Germany had a lot of catalog work." Melania talked to friends about New York, where models earned the most. But getting someone to sponsor a work visa was not easy, and the competition for one was steep, since many models wanted to go.

Today, it seems as if Melania left few traces in Milan. There are different explanations for the lack of information and also why so many people are so hesitant to talk about her. "I *choose* to forget," said one person, explaining why he denied knowing her until I showed him a picture of the two of them together. The early 1990s were particularly tumultuous in Milan. Italy was reeling from a massive political corruption scandal that would lead to the indictments of more than three thousand people and realign the nation's politics. The arrests began the year Melania arrived. At the same time, some modeling firms were also being investigated for not paying taxes, for ripping off models, and for not getting proper immigration papers for their foreign models. But Borgogelli, who worked for her first agency, also offered another reason. He said being associated with Melania is not a credential to highlight. "She was not a big model. Yes, she did some catalogs. But for agents, you want to say, 'I can make you a supermodel,' not, 'I can make you the wife of a rich man.' It's better in the industry to be known as 'I can make you Cindy Crawford' rather than the wife of [former Italian prime minister Silvio] Berlusconi or Trump."

• • •

MELANIA'S JOURNEY to New York took her through Vienna and to the office of Wolfgang Schwarz. He scouted for John Casablancas's Elite agency and also ran his own modeling firm. Like others before him, Schwarz saw that Melania had an "amazing smile" and beautiful eyes, but he also said that she had trouble connecting with some clients because her English was "very poor." German is the official language in Austria, and he presumed she did not speak German, or at least not well, because he didn't hear her speak it. She did, however, land a competitive job, a television commercial for Lauda Air, the holiday airline started by Austrian Formula One world racing champion Niki Lauda. The casting director wanted someone with a smile and a big, hearty laugh, and Melania delivered. She appeared in the TV commercial and on huge billboards dressed in a flight attendant uniform and wearing a red baseball cap that said PARIS. She was on screen for less than three seconds and did not speak, but Schwarz remembers that she was paid thousands of dollars.

Around age twenty-three or twenty-four, Melania was earning enough money and getting enough work to live in Paris. She shared a flat not far from Notre Dame Cathedral with a younger model, a blonde from Sweden named Victoria Silvstedt, who at nineteen had represented her country in the 1993 Miss World pageant. Silvstedt described their place as a small apartment. There was no elevator in the sixth-floor walk-up, so she and Melania used the stairs for exercise. "This was the time before cell phones. We were in a different country without speaking the language," Silvstedt told *Women's Wear Daily*. "I don't think I could have asked for a better roommate, actually." But she added that those years were tough. In interviews in Europe, Silvstedt said that the subway trips to auditions were endless and sometimes to rough parts of the city. She credited her tight family for getting her through it and said she could see how close Melania was to her family, too.

She and Melania were constantly worried about calories and weight gain. She remembered opting for simple dishes, like tuna out of a can, instead of heavy French meals. When they splurged one night, Melania said, "Come on, we'll run down the stairs, so we do not gain weight.'" Silvstedt remembered Melania "never wanted the attention. She was always very quiet." But she kept working. "She was motivated by the idea of helping her family financially," Silvstedt added. "Melania was very in control. Much more calm than me." She said Melania's work ethic inspired her, and that they both kept going to the next casting.

Silvstedt recalled that Melania would talk about screen legend Sophia Loren. "Obviously, she was her style icon," she said. "I want to do something great," Melania told Silvstedt one day. "I want to be bigger than Sophia Loren." Silvstedt added that the idea of aiming to be even *more* famous than one of the greatest Hollywood stars was remarkable.

A decade later, when she was Donald Trump's girlfriend, a *Vogue* article on Melania linked her to Loren: "When you spend time around Melania, you hear a lot of celebrity comparisons, 'She's like a young Sophia Loren' being one of the most frequent." Trump himself seemed to be fascinated with Loren; before he met Melania, he claimed the actress bought a place in Trump Tower when it opened in the 1980s, although Loren denied it. Newt Gingrich, who met Melania when he was a contender for vice president, chimed in at inauguration time: "Melania Trump is simply the most beautiful first lady in American history." And, misspelling Loren's name, he tweeted: "She brings a Sophia Lauren look to the White House."

Silvstedt would be selected as *Playboy*'s 1997 Playmate of the Year and the face of Guess Jeans. "It's kind of surreal," the Swedish model told *Inside Edition*, when asked what she thought about her former roommate being first lady. "But I guess, you know, that's America. Anything is possible in America, right?"

Melania, who was moving around Europe following the jobs, said she got a visa to come to New York with the help of an Italian agent in Milan who was scouting models. That man was Paolo Zampolli, a wealthy Italian who became executive vice president of a model management office in New York. Zampolli and Melania were born a month apart in 1970, but they grew up very differently. His father owned Harbert, a toy manufacturing company that sold the Easy-Bake Oven, Star Wars figures, and many popular toys. He said he was distantly related to Pope Paul VI, grew up skiing in the Alps, and frequently yachted off the island of Ibiza, a playground for the rich. When Zampolli was eighteen, his father died in a skiing accident, and the family business was sold to a company controlled by Silvio Berlusconi, who would become Italy's prime minister.

Like other wealthy young men in Milan, Zampolli hung

around the city's vibrant modeling and party scene. He threw parties and met everybody, including John Casablancas, the legendary creator of many models' images and careers. Zampolli, who dated several models, got into the modeling business himself and began scouting for women to bring to New York. He said in an interview that when he met Melania, she was beautiful and, unlike many other models, she was "stable and focused." His New York agency, Metropolitan, arranged her visa to the United States. Melania, tight-lipped about many things, has been particularly silent about whom she dated before she arrived in New York, but several men have publicly said that they dated her. As she was preparing to move to New York, people who knew her said that a Frenchman had called a few people, frantically trying to reach her, telling one that she had abruptly returned the car he had given her as a present. Her reason, it seems, was simple: she was moving on, heading to the city she had been reading about for years.

Melania and New York roommate Matthew Atanian

CHAPTER 4

Making Her Way in Manhattan

IN EARLY 1996, fashion photographer Matthew Atanian was swimming in the indoor pool at Zeckendorf Towers, the Gramercy Park apartment building where he lived. A man approached him as he stepped out of the water and said, with disarming bluntness, "Hello, my name is Paolo. How do you have so many beautiful girls?"

Atanian had seen him before in the building. He was about Atanian's age, in his midtwenties, a handsome guy with slicked-back dark hair. Atanian had noticed that when the man swam laps, he was careful not to get his perfectly combed hair wet. Atanian was amused by the question. He photographed all kinds of beautiful models, many of whom were friends; they visited him at the Zeckendorf and looked gorgeous around the swimming pool. Atanian learned that Paolo's last name was Zampolli and that he worked at Metropolitan. He had a taste for limos, exclusive nightclubs, and extravagant parties. Atanian was from Worcester, Massachusetts, and even in New York, he remained a low-key New Englander. In spite of their differences, the two men struck up a friendship. Another day by the pool, Paolo had a proposal. "Matthew, you need a roommate? I bring you a nice girl, not like the sixteen- and seventeen-year-olds in the model house. I bring you real girl. And she's clean and normal and nice."

It made sense to Atanian. His last roommate had just left, and he needed help with the rent. He understood the transient life of models, especially the ones arriving from overseas, and agreed to take in the new arrival, Melania Knauss.

Atanian remembered being surprised when Zampolli first brought Melania to his apartment. She was well past the traditional age for aspiring fashion models. And she was a curiosity. He liked her. She moved into a makeshift bedroom carved out of a small dining space and tucked behind a Styrofoam wall in their apartment. The previous tenant, Atanian's pal who was a drummer in a rock band, had erected the faux wall between the kitchen and the dining area to create just enough room for a futon.

To get to her space, Melania had to walk through the compact galley kitchen of the 1,200-square-foot apartment. Atanian let her hang her clothes in a small coat closet. They shared the bathroom, which was off the living room, their communal hangout space. There wasn't much privacy, which was awkward when Atanian brought girlfriends home. It was less a problem for Melania, who never brought anyone home.

Melania's dream was visible many mornings from her kitchen

window, where she could see the supermodel Paulina Porizkova, then the wife of Ric Ocasek, the lead singer of the rock group the Cars, exercising in her apartment. Five years older than Melania, Porizkova was part of the first wave of supermodels and in 1984, at age eighteen, became the first Central European woman ever on the cover of *Sports Illustrated*'s famous swimsuit issue. Born in Czechoslovakia, she was a lodestar for a generation of models from Central and Eastern Europe—and she had even married a rich, famous American man. Porizkova seemed to be living a fantasy life, outside the window of Melania's little cubby. Going to casting calls and reliably paying her share of Atanian's monthly rent, she saw success all around her. It was so close, yet it wasn't hers.

Zampolli told me that he paid for Melania to fly to New York in the summer of 1996, when she was twenty-six. A lawyer working for Melania said she initially arrived on a visitor's visa in August 1996 and by October she had been granted an H-1B work visa. Zampolli said that he arranged for the visa so that she could work for him at Metropolitan. Models are eligible for an H-1B if they can show "distinguished merit or ability" in their field. Those visas were much easier to obtain in 1996 than they are now.

Paolo Zampolli has been a rare constant around Melania for more than two decades. He said that two years after she arrived in New York, he introduced her to Donald Trump. Zampolli worked for a while in international development for Trump real estate projects. He also started his own real estate firm and in 2006 was in the news for using catwalk models to help sell Manhattan's priciest condos and penthouses. The Italian is now an ambassador to the small Caribbean island of Dominica. He maintains extraordinary access to the White House and Mar-a-Lago. His Instagram account is proof of that access, featuring players in the ever-changing landscape of Trump World: Mike Pompeo, Wilbur Ross, Ben Carson, Rudy Giuliani, Kellyanne Conway, John Kelly, Rod Rosenstein, and even Fox News superfan Jeanine Pirro. He posts photos of himself with Trump, Melania, and Barron. He has been photographed in the Rose Garden and at Thanksgiving turkey pardons, and he displays online his engraved White House invitations. He is a special planet orbiting close to the Trump sun.

Zampolli often seems to act as if he is Melania's image manager. He has been frequently quoted in news stories about Melania and seems to be one of few friends permitted to discuss her publicly. He talks and talks, often with his amiable smile, but always fiercely defending her, jousting with anyone who would question her or Trump, sometimes even threatening lawsuits.

Over the last two years, I always felt Zampolli's presence close by. My conversations with people in New York, Paris, Milan, Vienna, and Slovenia seemed to find their way back to him. Zampolli's allegiance is total. "Mary u know i love my President more then the mother of my child," he told me in his typically exaggerated style in an email in 2019. He also offered some advice for this book: "the title should be OUR Magnificent FIRST LADY."

He seems to have advised some people to make sure their memories are foggy. Atanian, now retired and living in Massachusetts, told me that Zampolli told him to "bury" the old days.

Atanian said that he'd always liked Melania and that she "didn't do anything wrong." Despite Zampolli's insistence, Atanian talked to me freely and candidly. "Now he is a politician," he said. "Before he was just a model agent."

From the moment Melania arrived in New York, Zampolli was always in her life. But even with his help, the New York modeling scene was a tough slog. On many nights, from her tiny makeshift bedroom, Melania Knauss would pick up the phone and dial the numbers she knew by heart: 011 to call overseas, 386 for Slovenia. Then her parents' phone number in Sevnica.

As she sat and waited for the distinctive European ring, she could gaze out the window of the tenth-floor apartment and see the glittering lights of Manhattan high-rises. Melania had arrived in New York just as Mayor Rudy Giuliani (who later became Donald Trump's personal lawyer) was making good on his promise to clean up the city. Times Square peep shows and sex shops were replaced by family-friendly stores like the Gap and the Disney Store, as well as movie theaters and restaurants. Crime was down; tourism and the stock market were up. The New York Yankees were marching toward their first World Series championship in almost twenty years, led by American League Rookie of the Year Derek Jeter.

After 11:00 p.m., the international calling rates fell dramatically. It was dawn in Slovenia, and Melania could talk to her mother before she left for her shift at the factory. One old friend said the combination of Melania's "persistence" and her mother's guiding hand helped her not lose sight of her goals. "So many other girls starting out in modeling in those days—eighty, ninety percent—would get confused, party too much, start dating left and right, never made anything of themselves. She was never like that."

It was hard to be an ascetic in the hypersexualized world of modeling and fashion. But Melania came close, Atanian recalled. She was no recluse, but her taste ran more toward spending evenings watching *Friends* or reading fashion magazines. He admired her steady routine, which included eating seven fruits and vegetables a day. She didn't drink alcohol. She walked around the house with weights on her ankles to keep her legs toned. Her focus seemed clear: to become a success. Melania was resolved and determined, to the point of sometimes seeming a little cold to those outside her small, closed circle.

Her late-night calls with her mother provided regular pep talks and strategy sessions with the most important influence in her life. Her mother gave her a lift as she navigated a competitive industry in a competitive city. Atanian had seen a parade of successful models through his camera lens, and he thought Melania didn't seem to have "it." Atanian recalled an old girlfriend who had modeled for Benetton and J.Crew. When she relaxed, she would often wear jeans and a man's dress shirt with the sleeves rolled up, and "she looked like she had just walked off a set." Melania, on the other hand, would try a similar style, and, to Atanian, it just didn't look right. "She just couldn't wear them in the same way," he said. "That to me describes what the 'it' is."

Every time a male friend met his beautiful Slovenian roommate, Atanian heard the same question. "You're hitting that, right?"—asking if he was having sex with Melania. "I'd say no, I don't feel any attraction to her whatsoever," Atanian said. "And they'd always look at me in disbelief. Like she was so good looking that I'd be crazy not to try to get involved with her. No one ever would believe me when I'd say we were just friends." And Melania routinely rejected the periodic advances of Atanian's friends.

He was used to Melania walking around in her robe and bedroom slippers the same way Rachel and Monica, the characters played by Jennifer Aniston and Courteney Cox, did on the hit TV sitcom *Friends*. They would order Chinese takeout. It was very much like dorm life. Sometimes he would take her picture as she modeled clothes her mother or sister had made for her, or in whatever she happened to be wearing. "It would be like, well, you're a model and I'm a photographer, so let's do what we do," he said.

Atanian's photos show a beautiful young woman, often without makeup, with no high-gloss finish. It wasn't lost on either of them that Atanian was in a position to help a struggling young model. He did a lot of work for the magazine *Marie Claire*, and she would ask him, "Matthew, when can you send me through to casting?"

He told her that he had no control over such things, which wasn't true. He simply didn't want to see her get hurt. There was a wide gulf between commercial modeling and editorial modeling for high-end fashion photos in *Vogue* and *Harper's Bazaar*, or even *Marie Claire*. "Melania was commercial at best. She was never going to achieve her dream of doing editorial," Atanian told me, adding, "A true editorial model has a certain relationship with the camera lens, in her face and in the way she moves, as if the model gives life to the photograph with her sheer power and chemistry. There's just something in the picture that you can't describe, but certain models have it."

Atanian, who now watches Melania on TV, believes that today she is still trying to assert herself as a supermodel, down to her stiletto heels and expensive clothes. "She always thought if something had a big price tag on it, it was beautiful. I learned from my mom, you can get something from Marshall's, and if the right woman wears it correctly, it's stunning. That's how I can best describe an editorial model. She can transform the clothes, not the other way around. Melania just could never do that."

A woman who worked as a booker for Zampolli at the time remembered Melania's first year in the United States. A "road mom" to many newly arrived young models, she helped them with doctor's appointments; some needed dentistry or wanted other cosmetic changes. She lent young models money and offered a shoulder to cry on—but not to Melania. "Melania was fully formed" and not in need of much help. "When she came, there was an air of she was a star already." She was dressed exquisitely and expensively, not a hair out of place, no need for money, no complaining, no need for a place to live, no sense of struggle at all. "She was a completed product—she was very polished, *very* polished." Even when this booker went to see Melania very early in the morning at Zeckendorf Towers, she would find her dressed in nice pajamas, not a T-shirt or anything less than perfect. Melania was formal—polite and sweet, but distant. "She never let her guard down."

She also spent a lot of time alone. "She wasn't friends with anyone, and you have to understand how unusual that is," the woman added. Also, despite having worked for years in Europe, she had remarkably few photos in her portfolio. It was filled with "test shots"—professional photos, not published work.

ON A cold late fall day in New York while she was still living with Atanian, Melania agreed to a nude photo shoot that would cause ripples in the presidential campaign twenty years later. It is common for models to do nude photo shoots at some point during their career, and Melania was no exception. This job entailed posing for *Max*, a racy French magazine. Not only would she be naked, but she would also be asked to strike suggestive and provocative poses with another woman, a Swedish model named Emma Eriksson.

The photographer was Jarl Alé de Basseville, an eccentric personality who was briefly married to supermodel Inés Rivero, and for years dated actress Kiera Chaplin, granddaughter of screen legend Charlie Chaplin. "I always loved women together, because I have been with a lot of women who desired the ménage à trois," de Basseville said of the shoot. Born in France, he knew many well-connected and wealthy people in the worlds of fashion, photography, and art.

Melania was not paid for the shoot, de Basseville said—a common arrangement for lesser-known models to gain exposure that can lead to other work. In a 2018 interview at the Café de Flore on the Boulevard Saint-Germain in Paris, de Basseville told me that on the day of the shoot, Melania arrived at a rented apartment near Twenty-Sixth Street and Sixth Avenue in the afternoon. He remembered her as being "cold" during the shoot, not bantering much with him or the makeup artists and stylists in the room, but being professional and hardworking. Emma Eriksson later described Melania to reporters as quiet and shy. She said that the two of them hardly spoke during the shoot, which involved them lying together nude in several poses, cheek to cheek, with their arms around each other.

A second series of photos, taken at night on a rooftop, shows Eriksson wearing a black bustier and stockings and holding a whip. In some of the photos, Melania wears a tight-fitting floor-length gown by designer John Galliano, who became head designer at French fashion house Christian Dior. When Melania married Trump in 2005, she wore a Galliano dress.

In other photos from the de Basseville shoot, Melania wore white lace panties under an open coat. Some shots depicted the two women embracing lustily; in one, Eriksson appears to threaten to whip an anxious Melania. Full-length nudes of Melania show her holding her hands coyly in front of her crotch.

Max handed the photos to Ann Scott, a young French novelist and former model, and asked her to create a story to accompany them, an erotic fairy tale of sex and domination between two women, told from the point of view of Melania's character. In Scott's steamy fiction, the two women meet at a party and are drawn to each other. "Sitting on the edge of the bed, I timidly lifted my buttocks one after the other to let my underwear slide off . . . I opened my thighs and closed them around her waist. She began to pinch the tip of my breast between her fingers while her mouth tightened around the other . . . She slid along my stomach and placed her cheek on my hip. She stayed that way drawing circles around my belly button. Pensive. Then she went lower, propped up my hip with her shoulder, then plunged with her mouth and took me . . ." The story had nothing to do with Melania Knauss. It was very possible that she never saw the text or even knew exactly how *Max* would use the photos. But there she was, tantalizing the magazine's readers.

The florid two-girl fantasy was laid out in an eight-page spread in *Max*'s February 1997 edition, which featured Cindy Crawford on the cover, her breasts covered by a small sweater, naked from the waist down, with nothing but a sheet between her legs. In the end, it was more reminiscent of the pages of *Penthouse* than of the art de Basseville said he intended. The *Max* photos remained a little-known part of Melania's past until her husband decided to run for president. By then, de Basseville had run into trouble with the law and spent time in federal prison on charges of conspiracy to launder money and distribute Ecstasy. Journalists began contacting him for the photographs. The *New York Post* unearthed the photos, including several of the full-length nudes of the GOP front-runner's wife, and published them on Saturday,

July 30, 2016. Melania appeared nude on the tabloid's cover, her nipples obscured beneath blue stars, under the headline "The Ogle Office." The next day, another cover featured Melania's nude embrace of Eriksson. "Melania Trump had an impressive body of work long before she met The Donald," the *Post* noted drily.

The *Max* photo spread didn't catapult Melania's career, but she kept looking for ways to break through. Two women who worked with her at Zampolli's agency said she always showed up for a casting and did get selected for some lingerie ads and catalog work. But there were also days when she would come into the agency and be given the time and place to audition but not get the job. Yet Melania always seemed unfazed. The office was awash in rumors that she had some wealthy boyfriend, maybe in Europe, helping her. People thought that this also explained why she never seemed interested in going out and was not pressed for money. Atanian, her roommate, had no memory of her mentioning a Paris boyfriend. He noticed that she did occasionally go to dinner for a few hours with wealthy older men who drove nice cars, including a lawyer with a Porsche, but she always came back home.

Atanian had always wanted a Ferrari, and Melania knew it, so for Christmas, she bought him a Hot Wheels selection of five toy Ferraris. She talked to him, posed for candid photos, shared stories about her family. But never confided anything too personal.

Federico Pignatelli, a wealthy Italian living in New York,

said that Melania called him "the very first day she landed in New York." They had a connection: his mother was from Slovenia. Pignatelli owned Pier59 Studios, a vast space in Manhattan. Some 2,500 ads a year were shot in his studios. For Melania, new to New York, Pignatelli was a fantastic contact to make. During an interview about his efforts to improve working conditions and rights for models, he mentioned that he knew Melania and had been struck by her poise. But what stood out for him, he said, was that "she was not one of these models that would just talk and talk and talk. She would only talk when she really had something to say."

He said that she had the same serious work ethic that many young models from Central or Eastern Europe had at the time. "They were beautiful women and they were hungry to work," said Pignatelli. "They were very disciplined; they really wanted to make money, and they were working very hard. Other models were a little bit less motivated." Melania's biggest problem was that she arrived in New York at age twenty-six, "a little too late for New York." Pignatelli added: "Her career was really cut short by her meeting Donald Trump." But he said that while that may have hurt her career, it gave her a family and a life that is "enviable, honestly."

Melania's gateway to New York modeling was Zampolli, but he had limited experience in big-time model management. He also soon had a serious falling-out with Thomas Zeumer, the president of his modeling firm. In a sworn affidavit, one of Zampolli's bookers, Michele August, said that Zampolli knew "next to nothing about this business, and indeed was supposed to sit next to me to learn how the business operates, but he never did so." She called Zampolli a "pure neophyte" who never "made any positive contributions toward the day-to-day operation of the business." Others said similar things under oath.

Zampolli loved the glitz. He threw lots of parties and drove a Rolls-Royce. His models were invited to dinners, gallery openings, and high-profile social events. The restaurant Cipriani would offer half-price meals to models so they would linger at the bar. "We always had dinner parties, always at Cipriani—we were always out," a booker told me. "People want to be around beautiful people. Someone would pick up the bill, I don't know who did. It was a way to see and be seen."

Zampolli told me that he met Donald Trump before Melania came to the United States. He was typically vague about the details. By the time Melania arrived in New York, Zampolli was already doing Trump-like work in courting the gossip writers at the *New York Post*'s Page Six. He would tip off reporters to celebrities at parties and then often appear in the newspaper photos next to them. He saw how Trump would use lavish parties, head-turning models, and outlandish stunts to get press attention and realized it could work for him, too. By my count, Zampolli has had more than one hundred twenty Page Six mentions since 1996.

In 1998, *Playboy* magazine named Trump and Zampolli two of "New York's Top 10 Playboys." These were ten men who the magazine believed "personify life, liberty and the pursuit of dreams." It was quite a list, including Derek Jeter, Leonardo

DiCaprio, Mark Wahlberg, Sean "Puffy" Combs, and a Tribeca hotel owner who rented rooms to models only.

Melania, too, had finally gotten a break, the one that she hoped would build her career. Sitting on a red velvet couch in a dark lounge, apparently wearing little more than two rings, a thick diamond bracelet, and a stone-cold "what-are-you-gonna-do-about it?" look, Melania was nine stories tall, gazing out from a billboard on the side of an apartment building in Manhattan's Times Square during July, August, and September of 1997. She held a martini in one hand and a Camel Light cigarette in the other, a wavy wisp of smoke curling up toward the ad campaign's teaser language: "What You're Looking For."

In addition to the billboard, the ad ran in *Rolling Stone* and other magazines, as part of a campaign for the R. J. Reynolds Tobacco Company. The cigarette campaign was created as an alternative to the "Joe Camel" ads that R. J. Reynolds had run for years, which had come under fire as being geared toward kids. "Camel is embracing night life and sophistication and an urban feeling," company spokesman Richard Williams told the *New York Times*. Dr. Robert Jackler, a researcher at Stanford University who studies the impact of tobacco advertising, told me "sex sells" and Melania's cigarette ad is "seductive, sexually charged, urban sophisticated, edgy." Melania was part of a particular subset of models the campaign was looking for. For a change, bookers weren't focused on teens or models with the hollow "heroin chic" look. By law, models had to be at least twenty-five to advertise cigarettes. (The following year, most cigarette advertising was banned entirely in the United States.) R. J. Reynolds was taking no chances, and initially said it wanted models over thirty for its new adult-oriented campaign. But as one person involved in the campaign said, "It was hard to find a model over thirty who didn't look like a mom."

"There were certainly hundreds of twenty-five-year-old girls who wanted that job," said an art director who worked on the campaign and was with Melania at the photo shoot. Melania had turned twenty-seven that April. "She exuded a lot of sexiness, but there was also a bit of composure and restraint to that," the art director said. "It wasn't sex-sexy, it was just sort of beautiful sexy." She said she couldn't tell if Melania was a smoker or just a good actress who made it seem like she was a smoker. "She played the part very well," she said. "She smoked for us and she made it seem like she was doing it naturally."

The photo campaign, shot by famed fashion photographer Ellen von Unwerth, was seen by the cigarette maker as a major success. One fan of the photo was clearly Melania herself. In April 2010, Regine Mahaux, a Belgian who frequently photographs the Trumps, was in their Trump Tower apartment. One photo Mahaux took was in what appears to be Melania's dressing room, and in the background it shows that alongside roses and perfume on her vanity counter is a framed shot of Melania, about 8 × 10, from the cigarette ad that once towered above the crowds near Times Square.

•   •   •

A FREQUENT question in the worlds of modeling and fashion is whether models have had plastic surgery, including breast augmentation. In 2016, Melania denied having any surgery on her chest or face. "I didn't make any changes . . . I'm against Botox, I'm against injections . . . It's all me. I will age gracefully." Three photographers who have worked with Melania told me that Melania did. Atanian said that in January 1997, she returned from a Christmas trip to Europe looking more buxom. After a model who knew Melania well got her breasts enlarged, she booked many more jobs and earned a fortune. The careers of many models changed after they had surgery. A half-dozen New York bookers, including some who worked for Zampolli when Melania was at his agency, told me they each had cosmetic surgeons on speed dial for their models, often sending them to Chicago, Washington, D.C., and other cities where the prices were cheaper than New York City.

Atanian said that Melania lived with him for a year, and that he noticed during their last months together that her calls to her mother became less frequent and that she began going out more. He then left New York, returning to Massachusetts to take care of his ailing mother, and Melania found a new place to live. Atanian recalled that she moved to a one-bedroom apartment in a brownstone off Park Avenue, just south of Grand Central Terminal, on a cross street in the Thirties. He said that he talked to her on the steps there once, and that they stayed in touch and spoke on the phone off and on until the following year, when Melania's life changed forever.

Donald Trump and Melania Knauss in 1999

CHAPTER 5

"He wanted my number, but . . .
I didn't give it to him"

ON SEPTEMBER 8, 1998, a half-dozen Slovenian journalists waited in the opulent living room of Suite 211 at the Hotel Lutetia, a luxury landmark in the pricey Saint-Germain-des-Prés neighborhood of Paris. They could see movement and shadows through a translucent glass door. A hairdresser and makeup artist were applying finishing touches to the mysterious woman they had been summoned to interview. Days before, editors at Slovenia's main publications had received phone calls offering journalists a free flight and an elegant meal in Paris along with a group interview with a "world-famous" fashion model born in Slovenia. Now, after flying six hundred miles in a private jet, they were waiting to meet Melania Knauss.

Most of the journalists had never heard her name. Nor did they know who had organized the event, but a free trip to Paris, and a visit to a hotel where a bottle of water cost more than a

Slovenian meal, was hard to turn down. Finally, a fashion photographer named Partho Ghosh appeared. "No photography, please," he said, insisting that anyone with a camera leave it in the hallway. The journalists pondered the concept of a camera-shy model.

Big-name celebrities sometimes banned cameras at interviews because a candid shot risked being unflattering. They preferred handing out preselected glossy photos, but no one handed out any such photos, although they did share one magazine cover, from *Harper's Bazaar En Español*, which featured a natural-looking Melania in a sheer black camisole. Though not as prestigious as being in the U.S. *Harper's Bazaar*, the cover was an important early accomplishment for Melania.

A young public relations executive, Tamara Deu, asked the journalists to focus their questions on Melania's career, adding, "No personal questions." Finally, they heard the words "Melania is coming!"

One reporter, Sebastijan Kopušar, was shocked. He had seen this woman in the hotel lobby a short time before. But she had looked like the "girl next door," and nothing like the model standing before him. *Who the hell is Melania Knauss?* he thought. "She went from normal to being a woman with this professional facade, with full makeup and without any emotions," he said. It was as if she had put on a "uniform and was completely something else."

Melania greeted them in Slovenian and began talking about herself. Her confidence was as striking as her big blue eyes, and she spoke to the journalists for hours. Within weeks, Melania's name would appear in the New York tabloids' gossip columns;

she was identified as the date of wealthy New York businessman Donald Trump. But this moment in Paris was all hers.

While the pitch had been to meet "world-famous" Melania Knauss, the journalists didn't take her too seriously. One reporter bluntly asked, "Since no one in Slovenia actually knows much about you, could you first give us some basic information about yourself?"

She laid out her story: She was born and raised in a small town. At nineteen, she won a contest at Rome's Cinecittà film studios. She left the architecture program at the University of Ljubljana before the end of her first year of studies to pursue modeling. She had lived in Milan, then Paris, and "for the past two years, my address is on Park Avenue in New York City."

At times, her story seemed to veer into exaggeration or pure confection. She described a luxurious life as one of the highest-paid models in the world and added that she was "among the top 50" internationally, according to multiple articles published right after the press conference. "I know some of the top models personally, as well as other famous personalities, like Elton John, Jon Bon Jovi," Melania said. "Sometimes we get together, or we see one another at various events." The Vienna office of Elite models was representing her, she said, and "other big agencies are trying to get me. People all over the world know my name and my work."

A reporter, incredulous, asked for confirmation of the fact that she was one of the highest-paid models in the world.

"Yes, yes, I am," Melania replied.

She also announced that she was heading to Hollywood. She said that she had just been selected for a role in a movie starring

Mickey Rourke. "It's all been agreed to and we will start film-ing shortly," Melania said. No, she wasn't nervous about her big-screen debut. "I have spent so much time in front of a camera; I am immune to stage fright," she said.

The conversation continued over a meal of fig salad, grilled eggplant, and mushroom risotto. As waiters poured glasses of Bordeaux for the reporters, Melania talked about the thrill of her movie deal. "I am really excited," she said. The foreign correspon-dent Boštjan Videmšek, who sat beside her, mentioned that Kim Basinger, who started out as a model, had just won an Academy Award. He noted also that it was a movie with Mickey Rourke— the erotic *9½ Weeks*—that had initially gotten her noticed a de-cade earlier. So, he said, maybe Melania was also on her way to winning an Oscar. "Slowly, slowly," she replied with a smile.

Melania said she did not have a favorite designer, preferring clothes she created herself, and, yes, maybe she would start her own clothing line one day. She mentioned that she had traveled to daz-zling capitals and gorgeous beaches. The Caribbean island of An-guilla "takes my breath away." New York City received her highest praise. "It's paradise," she said. "This is the city I have fallen in love with." Someone asked her if she had acquired U.S. citizenship. "No," she said. "Would I be happy to have an additional citizenship? Why not? The more you have, the more doors in the world might be open to you." She said that, with the exception of her parents and sister, she had lost contact with just about everyone else in Slovenia.

Melania spoke Slovenian throughout the press conference, the meal, and in individual interviews. No one heard her speak

French that day, to a waiter, or to anyone. Occasionally, English words or phrases would pop up. Reporters who were there recalled her sounding smart and savvy. But every so often, her voice and vocabulary changed, and suddenly the worldly sophisticate also sounded young and innocent.

As she sat for a separate Slovenian TV interview, and with the camera rolling, Melania let her blue-gray suede jacket slip off, one shoulder at a time. She acted like she didn't even notice. Her shoulders were suddenly bare, her silky camisole low-cut. "Were you ever asked to be a seductive woman?" a reporter asked. "Or, if you were asked, how do you do that?"

Melania paused. "Well, yes, it happens," she replied. "You can do that with your eyes. You talk to the photographer and figure out what to do together. He tells you what he wants. And you have to feel it inside so you can express it, because a photograph shows everything."

"Yes, I have posed nude. I have a good body and I am not ashamed of that," Melania replied. "As long as it's not pornographic, I have nothing against it. People have asked if I would ever pose for *Playboy*. Everything is possible."

She was more evasive when it came to specific questions about love and money, replying that she only discussed her earnings with her agent and ducking all questions about who she was dating, saying only that, yes, she "finds time for love."

"Who is the most famous person who has asked you out on a date?" Videmšek asked her during one of the day's multiple interview opportunities.

"I am not going to answer that," Melania replied.

"Please?" he persisted.

"Sorry!"

When asked to name her best qualities, she described herself as attentive to detail, professional, and always straight with people: "I always say what I mean about someone or something." Her advice for any young woman entering the fashion industry? "Rely on your own self." At another point she said, "Luck is important because you have to be at the right place at the right time." She noted, "You can get a phone call, somebody can notice you, offer you a role, so you never know. Doors always open."

When interviewed twenty years later, nearly everyone who had been in that hotel room said that they still are not sure what Melania was trying to accomplish, or what to make of her. Several described her as natural and completely at ease, and then at other moments, scripted and robotic, somehow both fascinating and boring in the same afternoon. One journalist wrote at the time that at one point, Melania was so uninteresting that the maids in the hotel "must be yawning."

If Melania seemed like two different personalities that day, at least part of the explanation may be found in how she described modeling: "In a way it's like acting, you turn into a different person." There was certainly some acting in Melania's performance. I could find no one who would have considered her among the top fifty models in the world. Models.com, which ranks models, said that she was never in the top tier. Wolfgang Schwarz, the modeling agent based in Vienna who helped book Melania for jobs, also did not understand how she could boast of being world-famous. She was, said Schwarz, one of hundreds of models working for him. Yes, she was making money, "but she was not a girl with this amazing aura that everyone was fascinated by."

She had indeed auditioned for a movie before she flew to Paris. The film was about the life of a hit man, slated to star Mickey Rourke. She had been approached by director Craig Singer after he had spotted her Camel cigarette billboard. He tracked her down through her agent, and they met at a Roy Rogers restaurant on Seventh Avenue—not glamorous, but convenient. Singer found her "stunning." He asked her to audition. At a callback, Melania was given a line to read, a description of a restaurant called Bones. The script said, "Bones—swanky, swanky."

After she read those words, Singer said he knew he couldn't cast her. "She said it with such a thick accent. She was very professional, very lovely, very nice. I was rooting for her. She was gorgeous, but the accent was a deal breaker." Melania, according to Singer, never received an offer, and the part ultimately went to Debbie Harry, the former Playboy bunny and lead singer of the pop group Blondie. Michael Rapaport would replace Rourke as the lead, and in 2003 *A Good Night to Die* would be released.

But the Slovenian journalists reported what Melania told them—that she was headed to Hollywood, a star in the making. "She stepped through the doorway. Tall. Beautiful. Elegant. Classy. Delicate movements. A professional smile on her face," Sebastijan Kopušar wrote in his newspaper dispatch. He noted, too, that she smelled "like heaven on earth." The reporter Hermina

Kovačič was another who noted Melania Knauss was going to be a Hollywood actress—and she also wrote that Melania would be an unusually guarded one: "She told us something about her life story, but she did so in self-controlled and carefully selected words, heavily influenced by English, but she said nothing of her private life." Kovačič also noted that Melania viewed acting as a "step forward" in her career. "She thinks she would like working as part of a team. If you're a model, she says, 'you're alone.'"

The woman who knew the central reason why Melania was in Paris was Tamara Deu, a young executive at Scholz & Friends, a European advertising firm headquartered in Germany. She was the one who had accompanied the small group of Slovenian journalists from Ljubljana's Brnik airport. The Paris experience was "meant to give the journalists a feeling of pure enjoyment and a feeling of being a part of the jet set," she told me. The reporters asked questions, but Deu had been instructed to give them very little information. A bit of mystery was intended to heighten interest.

What was really going on was more mundane. A cigarette company had hired Melania for an ad campaign and wanted to raise her profile. After her success with Camel, Melania had been selected to appear in advertising photos for a Slovenian cigarette called Boss, according to people who worked for Boss and documents related to the trip. The more "Melania is a star" headlines generated by the press conference, the better for the cigarette maker with plans to make Boss an international brand. Melania would be positioned as a star by the time the ads appeared in Slovenia and other countries. A mock-up of a planned ad showed

Melania with a blue streak down the left side of her face. That line on her cheek matched the blue line on the Boss cigarette box. Marlboro had the Marlboro Man, a model in a white cowboy hat. Boss would have Melania in a silky dress.

There was no mention of the cigarette ad during the press conference, apparently because France had such strict laws on tobacco advertising that even a press conference to launch a foreign cigarette would not have been permitted at the time.

Like others, Deu says that she had heard rumors that Melania was dating Trump when she met her in Paris. She remembered admiring Melania for not wanting to discuss her private life and focusing on her own career. "She didn't want to talk about Trump, although two journalists asked about their liaison," Deu said. "I was actually surprised at those questions. And I had a strong feeling that she might have been surprised as well."

"She made it clear she was not going to tell them anything personal," Deu said. The plan was to showcase "the elegant Melania," a Slovenian who had become a success abroad. At certain moments, as the questions continued, Deu said that there "was a feeling that the whole trip to Paris could go to pieces—but Melania actually saved it." She stayed on message and was "calm and polite the whole time." What she couldn't save was the cigarette campaign. Within a year, European governments began adding new restrictions on tobacco advertisements. Instead of being in magazines and billboards across Europe, Melania, according to Schwarz, her Vienna agent, collected her fee—he recalled it was around $60,000—and was done.

• • •

THE PARIS press conference stands out because in almost every other setting, Melania was not someone who bragged about or even drew attention to herself, according to many photographers, agents, and bookers who worked with her. But in Paris, she came across as a diva who name-dropped celebrities, exaggerated, even made things up. She seemed to suddenly be a different person— perhaps like an American real estate mogul named Donald Trump. In his best-known book, *The Art of the Deal*, which was translated into multiple languages and was available around the world start- ing when Melania was seventeen, Trump talked about the value of exaggerating, of calling even the ordinary, "the greatest!"

"The way I promote is bravado," Trump wrote. "I play to people's fantasies. People may not always think big themselves, but they can still get very excited by those who do. That's why a little hyperbole never hurts. People want to believe that some- thing is the biggest and the greatest and the most spectacular.

"I call it truthful hyperbole. It's an innocent form of exaggeration—and a very effective form of promotion."

Trump and Melania said that they met just after this Paris event, during Fashion Week in New York, which started later in September. But several people, including Wolfgang Schwarz, also said that they had heard Trump's name associated with Mela- nia earlier. "Gossip travels quickly in the modeling world, and the word was that Melania was dating Trump," he said. "People were saying, 'Keep it quiet.' No one spoke openly about it." Others who knew Trump said that when he met Melania, he was separated but not divorced from Marla Maples, and he did not want stories saying he had once again left a wife for another woman. But a friend of Trump's said that if there is any discrepancy about their first meeting, it may be nothing more than "Donald insisting on having a dramatic story, even if there isn't one."

Although New York's Fashion Week attracts models from around the world and cameras and photographers are everywhere, Zampolli said he has no photos of the party at the Kit Kat Club where he introduced Melania to Donald Trump. Trump has said that while a famous model was next to Melania, he was so thunderstruck he couldn't take his eyes off the beautiful Slovenian. "I went crazy!" Trump told the CNN talk show host Larry King. "There was this great supermodel sitting next to Melania. I was supposed to meet the supermodel . . . But I said, 'Forget about her. Who is the one on the left?'"

"He wanted my number, but he was with a date, so of course I didn't give it to him," Melania later told *Harper's Bazaar*. "I said, 'I am not giving you my number; you give me yours, and I will call you.'"

"If I give him my number, I'm just one of the women he calls," she said in a separate interview with *GQ*. She said she wanted to test him, to see if he would only give her an office number, and was impressed when he instead shared his private numbers—several of them. Curiously, despite all the interviews they gave, I could find no reference to this story of their meeting until they began discussing their wedding plans six years later. (Zampolli has said that the model next to Melania may have been Inés Rivero, then twenty-three and a Victoria's Secret Angel, who had been married to the same photographer who had shot the nude photos of Melania, but Rivero does not remember this.) Edit Molnar, a former girlfriend of Zampolli, told me in 2015 that she remembered Trump asking for Melania's number and Melania being adamant that she would not give it to him. "You don't fuck around with her," Molnar said about Melania. "She is perfectly clear about what she wants." Molnar, who had been living in Paris, has not given any interviews in recent years.

Interestingly, even though Zampolli said a few hundred people were at his Kit Kat party, I could not find former Zampolli bookers, models, or photographers who remember it. But I did find several people who remember a party at the same club that week thrown by Jill Johnson, the former model and founder of *Tear Sheet* magazine. Three people who attended her 1998 Fashion Week party said both Trump and Zampolli were there. Zampolli said he could not recall the exact date of the party where Melania and Trump met. But whether the story of Trump and Melania's meeting is the truth, it is now their truth. And while Trump made it sound like a fairy-tale beginning, Melania would not be the only woman he would date.

In the New York scene, Trump was known as a "modelizer," one of those men always hanging around models. He filled his parties with them and loved having his picture taken with them. He befriended top fashion photographers who were model magnets. He hung out with the owners of modeling agencies, including John Casablancas, the founder of Elite, who made Trump a judge in his Look of the Year competition. There, and at the Miss

Universe beauty pageants, which Trump had purchased in 1996, he met hundreds of gorgeous young women.

Trump was not, however, a perpetual bachelor. For most of the last twenty years he had been married. At age thirty, he had married Ivana, and he was still married to her when he started dating Marla, who would become his second wife. Now, at fifty-two, as he waited for his second divorce to be finalized, he enjoyed acting like a playboy. He craved publicity and saw its value for his brand. When he showed up at a gala or movie premiere with a new date—as he often did in 1998—he got ink. The more famous or photogenic the date, the bigger his photo. Trump boasted about his exploits, and was known to plant tabloid stories about the parade of women—Gorgeous! Young! Famous!—who found him irresistible. Many of these stories, like an earlier claim that the pop star Madonna was after him, were simply not true. But the tabloids ran with it, and the publicity was good for his image.

The same week that Melania was in Paris for her press conference, Trump invited one of the hottest models in the world, Kylie Bax, a twenty-three-year-old from New Zealand, to sit in his box at the U.S. Open tennis tournament. With a flair for the dramatic and a desire for maximum visibility, Trump arrived late for a finals match. The rest of the crowd was seated, and it was easy to notice Trump, wearing a red hat, which he told friends made him easier to spot, walking in with a tall blonde. The next day, Trump made the gossip columns, the rich guy with a model less than half his age. With Bax on his arm, "every head in the stadium turned towards him," the *Independent* of London wrote.

The article described Bax as "the hot model of the moment" and made it seem that she, too, was interested in Trump. But she told me that she was never romantically involved with Trump. He was famous for tipping off photographers about where he and his latest bombshell "date" might show up, but she did not know that at the time. This was the world Melania was walking into.

Melania has said that she didn't know much about Trump on the night she met him. "I had my life, I had my world," she told *GQ*. "I didn't follow Trump and didn't know what kind of life he had." But as a voracious reader of news and magazines, it's hard to imagine that she knew little about the man who was so often in the news and was a fixture in the modeling world. Her sister had recalled seeing Trump on CNN when she and Melania were still living in Slovenia. Trump was also friends with Zampolli, Melania's agent. Pignatelli, the owner of Pier59 Studios, said that Trump was well known as "a very rich man, a good-looking man, the boss, the airplanes, the this and that, and beautiful Palm Beach."

Everyone may have known Donald Trump, but it was the unknown Melania who quickly got the upper hand. Seeming aloof, or impervious to Trump's charm, made her more intriguing to him. Another old friend said that Melania knew that indifference was the best way to hook Trump—and was savvy enough to know that he coveted things he couldn't have. "She was willing to walk away. It piqued his interest," the friend said. "She is smart, strategic, and plays the long game. She knew Trump liked the chase. It made her more interesting."

Melania was attracted to Trump for more than his obvious

wealth and connections. Donald Trump had a better reputation than many of the other men who dated younger models. Trump was not considered one of the "horribles," as the models referred to the lecherous older men who always seemed to be hanging around, according to bookers. Trump loved the models' physical beauty and constantly flirted with them. But Jay Goldberg, one of Trump's lawyers during this time, told me that Trump was too in love with his next business project to think much about women. "I never heard him speak romantically about a woman. I mean, I heard him speak romantically about his work." Goldberg said at the end of a full workday, despite any manufactured playboy image, what made Trump happy was chocolate: "Give him a Hershey bar and let him watch television." He brought his dates to the most exclusive events, didn't drink or do drugs, and was so preoccupied with his own life and work that he was not very demanding of a woman's time. "He was in love with himself, and for a lot of these models there were rich men who were so much worse," a well-known booker said. "Think about the older guys who want to be around young, beautiful women. What do they want? Some of these rich guys, or those with power, were really awful to the women."

Trump had another upside: anybody who hung out with him drew tons of press attention. Aspiring models could do worse than to be seen in the New York press with such an influential man. As Trump and Zampolli alerted their friends at the gossip pages to Trump and his latest gorgeous "gal pal," Melania was in for the ride of her life.

On October 5, 1998, members of the Kennedy family glided

across marble floors under the soaring vaulted ceilings of Grand Central Terminal. John Kennedy Jr. appeared in his tuxedo, with his wife, Carolyn Bessette Kennedy, in a shimmering black strapless gown, long black gloves, and spiked heels. Caroline Kennedy, daughter of the late Jacqueline Kennedy Onassis, addressed the gala, celebrating the New York City landmark's renovation. Her mother had been a key supporter of the restoration, and was fondly remembered in remarks that day by her children and her sisters-in-law Eunice Kennedy Shriver and Pat Lawford. Also present to celebrate were Trump and, as the *Daily News* reported, "some delicious-looking arm candy, his latest date, a 5-foot-10 Slovenian model named Melania Knaus." *USA Today* noted her simply as "a slinky brunette, Melania."

Jackie O had been an icon for Melania and her mother. Later, when Trump entered politics, Melania said Jackie would be her role model as first lady. And now, there she was shaking hands with Jackie's children and chatting with her family.

Soon after, the *New York Post* weighed in. "DONALD Trump just scored big on the beauty exchange. It seems his companion of the last several months, Norwegian stunner Celina Midelfar, is suddenly nowhere to be seen—but Austrian model Melania Knaus is. On Tuesday night, the pair were canoodling at Moomba where they shared a table with embattled Fashion Cafe owner Tomaso Buti and his wife Daniela Pestova; apparently this wasn't their first date. A friend of Trump says Knaus, who's best known as the girl in the Camels billboard in Times Square, is mad about him. But he sees lots of people."

Melania flew on Trump's private jet to Paradise Island in the Bahamas for a party said to cost $7 million; other guests included Michael Jackson, Leonardo DiCaprio, Julia Roberts, Denzel Washington, and Oprah Winfrey. Jimmy Buffett sang "Margaritaville" barefoot on the beach at the celebration of the opening of the Royal Towers Hotel. Melania and Trump arrived with thirteen pieces of luggage for the party and the couple ended up dancing near Ivana Trump and her boyfriend.

Trump also brought Melania to Washington, D.C., for a black-tie gala fundraiser for the Larry King Cardiac Foundation at the Four Seasons Hotel. Celine Dion sang. Caviar was served. A Minnesota businessman bought a dinner with Trump and King for $15,000. Trump, still waiting for his divorce to be finalized, told a *Washington Post* reporter that he was "sort of eligible . . . but not officially." In addition to Melania, he brought his mother, his two sisters, and his brother. "He's the greatest man I've ever known, the smartest!" Melania told reporters that night. "Wow," replied Trump, beaming.

MELANIA APPEARED just as Donald Trump's fortunes were soaring. After a string of embarrassing bankruptcies, he was back. His name was stamped on everything from buildings to his plane to a magazine, *Trump Style*. He was expanding his brand internationally. His name and face were fixtures in supermarket and pharmacy checkout lines, thanks in part to his buddies at the *National Enquirer*. Just before he met Melania, the *Enquirer* declared Trump "the sexiest billionaire alive." Its "poll" said that Trump had won 70.3 percent of women's votes. A twenty-six-year-old woman reportedly said of Trump, who was exactly twice her age: "His pouty lips make my knees quiver." Ralph Lauren came in a sad second at less than 10 percent, and Ted Turner, Bill Gates, and the filmmaker George Lucas were far down in the pack. The supermarket tabloid was a ridiculous rag to many. But Trump recognized its reach and that its stories occasionally had a political impact, including photographs and reports about Senator Gary Hart's extramarital affair, which sank his 1988 Democratic primary run for the White House.

After Marla, Trump vowed he'd never marry again. Friends said that he loved and nurtured his reputation as a single-again playboy. But being around all those young women was partly illusion. When I reached Kylie Bax by phone in 2019, she told me, "There was a group of us who hung out, and he would say to me, 'Come on, let's get a picture. We would walk down the red carpet together. It was all in fun."

Now Melania was the object of Trump's attention. She wanted to be far more than just fun for Trump, or a shiny object for a quick photo. She seemed to be studying his habits, the games he played, and how to deal with his complicated relationship to marriage. One thing Trump had learned was that while one attractive woman got him attention, two women fighting over him got him more. In December 1989, his girlfriend, Marla Maples, confronted his wife, Ivana, in a restaurant in Aspen: "I love your husband. Do you?" "Get lost," Ivana shot back.

The exchange escalated into a full-blown media circus. "I

couldn't turn on the television without hearing my name," Ivana wrote in *Raising Trump*. "This young blonde woman came up to me out of the blue" and "shattered and shocked" her. But it wasn't out of the blue. Trump had invited Marla to Aspen and put her up in a hotel room near his wife and kids, all but guaranteeing a confrontation. The public war between Ivana and Marla embarrassed Trump's three children; Don Jr. said he didn't talk to his father for months. But Trump saw how it could also help him, as he explained on Howard Stern's radio show. "I was standing in the middle of these two. I was screaming and there's five hundred people up at Little Nell's, and there's this big fat bald-headed guy, nice guy, standing there. He must've weighed four hundred pounds. And he said, 'You know, it could be worse, Mr. Trump. I haven't had a girl in over twenty years.'"

Now at the end of another marriage, Trump seemed to be using similar tactics in the summer of 1998, when the *Enquirer* wrote, "Two world-class beauties created a scene over him during a recent party in the Hamptons." Two of Trump's companions— Norwegian heiress Celina Midelfart and Victoria's Secret model Kara Young—were in tears at the oceanside mansion party because they both wanted him, according to the *Enquirer*.

Trump arrived in a helicopter, without either woman, knowing both would be there. As he was leaving, he was overheard saying he wanted to tell the tabloids that he was at the party with two women. "We gotta get this out! We gotta get this out!" He knew the names and phone numbers of the people who produced New York's gossip and lifestyle columns. Photographers were grateful that he tipped them off to A-list gatherings. If a celebrity was staying in his Plaza Hotel at the edge of Central Park or having a drink at the bar, Trump knew. Sometimes he not only told photographers but dashed over to his hotel from Trump Tower a couple of blocks away to get in the picture. Over the years, he fueled reports that he was dating skater Peggy Fleming or having a tryst with model Carla Bruni (who would marry French president Nicolas Sarkozy). Both women denied dating him.

"He doesn't check his pulse to see if he's alive. He checks the papers and the internet so he can know that he exists," former *Daily News* gossip columnist A. J. Benza told Lloyd Grove for an article about Trump's complicated relationship with the media.

As he became more famous, Trump also didn't have to work that hard to manufacture attention. He was on many people's A-list, and many A-listers were on his. Donna Summer sang at Mar-a-Lago on New Year's Eve for a crowd of guests that included billionaire financier Ron Perelman, film director Penny Marshall, and actress Sharon Gless. Trump brought Melania backstage at a Ricky Martin concert at Madison Square Garden. She sat in the front row at a Mike Tyson fight in Las Vegas. She mingled with stars at the World Series and attended galas, wearing dresses that cost more than cars.

She accompanied Trump to the music video cable channel telecast *VH1 Divas Live '99* after-party, held at Cipriani; also in attendance were Whitney Houston, Wesley Snipes, Ashley Judd, and Russell Simmons. She joined Trump at an AIDS fundraiser with Matt Dillon, Conan O'Brien, and Stella McCartney. She attended the American Fashion Awards alongside Bette Midler, Anjelica Huston, and Sarah Jessica Parker. Trump and Melania were photographed at the MTV Video Music Awards at Lincoln Center, where a clearly proud Trump encouraged photographers to capture the back of Melania's revealing dress.

They flew in Trump's private jet to California, Florida, and the Kentucky Derby. They chatted with Supreme Court Justice Clarence Thomas at the Daytona 500. At a birthday party for Jennifer Lopez, news reports said Trump and Melania helped J. Lo cut her three-tiered pink cake at a New York club, in front of Leonardo DiCaprio, Derek Jeter, Marc Anthony, and Queen Latifah. They helicoptered to the Hamptons for parties, then flew back to Manhattan so Trump could sleep in his own bed. The tabloids cranked out a steady stream of gossip items on Trump.

Melania was a bit of added mystery. She had appeared out of nowhere. Her last name was often misspelled: Knaus, Kanauss, Knauff. And she was called Austrian as often as she was called Slovenian. Trump was telling people she was from Austria. The Republic of Slovenia was not even a decade old at the time, and many Americans had never heard of it.

But Melania was getting recognition. In May 1999 she posed for two photos in *Town & Country* magazine with models from the UK and Mozambique under the headline "Lady Luxe: The season's haute couture is as stunning as the worldly young women who wear it." The gushing text said, "For Melania Knauss, a New York–based model, whose charmingly accented English betrays a childhood spent shuttling between a mother in Slovenia and a father in Vienna, 'Glamour is something you feel inside, which goes with you no matter where you are or what you're wearing.'" She wore a Chanel haute couture off-white satin dress embroidered with pastel sequins, and $37,350 yellow-gold earrings with pearls by Mauboussin. On another page, she wore a Jean-Paul Gaultier satin dress adorned with ostrich feathers, along with a gold and diamond necklace worth $510,000. The photo shoot was styled by Lucy Sykes, a British fashion guru, socialite, and author who was friendly with Donald Trump.

In February 1999, Trump had launched his own agency, Trump Model Management, later called T Management. One early model signed was nineteen-year-old Paris Hilton. Another was Melania Knauss. On April 25, the day before Melania's twenty-ninth birthday, the *Daily News* reported: "Donald Trump didn't have to look far to snag a model for his fledgling agency, Trump Management. Donald's gal pal, Slovenian stunner Melania Knauss, just jumped from Elite." Trump said about Knauss joining his agency: "If I couldn't do that, then I don't know what I could do for her."

After he opened his own modeling agency, it became even easier for Trump to order up models for his parties the way others ordered flowers. Models working in South Beach in Miami were driven to Mar-a-Lago in vans for Trump events, where women in their twenties outnumbered the older, richer men. Trump boasted about Melania much the same way he had about his first wife, Ivana, whom he promoted as a famous model and a skier for the Czech Olympic team. While she did model and ski,

Trump's description was embellished. Similarly, Melania became a "supermodel" in Trump's telling.

He told people that Melania brought him good luck. Sometimes he brought her to business meetings in provocative dresses—many businessmen in New York have a story of Melania being the only woman in the room. She helped him, and he helped her. Melania's modeling day rate doubled, from $5,000 to $10,000, according to noted financial journalist Christopher Byron, who in March 2000 profiled Trump in *George* magazine. The magazine was started by John F. Kennedy Jr., but he died in a plane crash in 1999, and the Trump cover was a controversial move by his successor. Byron reported that because Melania was represented by Trump's agency, 20 percent of her fees went to Trump, who also collected additional fees from publishing companies and others who hired her. So Melania and Trump made money for each other.

Trump's connections didn't hurt. In April 1999, Melania appeared on the cover of the glossy Florida magazine *Ocean Drive*, wearing a bikini and a pout. The article described her as a "raving beauty"; it was written by Sandi Powers, a Trump friend whose husband, Jerry Powers, was the magazine's chairman and CEO and later became the publisher of *Trump* magazine. The owner of *Ocean Drive* was another Trump friend, Jason Binn, whose *Hamptons* magazine in New York would feature Melania on the cover three times. Binn described Trump and Melania as a "great team," and said Trump was always telling everyone how gorgeous she was. "She really loved him for him," Binn said. "She didn't need to be at the parties. She wasn't begging for covers or fashion shoots—she just wasn't that person." Nevertheless, becoming a top model had been Melania's dream, and now it was coming true.

IN MARCH 1999, Melania was on billboards appearing to wear nothing but a watch—a Concord watch. The Swiss luxury brand's timepieces retailed for as much as $15,000. Melania was the new face of the Concord marketing campaign "Be Late," which stressed that time was the real luxury. Be Late centered around a series of personal moments—a soak in a bubbly bath, a sensual embrace in the shower, a loving cuddle with a baby—all times when it was "worth being late." The campaign won praise in the advertising world.

The ads were plastered on New York City buses and Midtown billboards and across the pages of all the major glossy magazines: *Vanity Fair*, *GQ*, *Vogue*. A Trump friend, Peter Arnell, a photographer and branding guru, had suggested Melania to the campaign's creative director, Scott Woodward. "We were in a casting meeting," Woodward told me, "and Peter said to me, 'What do you think about Donald's new girlfriend, Melania?'"

Woodward liked Melania's photos and thought that she was even more attractive in person. "There was a magnetism, very quiet, very dignified," he told me. Woodward also knew that Trump attracted press attention, and so he told Arnell that if he could guarantee that Trump would accompany Melania to the ad campaign launch party, he was happy to cast her in it: "If he comes to my launch party, a thousand percent yes!"

The shoot, in the penthouse of the Mercer Hotel in SoHo, lasted all day. In pre-Photoshop days, it was difficult, if not impossible, to fix even tiny imperfections—a pimple, the hint of a scar. Each shoot required hours posing with a camera lens and people examining every detail of a model's appearance. Melania was patient and never demanding.

But then Trump arrived unexpectedly. The last scene was being shot, and it involved Melania and the male actor Sascha Eiblmayr embracing in the shower—her arm extended to show the watch. Getting it right was tricky, down to trying to coat the glass walls in gauzy steam so that the photo was provocative but not overly risqué. As the camera clicked, Woodward was focused on trying to get the perfect shot, asking Melania to change the position of her wrist on the glass door, or telling Eiblmayr exactly how close to stand to Melania inside the shower. And that was when Trump arrived.

"We kept shooting. We were so close, and we had to get it perfect," said Woodward, who was relieved that Trump only saw Melania after she and Eiblmayr had exited the shower and covered up. Melania sent Woodward a handwritten thank-you. Today, he notes that the Melania he worked with two decades ago and the Melania now in the White House appear very much the same: guarded, and with the ramrod-straight posture and movements of a European model. "I see her [acting the same] at Be Best events as I did in the Be Late campaign," he said.

Trump and Melania did appear for the ad campaign's reveal, held at a splashy launch party in September 1999 at a gallery in

Chelsea. As guests wandered through the lofty space, which featured bright white ceilings and an exposed brick wall, they could pause to gaze at a fifteen-foot-tall poster of Melania embracing Eiblmayr in the shower. The actor joked to a reporter that to keep his composure during the shoot he thought "about baseball, basketball, you name it." Eiblmayr also said that when Trump arrived at the photo shoot he quickly got out of the shower and put a towel around his waist and that Trump had joked to him, "It looks like I have some stiff competition."

The gallery event was part of a benefit. Woodward asked celebrities to donate personal items to be auctioned that night for amfAR, an AIDS charity. Muhammad Ali sent an autographed boxing ring bell, and TV personality Rosie O'Donnell donated her bowling ball and shoes. (This was years before O'Donnell's feud with Trump that led him to call her "a pig" and mock her in a presidential debate.) In an *AdAge* magazine profile of Arnell, Trump thanked him for having "the really great judgment to cast my girlfriend, Melania Knauss, in one of his big watch campaigns."

Sixteen years later, when Trump announced his presidential candidacy, the Concord campaign images were no longer easily found online. It is not clear why they seem to have vanished, but celebrities often hire "reputation managers" to remove or bury unflattering or embarrassing photos and stories.

Several photographers who were hired to shoot Melania wearing bikinis, lingerie, or less say that they have been warned by people representing Trump not to print or sell the photos. Manfred Gestrich, a photographer who shot pictures of Melania in 1997, said that he had been contacted by other photographers who told him that they had been threatened with legal action on Trump's behalf. Melania's former roommate, Matthew Atanian, said that he was warned not to publish photos he snapped around their apartment, even though, in his opinion, Melania looks great in them.

After Melania started dating Trump, she negotiated control over many of her photo shoots, so her permission was needed to publish the images. If she granted it, she was also paid royalties for their use. This is somewhat unusual in the business; most photographers typically retain the rights to any photos they shoot. Some famous photographers who took Melania's picture chose not to give up their rights but also told me that they are reluctant to upset her or the president by selling or publishing without her permission. Patrick Demarchelier, the high-profile French fashion photographer who was Princess Diana's personal photographer, did not give me permission to publish a 1999 picture of Melania wearing a tiny bikini and lying on a rug with the presidential seal, which had been published in *Talk* magazine. No reason was given when the request was turned down.

Getty Images holds a significant number of her photos. To use them requires a purchase. This arrangement is common with celebrities, although not with first ladies. But the Trump White House financial disclosure form in 2018 showed that Melania earned "between $100,000 and $1 million" from media companies paying her royalties.

Trump and Melania Knauss on
a 2000 *George* magazine cover

CHAPTER 6

First White House Run

ON JULY 12, 1999, Trump issued a statement indicating that he was considering a run for president as the candidate of the Reform Party, founded by Texas billionaire Ross Perot, who had run as an independent against George H. W. Bush and Bill Clinton. "My record of accomplishment in business and my outspoken views on trade, education, and other issues have led many people to believe I would be a strong candidate and a strong president," Trump said. "While I have not decided to become a candidate at this time, if the Reform Party nominated me, I would probably run and probably win."

Many political observers wondered if Trump was kidding. He had concluded his statement with an uncharacteristically self-deprecating joke: "If I won, I would ask for an immediate recount." Reform Party head Russell Verney even asked, "Is this a joke?" adding, "I have never once heard his name mentioned in the Reform Party."

But for Trump, it was serious. His ninety-three-year-old father, Fred Trump, had died three weeks earlier. Trump had a troubled relationship with his father, but considered him a great man, and himself his proven heir. What was a natural higher rung for a successful businessman? Politics. In a 2016 interview with the *Washington Post*, Trump was asked if his father's death had prompted him to run for president. "I would imagine perhaps it did, but maybe inwardly," he said.

Trump's political musings opened a new chapter in Melania's life. She now had to consider the possibility of being a political partner. A common narrative about Melania is that she simply wanted to marry a wealthy man, and that she was horrified when Trump entered politics in 2015 and disrupted her comfortable world. But there is ample evidence that from the very beginning, Melania not only accepted and embraced Trump's political aspirations but was also an encouraging partner. In interviews and public appearances at the time, Melania was fully supportive of Trump's running for president. "You see the reaction on the street when we go to something, it's amazing!" she told *USA Today*. One Melania friend said, "I know Americans think that she's dumb and she just went for money. It's really not that. She always wanted more than money."

Relatively early in her relationship with Trump, a reporter asked her if she'd like to be first lady. "I think every woman, every girl would. Yes, I would, why not?" she said. "I will put all my energy in it, and I will support my man." On October 7, 1999, Trump went on *Larry King Live* to announce that he was exploring a presidential run with the Reform Party. That same week he and Melania attended a Dominick Dunne book party, where Melania said that Trump would be "the best" president.

At the same time that Trump was testing the waters, Melania was preparing to be featured in the pages of *Sports Illustrated*'s swimsuit issue, a career highlight. For the February 2000 issue, the magazine dispatched models to Hawaii, Malaysia, and Mexico. Melania was part of a group of seven models, including Kylie Bax, the New Zealand model, and Carré Otis, who was returning to modeling after her recent divorce from actor Mickey Rourke, with whom she had appeared in two films. The group flew to the Las Alamandas Resort, south of Puerto Vallarta, on Mexico's Pacific coast.

In charge of the shoot was high-profile fashion photographer Antoine Verglas, who said he met Melania through Zampolli in New York. Verglas was one of the best in the business, a top-shelf photographer who had shot Claudia Schiffer and Cindy Crawford. When I met him at his studio in New York in 2018, he told me that he always tried to have a "gimmick" for the swimsuit edition, such as having models wear nothing but body paint. In Mexico, the idea was to have the models play with inflatable toys. When he spoke of Melania, Verglas described her as other photographers did: exceptionally reserved, all business, pleasant, and friendly with everyone she worked with but not gregarious. She would have dinner at the resort and go to bed. "She was a different type of woman," he said. Verglas, who shot photos of Melania a half-dozen times over the next few years, said Trump told him he thought Melania should have been the cover.

"Trump was very happy when she got into the *Sports Illustrated* swimsuit edition," Verglas said. "He was struck by her beauty," and thought her picture should be everywhere. In her photo, Melania stands on a beach in a tiny bikini, nuzzling up to a six-foot inflatable whale propped up on its tail like her dance partner. As the Pacific laps up on the Mexican shore, she looks like she is about to kiss the big orca.

It is hard to overstate the prestige of the *SI* swimsuit issue. Cover alumni are a Who's Who of the modeling world, including legends Cheryl Tiegs, Elle Macpherson, Christie Brinkley, Kathy Ireland, Tyra Banks, Heidi Klum, Chrissy Teigen, Kate Upton—and celebrities outside that world: Beyoncé Knowles, U.S. soccer superstar Alex Morgan. For two years in a row, in 1984 and 1985, the cover had belonged to Paulina Porizkova, the Czech supermodel Melania could see exercising as she looked out Matthew Atanian's kitchen window.

Six months before Melania's *Sports Illustrated* shoot in Mexico, the Trump-owned Miss Universe pageant held its 1999 competition in the Caribbean nation of Trinidad and Tobago. Trump often invited his pals to be judges, and that year he asked Kylie Bax and world heavyweight boxing champion Evander Holyfield. Perhaps more important, he invited Diane Smith, the influential *Sports Illustrated* senior editor in charge of the swimsuit edition. Within months of the Miss Universe pageant, Melania, Bax, and Holyfield all appeared in the 2000 swimsuit issue. (Male sports stars are sometimes featured posing with the bikini-clad women.)

A few weeks after the fall photo shoot, in late 1999, *Sports Illustrated*'s top editor, Bill Colson, received a phone call out of the blue: Donald Trump wanted to have lunch. Colson had never met Trump, and he thought it strange to be summoned by the celebrity developer. But everybody knew Trump was interested in sports, particularly golf and tennis, so perhaps it made sense that he wanted to chat with the editor of the biggest sports magazine in the country. Colson met him at Jean-Georges, the high-end restaurant housed in the Trump International Hotel and Tower on Central Park West. Colson engaged Trump on sports, and they chatted. But Colson said it soon became clear why he was there.

"Did it go well with Melania?" Trump said.

At that moment, *Sports Illustrated*'s editors were busily culling thousands of photos down to fewer than a hundred that would appear in the magazine's pages. Trump wanted to know if that would include photos of Melania. "I told him, I guess she's going to be in the issue," Colson said, assuring Trump that the magazine wouldn't have sent her all the way to Mexico if they didn't intend to use her photos. Colson said that Trump didn't pressure him or argue for Melania. But Colson said, "I knew what he wanted."

Colson was not involved in the issue's details, although as managing editor at the time, he had final say over the cover photo. He told me that he never met many of the women who appeared in the magazine, and he left the interior layout entirely to Diane Smith and her team, the fashion experts. He was a sports guy.

He never met Trump again.

• • •

A MONTH after the *Sports Illustrated* photo shoot in Mexico, Antoine Verglas had another idea that would land Melania a major magazine cover. He could see it in his mind: Bond girl. On a helicopter, maybe a private jet. Even a limo. Some sort of sleek luxury ride where the photos would channel the iconic Bond girl mix of sex and money, with a touch of that over-the-top Bond-style camp—shaken, not stirred.

The model would be gorgeous, wearing nothing but lingerie and showing as much skin as possible, dripping in jewels, maybe with sunglasses, maybe a gold-plated gun. Maybe handcuffs? Dangerous, icy-cool, and smoldering.

Verglas knew the model he wanted. He'd call his friend Paolo Zampolli, and he'd ask for Melania Knauss. Melania would be perfect. Those long legs, the cheekbones, the bright blue eyes, the Eastern European aloofness. Verglas was sure that Melania had the special something to pull off his Bond girl photo fantasy. "Of course, I could have found another pretty girl, but then it would have been more complicated for me," Verglas said. "It was fantastic that she was the girlfriend of Donald Trump," and that he had a private jet they could use in the shoot.

Verglas called Dylan Jones, editor of British *GQ*, with his pitch. He had the concept, he had the model, and she was the girlfriend of a man who knew how to wind up the media like nobody else. Trump's girlfriend on the cover of the magazine meant Trump would promote the magazine. "It was huge because she was Donald Trump's girlfriend," Jones said. "She wasn't particularly famous, but she was notable, a boldface name, because of Trump."

Two decades later, that *GQ* cover still stands as perhaps Melania's best-known, most frequently viewed work as a professional model. And for Trump, who was seriously mulling a presidential run, it was a chance to show off his attractive partner. It served both the personal image he had worked so hard to cultivate and the political image he was creating. Jones said that Trump was personally involved in the negotiations. "He was very keen to do this. It was his jet; he facilitated it all and he was very enthusiastic," Jones recalled. "It was a remarkably easy thing to organize because if somebody wants something to happen, it happens."

Verglas also wasn't surprised. Trump and Melania seemed incredibly supportive of each other. "They seemed like they were so in love," he said. "She was always looking at him like he was God, and he was looking at her like she was a goddess. Always saying, 'She's the best.' For him, she was the most beautiful girl on the planet, and he didn't understand why she would not be on the cover of *Vogue* and everywhere. I think he wanted her to be an extremely successful personality because that's who he is."

The details came together quickly, and the shoot was booked on the tarmac at LaGuardia Airport, where Trump kept his plane, a Boeing 727. And what a plane. It had a bedroom, dining room, shower, and gold plating everywhere—even the seat belt buckles were plated in 24-karat gold. Trump's name was emblazoned in large letters on the outside. It was perfect for what Verglas had in mind, as he realized when he and his assistant, plus a stylist and a hair and makeup artist, settled into Trump's gilded world. The stylist had carried the props aboard: a briefcase, handcuffs, a chrome-plated prop pistol, an armload of sparkly jewelry, stilettos, leather boots, thongs and other lingerie, and a fluffy white fur rug.

They'd arrived around nine, and Melania had rolled up shortly after, right on time and very professional. She came by herself. No assistant. No publicist. None of the trappings of the supermodel set. And notably, no Trump. As in Mexico, she remained quiet and professional throughout the shoot, although she had definite ideas about her Bond girl: nothing too far, not fully naked, nothing that felt exhibitionist. She was okay with sexy, but there was a line she wouldn't cross—unlike her more daring nude scenes with Emma Eriksson three years earlier, before she had met Trump. "She was definitely someone who was more modest and private" than many other models, Verglas said. "But she wasn't doing it under duress; she was completely complicit in the whole thing," Jones, the *GQ* editor, recalled. "I mean, they were fun pictures."

On the set, Verglas tried to create the most reassuring space possible. His assistant and the makeup artist were women. Even in photos where Melania looked totally nude, she was in fact slightly covered, just out of sight of the camera. "We wanted to do something that was extravagant, something that was kitsch," he said. "And in terms of sexuality, these photos did push the envelope. But they were very playful; they were ironic. She was meant to be this sort of barmy girl. It was overladen with cliché, but deliberately so."

They worked for at least eight hours. Most of that time was spent on setting up—getting the lingerie right, the hair, painting her nails gold. The actual photography was much quicker. With the right preparation, a good photographer can fire off hundreds of frames in twenty minutes and get the right look.

Melania's cover appeared more than a month before the *Sports Illustrated* swimsuit issue was set to release, in the January 2000 edition of British *GQ* for its "Naked supermodel special!" (Glossy monthly magazines would release in advance of the new month, a January magazine appearing in the final days of December.) The cover subhead promised interior photos of Kate Moss and other models in the nude, plus the "The GQ Bitch List: Who we hate and why." On the cover, Melania appears to be wearing only a diamond choker and bracelets as she stretches out on a soft, fluffy fur rug. "Sex at 30,000 ft: Melania Knauss earns her air miles," says the tagline. And the tiny type adds cheekily: "Melania Knauss: cleared for takeoff!"

Inside are additional photos of Melania, striking poses that Jones said were "deliberately over the top." Wearing stilettos, a gold dress cut to below her navel, and rose-colored sunglasses, she holds a chrome-plated pistol and is handcuffed to a briefcase filled with jewelry. In another image, she stands on the plane wing in a red bikini and knee-high leather boots, twisting to point her pistol. The photo spread ran to fourteen pages. In one picture, shot from below, she ascends the plane's steps in a silver thong. In the cockpit, in lingerie made of metal, a cyborg headpiece, and blinders, she straddles the controls. "We were just trying to make her look strong, sexy, determined," Verglas said. "It was perfect; she had the look, she had the attitude, she was not scared of going up on the wing of the plane."

GQ readers—the magazine had a circulation of 1.2 million— loved it, Jones recalled, and Donald Trump "was very enthusiastic afterward." Overall, "it seemed to be a huge success. Trump didn't see or didn't care about the irony involved in those pictures, where we thought they were kind of ridiculous." Jones didn't give Melania Knauss much more thought until 2016, when suddenly Trump was a serious contender for the U.S. presidency. One of the magazine's digital editors remembered the 1999 photo shoot, and he dug out the old photos. "It was such a long time ago that we'd forgotten," Jones said. "But now we got to chew the second bite of the cherry. These pictures were suddenly everywhere—it was such an extraordinary gift." Jones said that his staff estimated the photos online had been seen by about forty-five million people. Hard copies of the original magazine were suddenly selling for hundreds of dollars online. "I've got dozens at home, so that's my pension sorted," Jones joked.

He said that the Trump campaign called twice, trying to get *GQ* to stop using the photos, "which obviously was the dumbest thing to do because it just encourages me to publish." The magazine owns the copyright to all the photos, so neither Melania nor the campaign could legally stop publication of the images.

"They used the usual excuses when someone is attempting to do something they have no legal authority to do whatsoever: 'This is an invasion of privacy; these pictures were taken so long ago; they were no longer representative, etcetera, etcetera,'" Jones said.

Did the campaign have a point? Were the photos no longer representative?

"I'm not sure I can answer that," Jones said. "I have no idea what the first lady gets up to on Air Force One."

THERE WAS an increasingly political aspect to the Trump-Melania relationship. In November 1999, the two flew to Miami so Trump could address a crowd of Cuban Americans. At the Bay of Pigs Museum, he called Fidel Castro a killer and a criminal and said he would tell him, "*Adios, amigo.*" He also said he would like to build the first hotel in post-Castro Cuba. The older men who had fled Cuba took photos with Trump and Melania, who wore a sleeveless dress and stiletto heels. "We're having a good time, and I'm supporting him in everything what he's decided to do," the *Daily News* reported, quoting "the Austrian native."

That weekend, in a Miami hotel, Trump and Melania sat with Roger Stone, Trump's political adviser, and six members of the Reform Party, who were there to see what they thought of Trump. Phil Madsen, who worked for Minnesota governor Jesse Ventura, recalled that the meeting quickly turned into a hero-worship session by the Reformers: "They were just falling all over themselves about the opportunity to work with Trump, and it was embarrassing." Trump barely spoke. Melania sat at his side and didn't say a word. But they communicated. He handed her a towel. She handed him a glass. They showed the attentive little kindnesses of a couple. They paid attention to each other; they were warm. "These two really like each other," Madsen remembers thinking.

As the year came to an end, Melania's modeling career was in high gear and Trump's possible political aspirations were making news. He had a campaign manifesto, *The America We Deserve*, written with Dave Shiflett, waiting to be released in January 2000. Earlier, in the fall of 1999, *New York Times* columnist Maureen Dowd had asked Trump why voters should consider him: " 'To be blunt, people would vote for me,' Mr. Trump says. 'They just would.' Why? 'Maybe because I'm so good looking.' " Dowd wondered how he would do with the women's vote.

"I might do badly," he kids. "They know me better than anybody else. Women are much tougher and more calculating than men. I relate better to women. I go out with the most beautiful women in the world. Certain guys tell me they want women of substance, not beautiful models. It just means they can't get beautiful models."

He does not think Americans would mind a twice-divorced playboy in the White House. "Actually, I think people like it," he says about his racy love life. "It's a fantasy."

"Of course, if necessary, I could be married in 24 hours," he adds. "It would be very easy. Believe me."

Trump told Dowd that Bill Clinton "would go down as a great President" had it not been for the Monica Lewinsky scandal—but not necessarily for the obvious reasons. Trump's take: "People would have been more forgiving if he'd had an affair with a really beautiful woman of sophistication."

On the same day, *Time* magazine quoted a Trump adviser saying of Trump's "mostly male" voters: "They stay at our hotels. They play at our tables. They like his plane. They like his boat. They like his house. They like his girlfriends. They all love Trump."

Trump's political campaign strategy seemed to be that a hot model on his arm was more important than a stack of boring policy papers. Trump has always been obsessed by physical beauty. He prizes good looks and evaluates a potential girlfriend—or cabinet secretary—based on whether the person looks the part, as if he were casting a movie. He was rumored to have had a relationship with 1993 Playmate of the Year Anna Nicole Smith in the early 1990s. When she died, in 2007, he went on *The Howard Stern Show* and offered this tribute: "She was six feet tall, she had the best body, she had the best face. She had the best hair I've ever seen. Hair is my thing. I'm really into hair up right now, ok? . . . Now, when she opened her mouth, it was different. Let's face it."

Dave Shiflett told me that he was always struck when he got off the elevator at Trump Tower by all the beautiful women Trump had working for him. "They were so flawless that they looked like they were cooked up in his laboratory," he said.

The spotlight was suddenly now on one woman, Melania, the

potential first lady. The tabloids were filled with variations on the "Model First Lady" headline. "Could We Next Have a Super-model as First Lady?" mused the *Daily News*. "Possible presidential contender Donald Trump's first lady of the moment is Melania Knauss, a willowy, Slovenian-born knockout who has been The Donald's steady since September 1998 . . . 'It would be great to have someone glamorous and sensual in the White House,' said Elite model agency owner John Casablancas. The type of woman Trump likes is sexy, fun and light and would put politicians in perspective that behind the public image is a guy who likes what the average guy likes." The *Daily News* added, "Knauss would have little trouble talking to VIPs. She speaks French, German, Italian, English and Slovene."

But Melania made sure that the world saw her as her own woman, not just Trump's companion. She said that they didn't live together and that she maintained her own small apartment. "I have my career, he has his career," she said. "We spend a lot of time together. We understand each other very well. It's a great energy, a special chemistry between us." What about Trump's quip that he could be married in twenty-four hours if necessary? "He'd need to ask," she told the interviewer. But "yes, yes," she would wed Trump on twenty-four hours' notice. "You never know what could happen in life."

A constant media wild card was Howard Stern's show. On November 9, Trump and Stern were having another of their frequent radio chats. Trump mentioned that "grown men weep" when he walks into a restaurant with Melania. Stern called Trump "Mr. President" and played a snippet of "Hail to the Chief."

"Let me talk to that broad in your bed," Stern said. Trump said that she was in another room; he went to get her. "What's her name again? Melanie?" Stern said to his colleagues while he waited. "Starts with an *M*," one of them said. Melania got on the phone, and the exchange was memorable.

MELANIA KNAUSS: *Hi, how are you?*

HOWARD STERN: *You are so hot.*

KNAUSS: *Oh, thank you.*

STERN: *I've seen pictures of you. I can't believe it. You're a dream.*

KNAUSS: *Oh.*

STERN: *You are so hot.*

KNAUSS: *So you're coming out with us?*

STERN: *Yes, I am, baby. Let me tell you something—I want you to put on your hottest outfit.*

KNAUSS: *Okay, no problem.*

STERN: *What are you gonna wear?*

KNAUSS: *Oh, I don't tell you now. You will see.*

STERN: *What are you wearing right now?*

KNAUSS: *Uhh, not much.*

STERN: *Are you naked? Are you nude?*

KNAUSS: *Almost.*

STERN: *Uhhh. I have my pants off already.*

More banter, then:

STERN: *So what are you—you in love with Trump?*

KNAUSS: *Sorry?*

STERN: *Are you in love with Trump?*

KNAUSS: *Yeah, we have a great time.*

STERN: *You wanna marry him?*

KNAUSS: *Uhh, I'm not answering that.*

STERN: *You don't even care.*

KNAUSS: *Let's see. What?*

STERN: *You don't even care.*

KNAUSS: *Why?*

STERN: *You're perfect. And what do you do? You go over there every night and just have sex?*

KNAUSS: *That's true. We have great, great time.*

STERN: *Every night you have sex?*

KNAUSS: *Mm-hmm. Even more.*

Melania explained that she wears a thong bikini on the beach so that she doesn't get tan lines. Stern told her that she had "a very big chest for a model." Then she put Trump back on the phone.

STERN: *She's naked there, isn't she?*

TRUMP: *She is actually naked.*

STERN: *Oh Jesus, what a life.*

Stern called Trump "refreshingly honest" and brought up Trump's comments about Clinton and Lewinsky.

> STERN: *I was watching an interview with Donald and very seriously Donald said, "Listen, I don't think America was shocked by the Monica Lewinsky thing; they were shocked by that he wasn't with a supermodel, that he was with some big, fat chick." And even Donald couldn't believe it.*
>
> TRUMP: *Well, I did make the statement that there are those that say that if President Clinton was caught with a supermodel, he would have been everyone's hero. Now, of course, I would never say a thing like that, but there are those that say it.*

Stern closed with a prediction: "Donald Trump is a great friend of this show, and President Trump will be a reality."

> TRUMP: *Thank you.*
>
> STERN: *Thank you, Mr. President. Mr. President, go back to that girl.*
>
> TRUMP: *I will.*

Melania's credentials as a Trump-style first lady had just taken a massive leap forward. By early December, the *New York Times* was taking another look at Melania, in light of the "notorious interview" with Howard Stern.

The article described Melania as having an "Eastern European accent that can render scrambled eggs caviar," and went on to say:

Did Ms. Knauss do the interview naked?

"He did ask me what I'm wearing, and I said, 'Not much' and it was quoted that I am nude."

. . . But her boyfriend talked about their sex life on the air.

A shrug, a conspiratorial woman-to-woman grin. "It's the man thing, that's how the man talks."

The 1999 *Times* piece went on to say that Melania does not "admit to being bothered by the not uncommon suggestions of gold diggery that sometimes accompany young women who date wealthy older men; by a *New York Post* cartoon, after the Howard Stern interview, which pictured Ms. Knauss in bed with Mr. Trump, with a thought bubble in the form of a dollar sign over her head.

"The press could be sometimes very mean," Ms. Knauss says. "They love to make a joke, that's how they're selling the newspapers. But I think you can't be with the person if it's not love, if they don't satisfy you. You can't hug a beautiful apartment, you can't hug an airplane, you can't talk to them."

What would Ms. Knauss's role be should she and Mr. Trump ever end up in the White House?

"I would be very traditional. Like Betty Ford or Jackie Kennedy. I would support him."

A few days later, *Good Morning America* aired an interview with Melania. It seemed that she had practiced lines. She came across as all-in, Trump's political partner, even telling correspondent Don Dahler which first ladies would be her role models. As almost every media outlet had reported all year long, Dahler told viewers that she was twenty-six years old, when she was actually twenty-nine (Melania didn't correct him). And, like everyone else, he repeated, without question, the assertion that she spoke four languages.

DON DAHLER: *When he talks about being a playboy, does that bother you?*

MELANIA KNAUSS: *It does not bother me because it's like a man thing. It doesn't mean if somebody's talking, you know, but it—it's a man thing, it's a man thing. And sometimes very cute.*

DAHLER: *Can you picture yourself the first lady?*

KNAUSS: *Yes, I would be very traditional like Jackie Kennedy and Betty Ford. I will support him, I will do a lot of social obligations.*

DAHLER: *Now you realize that if you did become first lady, it probably wouldn't be ethical for you to give commercial endorsements to products, so your modeling career might be over at that moment. What would you think about that?*

KNAUSS: *I will stand by my man.*

DAHLER: *You will be willing to give up a modeling career?*

KNAUSS: *Yes, yes.*

Dahler said that Melania's agent had told him that "dating Trump has been good for her career." He noted that "over the past few months, Knauss landed a number of high-profile modeling assignments," including a Concord watch campaign and a Panasonic commercial. Then she repeated that she wasn't with Trump because of his money:

> DAHLER: *Have you been hurt by the comments that you're with him because he's rich?*
>
> KNAUSS: *No, the people they don't know me. People who talk like this, they don't know me.*
>
> DAHLER: *Well, you don't see many twenty-six-year-old supermodels on the arm of fifty-three-year-old car mechanics.*
>
> KNAUSS: *You know what, you can't—you can't sleep or to hug or to talk with beautiful things with beautiful apartment, beautiful plane, beautiful cars, beautiful houses. You can't do that. You could feel very empty, and if somebody said, you know, marry the man because he's rich and famous, they don't know me.*

CBS NEWSMAN Dan Rather invited Trump and Melania to sit for a joint *60 Minutes* interview. In a segment taped in December 1999 and aired on January 11, 2000, a visibly skeptical Rather grilled Trump about his unconventional views. Watching the interview in 2019, it is striking how little Trump has changed in both the words he uses and his demeanor. He's been reading off the same script for decades, with Melania nearby, glowing with admiration. When Rather asked about Senator John McCain's war record, Trump said exactly what he would say on the campaign trail almost two decades later: "Does being captured make you a war hero? I don't know. I'm not sure." He said other politicians are "dumber than a rock," and that George W. Bush "doesn't seem like Albert Einstein."

Trump boasted that 21,000 people had come to hear him speak at a California campaign event. Rather pointed out that the crowd had actually come to hear wildly popular motivational speaker Tony Robbins, and that Trump was the "paid entertainment," earning $100,000 for an appearance at the Robbins event. Video from that event shows that Trump delighted the Robbins crowd with this salty advice: "Get even. When somebody screws you, screw 'em back, but a lot harder, folks." Standing behind him on the stage was Melania, smiling and laughing along.

People who have tried to understand Melania have wondered if she was shocked by her husband's language or behavior during the 2016 campaign and into his presidency. But Trump today is much the same Trump Melania knew and fully supported in the 1990s. In an April 2016 campaign appearance in Milwaukee, Melania told the crowd: "He's a great leader. He's fair. As you may know by now, when you attack him, he will punch back ten times harder." The crowd erupted in cheers and chanted, "Trump! Trump! Trump!"

In the *60 Minutes* segment, Melania said little, but she played a key role by just being there. "As a person, as a man, what's the best thing about him?" Rather asked her. She sat next to Trump, wearing a turtleneck and cream-colored slacks.

"He's a loyal man," she said, smiling. Seventeen years later, addressing the Republican National Convention, Melania would echo those words, saying, "Donald is intensely loyal to family, friends, employees, country."

In their interview, Rather asked: "And what's the worst thing about him?"

She shook her head, still smiling. "I don't have the worst thing," she said.

"Well there has to be something. Nobody's perfect," Rather pressed.

Trump looked at Melania. She looked at him. They smiled at each other. "I don't have it," she said to Rather, with a little laugh.

JUST BEFORE Christmas 1999, the news broke that Melania was going to appear nude in the coming issue of British *GQ*. The *Daily News* called it "Trump's Bare Force One." Trump was coy about his involvement in the shoot, leaving the reporter with the false impression that he had been "blindsided" by the "sizzling spread." Trump said that Melania looked "gorgeous" and said he was unconcerned about the photos because *GQ* was "a highly reputable magazine." He added, "She sure doesn't look like Barbara Bush."

In late December, Melania told the *Washington Post*: "'I think America needs a new leader. It's good. It's a good idea. You need someone who is, mmm, talk straight and not—' And Knauss wiggles her hand around in imitation of a slithering snake."

On January 5, Trump appeared at Trump Tower to sign copies of his campaign book, *The America We Deserve*. Melania was nowhere to be seen.

They had just broken up.

Kara Young, supermodel who once dated Trump

CHAPTER 7

Melania or Kara?

THE NEWS that Trump and Melania had separated spread when the *New York Post* wrote about it on January 11 (the same day the *60 Minutes* interview aired), with the headline: "Trump Knixes Knauss: Donald-Dumped Supermodel Is 'Heartbroken.'" The story quoted unnamed people close to Trump—at the time, that was widely assumed to be code for Trump himself—saying that he had initiated the breakup. Regardless of the facts, the Trump spin was always going to be that he was the man in charge (and that he had "dumped" a "supermodel").

Two days later, Melania apparently counterpunched. A different *Post* writer filed a story sourced to a "pal" of Melania's— which at the time was interpreted to mean that Melania was playing Trump's game and speaking to the press herself. In this version of events, Melania had dumped Donald after discovering a towel smeared with another woman's makeup in his Trump

151

Tower apartment. She suspected he was cheating on her. In fact, according to someone who saw the two women, Melania had even crossed paths in the building with Kara Young, whom she knew had dated Trump. A Trump friend said that he had wanted Melania to find out that Young had been there, to see how she would react. Details of exactly when and how they broke up are still unclear, but afterward, Trump spoke of her to reporters as casually as if he had just let a favorite housekeeper go: "Melania is an amazing woman, a terrific woman, a great woman, and she will be missed."

Trump would read how others missed her, too. The *Globe and Mail* wrote, "Most of the construction workers canvassed at the base of Trump World Tower this week chuckled at the idea of their boss running for higher office, though their eyes grew wide at the thought of a Slovenian underwear model as First Lady."

The timing of the split meant that the Melania and Trump relationship lived on in a number of glossy magazines that were about to go to press—or had already. *George* magazine had committed to featuring Trump on its February/March issue cover, with Melania about to plant a kiss on his cheek. The headline was "The Secret Behind Trump's Political Fling." News of the Donald-Melania breakup caused some last-minute shuffling. Editors found a quick fix: they cropped the photo. It still showed Trump with Melania, but the picture showed only her lips, and she could have been any woman. Inside was an extended profile by Christopher Byron, the noted financial journalist who died in 2017. It delved into Trump's life, career, finances, and the general

American zeitgeist of a celebrity real estate developer considering a run for president.

Byron seemed especially impressed by Melania's arrival during his interview with Trump at Mar-a-Lago. He wrote, "This vision, emerging from nowhere, wrapped in a towel you could have fit in a Taj Mahal tote bag, trying to clasp it to her nakedness with one hand, while shaking my hand with the other, and saying, 'I'm so flattered to meet you. Donald has told me so much.'" In last-minute edits, the breakup—but not Melania's correct age—was worked into his story.

Even the beautiful 26-year-old model, Melania Knauss, whom he paraded around as his potential first lady until their recent breakup, is something of an illusion. The press has taken to describing her as a fashion "supermodel," in much the way they uncritically fawned over his first wife, Ivana, as a top model and an "Olympic skier," two images that Trump did much to help cultivate. But just as Ivana seems to have been, at most, a barely known model prior to hooking up with him, Melania Knauss was largely unknown prior to her yearlong romance with Trump. She earned a good living, to be sure. But her status as a supermodel, whatever that means, was bestowed by the media only after Trump began incessantly introducing her that way as she hung on his arm at public functions.

A bigger editing problem was the sidebar about Melania, written by Sean Neary, under the headline "Meet the First Babe." The original layout featured a full-page photo of Melania in a tiny black bikini and a half-page photo spread of women from Trump's past—his ex-wives and six women identified as girlfriends. The smaller spread was headlined "Dealer's Choice," with the women's faces displayed on gold poker chips. In the updated layout, Melania was demoted to just another poker chip, under a newly plural head-line, "Meet the First Babes." In the story that was not published, Trump described Melania as his "possible wife number three" and "a potential first lady." There was also a description of Melania and Trump in their apartment: "'Isn't she gorgeous?' glows her boy-friend, Donald Trump, as he puts his left arm around her, strate-gically placing his hand on her backside, where it remains for the next 10 minutes. 'As far as supermodels go—and unfortunately I know them all—she is the most beautiful.'"

According to a copy of the original version of the story that was spiked because Melania and Trump broke up, Melania raved about Trump and took a swipe at Hillary Clinton, who would be a guest at the Trumps' wedding five years later:

Knauss is already thinking about moving into 1600 Pennsyl-vania Avenue. "Mr. Trump would be a great leader," she says, settling into a plush couch. "And as first lady, I would serve the nation. I would help the country be a better place." Unlike New York Senate candidate Hillary Clinton—who, Knauss says, "should run somewhere else"—this would-be presiden-tial partner promises to take a back seat to her husband. "I will be social. That is the right thing for the woman to do," Knauss explains in her accented English. "I will campaign with him, support him, be there for him . . . "

Knauss says she would give up all the glamor to take on the duties of first lady. "It would be an honor," she says. "Life will not be that different if we go on to the White House. I will continue to do charity work and attend social events."

After the split, Neary did manage to get Melania on the phone to confirm the breakup and to update his story with her thoughts on Trump. His final published story was boiled down to a few paragraphs and noted: "Just two weeks later, sources close to Knauss say she dumped the 53-year-old real estate mogul after she began to suspect that Trump was cheating on her. 'I'm not going to stay home and cry,' Knauss told *George* in her first interview after the breakup. 'Other girls would do that, but not me. I am confident in myself and who I am.'"

Neary said Melania also offered a new perspective on politics. The story that ran quoted her as saying:

Before the breakup: "I will campaign with him and be there for him."
After the breakup: "I will have to follow the election a bit more closely and listen to all the candidates."

Neary said in a recent interview that he thought it strange that Melania repeatedly referred to her boyfriend as "Mr. Trump." But he remembered her as "lovely, personable, and intelligent," adding, "She seemed to be proud to be in the situation she was in, and of who she was with. She was in a position of power."

The Trump-Melania split also happened after an article in *Talk* magazine had gone to print. The February 2000 issue hit newsstands in early January and featured a two-page photo of Melania in a red bikini and stiletto heels sprawled across a carpet bearing the presidential seal with the words "A Model First Lady." Accompanying Melania was a smaller photo of Trump, sitting in front of an American flag while talking on a red phone.

At the time, Amy Brill, a young writer assigned to profile Melania, seemed to be almost winking at readers. The idea of Melania Knauss in a presidential campaign, let alone as first lady, seemed like a joke. But there was Melania, talking it up seriously, like a political spouse, without the slightest whiff of irony. Melania wore a robe for the interview, before she removed it and posed for the photograph in her bikini on the rug.

> "You play a role," Melania Knauss says, very quietly. "It's a beez-ness." She has an Eastern European honey whisper. . . . When Knauss speaks, she does so in the manner of a cat on the verge of sleep. But she can shed this pose in a heartbeat.
>
> In politics, "you need to know how to deal with people," Knauss says brightly. "You need to choose the right people to work for you. You need to make the right decisions and stand by them. And," she finishes, "you need to know how to run a beez-ness."

Brill asked Melania if she was very different from her boyfriend, and she said no. What about the age difference? "I don't feel the age difference because we are still so young in the mind, and it is so enjoyable. We enjoy the life." As to what kind of first lady she would be:

> "I would be very traditional," she says. This is something of a stump speech for her. She'd emulate Jackie Kennedy, Betty Ford. "I will do social obligations, social events. I will do charities. I love children. I think Make-A-Wish Foundation is great." Knauss trails off, sips a diet Coke carefully. There's Barbara Bush to consider, Nancy Reagan. Hillary, too. Hillary perhaps especially.
>
> "Jackie is traditional," says Knauss. "Hillary—she is not. She is the opposite." Knauss is thinking now: "I don't think it's wrong. I think Hillary is a great woman."

In this 2000 article, Melania raved about Trump's political appeal and ability to connect with people, saying his supporters were so fervent that they would scream his name when they saw him. In 2016, as people stood in line for hours and yelled his name at Trump rallies, Trump told others that his wife had long been a true believer.

In 2019, Brill told me that Melania struck her as "smart, polite, and savvy" during the interview. "She was quite intelligent," she said. "She was very measured and very thoughtful and very soft-spoken and very polite. It was sort of 'not a word out of place.' She's the opposite of a loose cannon." She said Melania seemed to view the two roles—model posing in a bikini, domestic icon for the nation—as completely unrelated. "She's a model—she does whatever she's told to do in front of a camera," Brill said. "Being a first lady is a different job where you do different things. I don't think she saw the irony at all."

Brill said she believes that Melania was speaking hypothetically about being the first lady and didn't really believe Trump would ever be president. But she also saw in Melania a "chess player," someone who seemed capable of doing whatever it took to "protect her position." Brill added, "She doesn't seem particularly vulnerable to me, ever."

Her article was accompanied by a memorable photo of Melania lying on a rug in what was meant to look like the Oval Office. The photographer was Patrick Demarchelier, famous for his photos of Farrah Fawcett and Brooke Shields, whose work appeared in *Vogue* and other premier magazines. For years, Demarchelier, who earned a mention in *The Devil Wears Prada*, attended dinners and parties with Trump. Melania has cited being photographed by Demarchelier as a career highlight and listed working with him on her resume as late as 2015. (More recently, his career suffered after seven women accused him of sexual harassment.)

The last of the magazines still reporting that Trump and Melania were together was *Tatler*'s April issue, which included an eight-page spread of Melania wearing seven different bikinis.

Photos in it were shot at Mar-a-Lago. Melania reclines on a putting green, she pouts beneath the palms, she struts on stone steps, she poses with a putter.

> Melania . . . the curvaceous Slovenian model, who first arrived on America's shores in 1996, saw her career skyrocket when she hit the campaign trail with Donald Trump . . .
>
> The 53-year-old billionaire maintains that he dumped her in order to focus on his presidential ambitions, while the 26-year-old brunette insists that it was she who dumped him. Apparently, she found out he was carrying on with an ex-girlfriend—another supermodel.

Tatler also quoted Trump's friend Lucy Sykes, the stylist on Melania's *Town & Country* shoot the year before, about their relationship: "He'd say things like, 'She's only with me because I'm rich,' and she'd say, 'That's right, honey,'" recalls Sykes. "She played him at his own game."

Tatler said Knauss "has profited from the association at least as much as Trump has. When she hooked up with him at the end of 1998, she was a little-known lingerie model. . . . It's surely only a matter of time before she's cast in the next Bond film. Watch this space."

At the start of 2000, Donald Trump was the one to watch. The opening of the new millennium was a time of triumph for Trump. At fifty-three, he was now fully riding the Clinton-era economic boom. He had carefully cultivated his image as a lady-killer, a business whiz, master of the "Art of the Deal." At the time, Trump was fascinated by Jesse Ventura, a professional wrestler and political neophyte who became governor of Minnesota by winning only 37 percent of the vote in a three-way race. Trump told people he suddenly realized that he didn't need all the votes to become president, he just needed enough to win. He floated the idea of running as a third-party alternative to "Gush and Bore," as he liked to call Republican George W. Bush and Democrat Al Gore.

The night the news of his breakup with Melania ran in the *Post*, Trump was out with thirty-two beauty pageant contestants at One 51, a Manhattan dance club. A few days later, he hosted more than one hundred Reform Party members at Mar-a-Lago— without his steady girlfriend. Even the sober *New York Times* wondered: "What about Mr. Trump's breakup with MELANIA KNAUSS, the Slovenian model he had been dating? The split was no longer a rumor, but a fact, Mr. Trump said. This raises a question: Will it be difficult to campaign without a significant other?"

Trump's love life now had a political element.

Marriage thus far had not been a success story for Trump. His first one, to Ivana, ended badly. The second, to Marla, included the sting of having Marla caught on a beach late at night with one of his security guys. People close to Trump said they had never seen him so furious and humiliated. In January, Maples announced that she was publishing a memoir, *All That Glitters Is Not Gold*, and that it was not expected to be flattering to Trump.

Trump is known for threatening to sue to try to stop books about him from being published. Marla's memoir never appeared, eventually being withdrawn "by mutual consent."

Jay Goldberg, Trump's friend and lawyer who worked on his divorce from Ivana, said marriage hadn't been an easy fit for Trump, who was always looking for the next thing. "I noticed in the relationship with Marla, the philosophy that there's nothing that destroys love except for marriage . . . that if you have steak every night, you get tired of it," Goldberg told me. "He was so in love with Marla when he was cheating on Ivana. Then once they got married, the fun of the chase was over."

Yet, despite his track record, some people advising Trump to enter politics were nudging him toward a third marriage. The argument was that there had not been a bachelor president in more than a century. But Trump had other options besides Melania, chief among them another beautiful model named Kara Young.

Trump had first met Kara in 1995; Marla Maples introduced them at the downtown Cipriani, where many models gathered. While having lunch with Marla, Trump had spotted Kara sitting at the counter with a friend. "Who's that?" he asked. Marla told him, "That's Kara Young, the Victoria's Secret model," and then introduced Trump to her. Two years later, when Trump's marriage to Marla was on the rocks, Trump and Kara started dating. She loved that Trump was a fun, sober alternative to many of the men she met. On an early date when she ordered a glass of wine, he ordered one too but left it sitting untouched. Kara was charmed, and they started an on-again, off-again relationship that spanned several years.

Kara was from San Francisco, the daughter of a white father and a black mother. She was wild and exciting, gregarious, confident, and willing to tell Trump when she thought he was full of shit. She knew everybody he wanted to know—when they took Tiffany, who was around four years old, to see *The Lion King* on Broadway, they ended up chatting with Whitney Houston. Kara was cooler than Trump, and he knew it. Kara was also already famous, and hung out with supermodels such as Cindy Crawford, Elle Macpherson, and Christy Turlington. While Trump was a major celebrity in New York, she knew people he didn't. He loved it when she introduced him to Naomi Campbell, Kate Moss, Robert De Niro, Jack Nicholson, and Puff Daddy (Sean "Puffy" Combs).

"With Kara dating him, he scored the ringleader of the super-models," said his friend Jason Binn, the publisher of *Ocean Drive* and *Hamptons* magazines. "That was his thought process. . . . All the girls listened to her. She was a rock star and all the girls loved her." Kara was struck by how much Trump loved attention, and how he loved to be out, to be seen, to be written about in the press. She used to tell him, instead of people always saying, "There's Donald Trump," he should leave them saying, "Where's Donald Trump?" Leave them wanting more, she told him: "It's more alluring if you don't go every single place or comment on every single thing."

Trump and Melania said that they started dating in September

1998, when they met at the Kit Kat Club. Kara is unclear about her exact timeline with Trump but said that they started seeing each other in 1997 and dated on and off for years. "He was an intoxicating person, and it's not easy to exit that orbit," she said. For a while, at least, both Melania and Kara seem to have been orbiting together—seeing Trump at the same time. "They were concurrent for months," said one longtime Trump associate. "I would see them. They were in and out of the office at the same time. Both of them. I'm sure they knew about each other, because Donald told me they knew about each other, so there's no doubt about that."

How much they actually knew about each other is unclear, but they certainly saw each other. They ran into each other at a casting call, and they saw each other at a few parties. But whatever equilibrium existed, it all blew up in late 1999.

Interviews with people who know both Donald and Melania offer some nuanced explanations. Several associates said that Trump wanted to end things with Melania, but he didn't want to drop the axe himself. Despite Trump's famous "You're fired!" tagline from his television show *The Apprentice*, he has a long history of avoiding direct confrontations; he doesn't like the dirty work. Some friends suspect that he stage-managed the end—that he arranged events so that Melania would see Kara or find evidence of Kara—to get out of the relationship without having to confront Melania.

But Melania didn't give up on Trump, even though she had lots of interest from other men while she was dating Trump. Once during their courtship, a friend recalled that Melania wanted to attend a premiere in Los Angeles. Trump was unavailable, so Melania was accompanied by the heir to a wealthy family. "He was younger, good looking, everything—and his family was much bigger and richer than Trump," the friend said. This man liked Melania and felt he had much more to offer her than Trump did. He was shocked that she showed no interest. As he put it, Melania couldn't be "flipped" to dump Trump and take up with him. She told him that she had zero interest in anyone but Donald. Their breakup didn't seem to change that.

Several people close to Trump have said that Melania understood him better than any woman he had dated. He had published several books, and as one friend said, Melania seemed to have read the whole shelf. "There is high maintenance. There is low maintenance. I want no maintenance," Trump wrote, in *The Art of the Comeback* (1997), coauthored by Kate Bohner. Melania certainly was that, and she also didn't make herself too available to the man who had said that nothing was more attractive to him than something he couldn't have. Trump had written years earlier: "The same assets that excite me in the chase, often, once they are acquired, leave me bored. . . For me, you see, the important thing is the getting, not the having." A friend of Melania's explained, "She always knows the direction where she wants to go. She's not scared to go to the next step, and for that you have to have a lot of brains."

•   •   •

THROUGH THE winter, Trump continued to play Hamlet, contemplating both women and avoiding a decision. And as he thought about his political prospects, there was a new question to consider: Who would make the best political spouse? Trump called his friends and reviewed the pros and cons: "Melania or Kara?" Some advised him that Melania could be great, because she was a head-turner and loyal—there would be no whiff of scandal, no drama, no tell-all book. But they also noted that she was an immigrant who spoke English with a pronounced accent, which might be a negative for some voters, and she didn't like to speak in public. Even New York tabloids, the bibles of all things Trump, were still confused in late 1999 about her background and reported it in different ways. The Associated Press wrote about how little was known about where she came from. "Knauss' past is as mysterious as her German-sounding name," the wire service reported. Some reports said that she was Slovenian; others, Austrian. Trump told some people she was partly Italian. "She's Croatian," said one modeling agent she worked for. "No, maybe she's from Slovenia?"

Kara was gorgeous, famous, and well respected, and she would add star power to Trump's candidacy. She was also biracial, which could be a plus or a minus, depending on the voter. Kara had been married and had a young child, and while she found Trump fun to be with, friends said that Melania seemed to be much more committed to being his partner for the long term. Melania praised him constantly. She had few friends and a small family and seemed focused solely on Trump. She was always impeccably dressed, her hair and makeup just so, never sloppy, always camera ready. "I don't even know if she goes to the bathroom," said one friend, laughing.

"She is always perfect, put together," the friend added. "For me their relationship is not bizarre. She's from a small town in a small country and that has always driven her to make the extra effort to stand out." The woman said that Melania proved to Trump that she was not like any other woman and "embedded that image in his eyes." Melania was careful to always shine but to never outshine her boyfriend. She continued to do exactly what Trump liked during their breakup period. She stayed in; she dated no one. "Would another girl do that?" a friend said. "She was smart. She knew how to get him back. If she wanted to get back with him—and she did—this was the way to do it: prove her loyalty."

Trump began telling people he was impressed that she turned down dates. He could go out and it would not mean much, but she couldn't—and she seemed to understand his rules. That's not to say that Trump's behavior didn't infuriate her sometimes. During the breakup period, Matthew Atanian recalled phoning Melania just to check in. "How's it going with Trump?" he asked. "Oh, I don't go out with him anymore—he's a pig," she replied, according to Atanian's recollection.

But she also still wasn't going out with anyone else. She waited.

"He asked me which girl I should choose, and I said Kara because I never really liked Melania that much," said one long-time Trump associate. "I could tell that was not the answer he wanted. He had made up his mind. He said Melania was 'central casting.'"

Phillip Bloch, who worked as the creative style director of Trump's Miss Universe pageant, met Melania around this time, when she accompanied Trump to a fashion show, causing a commotion. After watching Melania with him over the years, he believes it would be hard for Trump to find a better match. "She's glamorous and presents very, very, very well—and she doesn't say much." Bloch knew other women Trump dated, and he knew that Trump wanted someone who made him look good but who also wasn't "too showy." "She is very gracious and polite and steady. She's the complete opposite of him, really. Which is why I think that's kind of the secret to her success."

But even a year after they got back together, Trump was still talking about Kara.

On May 10, 2001, former *Daily News* gossip columnist A. J. Benza, who had gone out with Kara Young before she dated Trump, appeared on *The Howard Stern Show* to promote a book. Trump called in, and he and Benza ended up shouting at each other. "I had been very successful with your girlfriend, I can tell you that," Trump said, gloating. He added: "A. J. doesn't like Trump for one reason: I stole his girlfriend. I took her away like he was a dog." Benza threatened to whack Trump with a baseball bat, and Trump taunted him: "Any girl you have, I can take from you."

The Trumps in 2005 with photographer Patrick Demarchelier,
actor George Hamilton, and director Martin Scorsese

CHAPTER 8

"Aren't I lucky?"

TWENTY-ONE-YEAR-OLD Melanija Knavs stood on a sidewalk in Ljubljana at the same moment Jure Zorcic rode past on his Vespa. She was, he recalled, "extra beautiful," and he stopped to talk to her. It was not simply her eyes that made her so striking, it was "everything," including how she was dressed. Zorcic said he and Melanija briefly dated before she left for her modeling career in Italy. "Disciplined and quiet" is how he remembered her, saying that these are common characteristics for Slovenians. She was smart, too. "She was thinking a hundred times over."

He still remembers one outfit she wore: rich brown leather from head to toe—soft leather, like the kind found in expensive cars, accented with big gold buttons. He pronounced her "one of the nicest girls I have ever met. But why? Because always low profile, always." She did not drink, he noticed. She was not one of the party girls letting loose as the country shed its socialist past.

They met again about ten years later in New York. Zorcic, who had made the trip with his girlfriend, left a message for Melania Knauss at Trump Tower, since he knew she was dating Trump. Two days after he left the message, he said, Melania called him in his hotel room.

Zorcic and Melania met in the café at Saks Fifth Avenue at 10:00 a.m. A man who Zorcic assumed was a bodyguard was sitting in another section, watching. They talked about life in the United States, but nothing personal. After an hour, Zorcic asked for the check, and Melania said, "What are you doing? Forget it." She made sure it was taken care of. Then they walked to the street and Melania left in a limo—a long way from riding Vespas in Ljubljana.

But to Zorcic, she seemed still to be the same woman who had been raised in a "normal, middle-class family." Her life, surroundings, wealth, and fame had changed drastically, and he expected that she could not possibly have remained the person he once knew, but after their conversation, he felt that in some ways she had not changed much at all.

But as Melania became a more permanent part of Trump's world in New York in the early 2000s, she increasingly left her old life behind. The woman who enjoyed her small apartment and bought her furniture at Crate & Barrel became the woman who embraced Donald Trump's gold-plated universe. Even before she met Trump, Melania had perfected the art of sealing off different parts of her life. In my travels around Sevnica and Ljubljana, people who had at one time considered Melania like family said she never called once and had long since moved on. People who met her in New York knew virtually nothing about her years in Europe. Many of those I interviewed in Slovenia, Europe, and New York said that they felt it was as if she wanted to erase anything that had happened in her life before she met Donald Trump. "It's almost like she actually believes she was always Mrs. Trump," said one.

Trump is a master image maker and mythologizer. In his telling, his wife was a supermodel from the minute they met, and then she became Mrs. Donald Trump. One seamless yellow brick road.

In an interview with *Tatler* in 2005, Melania herself made it clear that she never discussed past boyfriends, and that she had largely severed ties with Slovenia. "I left 15 years ago. I don't have many contacts with people there—no schoolfriends. I go there because of my mum . . . the last time was about two years ago." It was an explanation she repeated often. As early as her 1998 Paris press conference, she had stated that she had lost contact with people in her home country, an odd thing to tell six Slovenian journalists.

In 2019, I discussed Melania's tendency to compartmentalize parts of her life with Stephanie Winston Wolkoff, who has experienced this behavior from both sides, first as one of Melania's close friends and part of her small circle in New York and later as an outsider, after a falling-out. Winston Wolkoff was one of Melania's few personal friends to attend her wedding, and they both raised young boys together. She had worked for *Vogue* and also organized the Metropolitan Museum of Art's Costume Institute Gala, the famous "Met Gala," which led the Trumps to select her as a primary organizer for many events at Trump's 2017 inaugural. She worked on planning the details of inaugural events, down to how thick the gold border on invitations would be. As she helped Melania think about how to use her office to help children, Winston Wolkoff held White House meetings with experts on social and emotional learning—but plans to focus on that never materialized. When a controversy erupted regarding how more than $100 million raised for the Trump inaugural was spent, Winston Wolkoff received significant blame. She felt scapegoated by others around Trump, and several working on the inaugural agreed. Melania never publicly came to her defense and that, she said, was "devastating."

Winston Wolkoff said perhaps it is no coincidence that Melania admires old-time actresses including Sophia Loren and Audrey Hepburn. Years ago, Hollywood studios could create whatever image they wanted to for their stars. It was much easier to sell a perfectly polished story to the public in the days before the internet and social media. And there was far less questioning of the personal stories that actresses told about their lives or the images they chose to project.

Her unsentimental streak has left a bad taste with other old friends. After they no longer shared an apartment, Atanian said that he and Melania would run into each other periodically but that the atmosphere was always chilly. He remembers when she introduced him to Trump—"Matthew, this is Donald Trump"— at a Halloween party thrown by Heidi Klum. "This is Matthew, my old roommate," she explained. Atanian said Trump barely acknowledged him. Soon, he said, Melania started treating him the same way. As she climbed higher up the social and professional ladder in New York, Atanian said that he felt as if she was pulling the ladder up behind her. She seemed to be wiping him from her history. He saw her and Trump one more time, at trendy Manhattan club Spy Bar. He said that she hardly spoke to him. "She was always a nice person," Atanian said, but he feels that she changed after she met Trump. "She'd just walk around hanging on to his arm, and that was it," he said.

But Atanian also didn't go out of his way to join Melania's new world. When she was first with Trump, Atanian remembers that he and Paolo Zampolli's girlfriend, Edit Molnar, joked about Trump's penis size. "Don't say this—he's a real man," Melania told them. She had a similar response when Atanian asked her about Trump's over-the-top gilded apartment in Trump Tower. According to him, her answer was, "Oh, it's so beautiful, so much class. This is the way real men live."

Atanian said that he and Melania stayed in touch for a while, but that at some point he called and found that her number had been changed. He called Donald Trump's modeling agency repeatedly and left messages for her. She never called back. They told him: "We gave her your message, man. If she doesn't call you, there's nothing we can do." Atanian heard similar stories from others. He recounted being in Salt Lake City to photograph the 2002 Winter Olympics and running into a photographer from Slovenia. He mentioned that his old roommate, Melania Knauss, was also from Slovenia. The photographer replied: "Oh, I went to high school with her. She's a snob. She doesn't talk to us or any of her friends."

Trump-era friends, however, recount a different experience with Melania. Donald Trump and Chris Christie, then the U.S. Attorney in New Jersey and later New Jersey's governor, often met for dinner in Manhattan. In 2002, for the first time, Trump said that he would bring his girlfriend, and he suggested that Christie bring his wife, Mary Pat, who worked on Wall Street. He told Christie that he was getting serious with this one. The woman who arrived with Trump was Melania. "Melania was the only one he ever brought," Christie recalled.

"I didn't know what to expect when I met her the first time," he said. "I'd heard of her obviously, because she'd been in the tabloids for dating him and for her own modeling career. So I knew the name, but I knew nothing about her. And by the end of the first dinner, it was clear to me that this was a really smart, really strong personality."

Christie added, "That first dinner, I remember getting into the car afterwards and Mary Pat saying, 'So she's gotta be that beautiful and smart.' Like she's a home run. We would go out to dinner usually three or four times a year." Christie noted that Melania was "up-to-date" on what was going on in the world, and readily discussed any topic that came up at their dinners, whether it was business, politics, or law enforcement. They also talked about their families. He recalls her being "incredibly relaxed," adding, "I don't think she felt like she was being observed, judged, that kind of thing, so she was very comfortable. We just hit it off."

The other thing that Christie noticed was how well Melania balanced Trump. "She was very good at slowing him down." When Trump would launch into a long commentary, making it hard for other people to say a word, Melania would gently put her hand on his arm. Trump would pivot and start asking his dinner companions questions, engaging and including them. "What became clear to me was that she was very influential with him and remains so. And she is also very candid, so if she doesn't like something, she says it. Now, she doesn't do it in a rude way."

Christie sees Melania as a good judge of people and a positive influence on Trump. "If she trusts you, if she's developed a trust for you, she is an extraordinarily warm person." One thing many people agree upon about this time: Trump was never boring and was generous with his homes and plane. Apart from his flirtation with the Reform Party, he was not personally involved in politics, and people laughed at his self-promotional, over-the-top style. It was entertainment. In the pre-Twitter era, Trump hung out with as many Democrats as Republicans. He took Melania to interesting places and introduced her to famous people. "She thought she died and went to heaven when she met him. She loved him. People say she just married him for his money—there were other rich men she could have married. She really loved him," said a woman who knew her at the time.

ON JANUARY 22, 2005, thirty-four years after she was born Melanija Knavs in a socialist country, Melania Knauss married one of the kings of American capitalism and became Mrs. Donald J. Trump. The ceremony was held at the Bethesda-by-the-Sea Episcopal Church, in Palm Beach, and a fleet of limos ferried the guests to nearby Mar-a-Lago for the reception afterward. Most of the three hundred fifty guests at their wedding were famous. Elton John sang. So did Billy Joel, who performed his own version of "That's Why the Lady Is a Tramp," calling it, "That's Why the Donald Is a Trump."

Some of the guests were not especially close to the Trumps but attended out of curiosity. Bill Clinton, who had left the White House four years earlier, was there, as was Hillary Clinton, then a U.S. senator representing New York and later Trump's rival for the presidency. (One guest recounted how people approached her at the wedding and encouraged her to run for president.) Rudy Giuliani, Arnold Schwarzenegger, and Benjamin Netanyahu, who had been prime minister of Israel and would later be elected again, were also among the guests. So were some of the country's most famous athletes, including Derek Jeter and Shaquille O'Neal. Also at the wedding was Jeff Zucker, then running NBC television programming, and now head of CNN, one of Trump's most frequent Twitter targets.

Anna Wintour, editor in chief of *Vogue*, *American Idol* judge Simon Cowell, and supermodel Heidi Klum were also in the crowd. So were a lot of media celebrities, including Barbara Walters, morning show figures Matt Lauer, Katie Couric, Kathie Lee Gifford, and Gayle King, longtime MSNBC host Chris Matthews, daytime talk show hosts Kelly Ripa and Regis Philbin, and CBS president Les Moonves. The names alone are a reminder that in 2005, Melania did not marry the polarizing person America now knows.

Melania invited very few people she had known before she began dating Trump. Her sister, Ines, was her maid of honor. There were no bridesmaids. Her parents were there and so was Paolo Zampolli, who introduced her to Trump.

Trump, as he boasted about the lavish plans for their upcoming wedding, said he was considering hiring two of the most sought-after photographers in the world, Marco Glaviano and Patrick Demarchelier, to shoot it. Neither was keen to act as a wedding photographer, and both knew Trump would likely turn around and sell exclusive rights to the wedding photos to make money. Glaviano quoted his fee to Trump—at least $1 million, according to other photographers who heard the story—infuriating Trump. Demarchelier reportedly proposed an even higher fee. Trump told Melania he didn't want either of them and to make sure neither photographer brought a camera—not the easiest phone call for a model to make to two fashion-world icons. But people involved in the wedding said Melania made the calls and shrugged any embarrassment off with a characteristic *You know how he is*. To this day, unless it involves another woman, she has shown a great ability to not be fazed by anything Trump does, explaining to others, "That's the way he is." But even then, she did set her own boundaries. Trump wanted to accept an offer from NBC, the network on which his television show, *The Apprentice*, aired, to broadcast their wedding live. Melania said no.

At the service, Tiffany Trump, eleven, handed out programs, and Ivanka read from the Bible. Don Jr. and Eric were their father's best men. Cameron Burnett, the young son of Mark Burnett, the producer of *The Apprentice*, was the ring bearer. Melania's mother brought her baptism candle from Slovenia, and the bride carried the family rosary beads. At Mar-a-Lago, an orchestra in white tuxedos played the classics: Gershwin and Porter and, naturally, "I'll Take Manhattan." Toasts were made with endless bottles of Cristal champagne. Trump told people the wedding was Melania's day, and she told *People* magazine: "I arranged everything." She had a wedding planner but selected everything herself, from the centerpieces to the candles lighting the walkways. Her dress was made of white satin and beaded with 1,500 crystals and her veil was sixteen feet long. Tiffany & Co. printed invitations that she designed. It was her fairy-tale wedding.

Appearing on the cover of *Vogue* is the holy grail for a model, and Melania landed on the cover in her wedding dress. She had chosen a design from Dior that she had shopped for in Paris with

Vogue's famous style guru André Leon Talley. On the cover was the headline "Donald Trump's New Bride: the Ring, the Dress, the Wedding, the Jet, the Party." Inside, the accompanying story was headlined "How to Marry a Billionaire." Writer Sally Singer, traveling with the Trumps on his private plane, captured an exchange between Melania and Trump:

> She says with a laugh, "Doesn't anybody care what the bride wants?" She turns to Donald. "You said, 'Do everything and I'll just turn up.'"
>
> "That's right, I did," Donald admits. "I'll just turn up in my suit. Black tie."
>
> "You're wearing a white tie," Melania informs him, "and a white cummerbund. They're already hanging in your closet."
>
> Donald laughs delightedly. "Isn't she spectacular? Aren't I lucky?"

Glamour magazine later listed the nuptials as one of the "7 most spectacular weddings of all time." Among the other six were those of Princess Diana and Prince Charles, Grace Kelly and Prince Rainier, and Jacqueline Lee Bouvier and John F. Kennedy. Getting mentioned alongside global royalty was seen as a patented Trump publicity move. To many guests, the wedding provided a glimpse of Melania's role in her relationship with her new husband: she was a star, but it was unmistakably a Trump production. It was the moment Melania became fully absorbed into Trump's world. Before a crowd of Trump family, Trump friends, Trump business associates, Trump sports and media pals, and Trump golfing buddies, Melania became a Trump.

Becoming Mrs. Trump meant signing a prenup. Questions about their financial agreement surfaced about a year after Trump and Melania started dating. "Donald Trump's name is synonymous with a lot of things, but not the least is the phrase 'prenuptial agreement.' Do you know what that is?" *Good Morning America* correspondent Don Dahler asked Melania in their early December 1999 interview. He seemed to be making sure Melania understood the question.

"Yes, I know what it is," she said.

"Given his history with acrimonious divorces, with bitter divorces, would you even consider signing one with him?" Dahler asked.

"You know, everybody has different opinions, so let's see what happens," she replied. This was chess in front of a national audience. Dahler looked surprised, like she couldn't be serious. "Different opinions about?" he asked.

"About the prenuptial agreement, about sign it, not to sign it. Everybody decides what—you know, what is inside of them," she said with a smile.

"So you're not ruling out anything?" he asked.

Melania paused for a couple of long seconds. She knew that in addition to an audience of millions, an even more important audience of one was surely watching. "No," she said.

Donald Trump had a highly public track record of protecting himself with ironclad prenups. When he married Ivana in

1977, she signed a prenup that was renegotiated several times. When they divorced, Ivana challenged their agreement in court, demanding $2.5 billion, half of what she estimated his net worth to be at the time, and asking for half was not outrageous. Actress Amy Irving had recently divorced Steven Spielberg, and her attorneys successfully argued in court that the prenup written on a napkin didn't count. Irving had been married to Spielberg for four years and ended up with almost $100 million.

There are varying accounts of exactly how much Ivana got. But in the end, the prenup largely held, and Trump kept the vast majority of his wealth. Ivana settled for $14 million in cash, the Greenwich mansion, an apartment in a Trump building, and access to Mar-a-Lago for one month a year (but she would later write that it was "too weird to go there," so she bought her own place in Palm Beach). Trump also agreed to pay $650,000 a year to support the couple's three children. When Trump married Marla Maples in December 1993, he had insisted on a prenup that gave him the option of an inexpensive emergency exit from the marriage if it lasted less than five years.

In a June 2019 *Vanity Fair* article, journalist Gabriel Sherman reported that he had been passed a copy of the Marla prenup. He said that she had originally sought a guarantee of $25 million, but that under the terms she finally signed, Trump agreed to pay her only $1 million if they separated within five years, plus another $1 million to buy a house. The document also said that Trump would stop making $100,000 annual child support payments for Tiffany when she turned twenty-one. And Trump's payments would cease earlier if Tiffany joined the military or the Peace Corps.

In addition, Sherman reported, Marla had agreed to an extensive confidentiality agreement saying that she wouldn't publish "any diary, memoir, letter, story, photograph, interview, article, essay, account or description or depiction of any kind whatsoever, whether fictionalized or not, concerning (or seeming to concern) the details of the parties' marriage." Jay Goldberg, Trump's longtime lawyer, told me that Trump kept one eye on the calendar. "He kept questioning me—how close are we to the five years? Like he wanted to divorce her, and he didn't want the five years to pass. I'd say, 'Donald, it's only a little more than four years.'"

Trump served Marla with divorce papers just under the deadline, allowing him to make an inexpensive exit from the marriage. They separated in May 1997 and their divorce was final in June 1999. "After giving Donald two years to honor the verbal commitments he made to me during our 12-year relationship, I decided to walk away completely under the terms of our prenuptial agreement that had been placed before me just five days before our 1993 wedding," Marla said in a statement at the time. Melania, who had lived through the last gasps of the Marla relationship, saw precisely how the prenup worked so ruthlessly well against Marla.

A few months before his wedding to Melania, Trump jokingly recalled his history with prenups with gossip columnist Liz Smith, saying that both exes had sued him but that he had prevailed: "And had I not had those prenuptial agreements, I wouldn't be talking to you today. Other than talking to you from the standpoint of a loser, perhaps. And even then we'd be having lunch at McDonald's instead of Le Cirque."

Smith asked if he and Melania had a prenup. "Yes, we do. And the beautiful thing about Melania is she agrees with it. She knows I have to have that. Nobody gets married thinking they're going to get divorced. But 55 percent of the people who get married do get divorced. You have to protect your life. Because the court system is unpredictable, and you can't have unpredictability and be a successful person. You have to have a prenup. But I would be shocked if I had to use it. I'd be very surprised if something went astray with this."

MELANIA KNEW from the start that Trump would be a hands-off father. He had often said that he was not the type of guy to push a stroller around Central Park, and his views hadn't changed in 2016, when I interviewed him in Trump Tower. He said that he raised great kids in no small part thanks to their mothers. While we were talking, Jared Kushner, wearing shorts, entered Trump's office, ready to review a campaign speech. Jared paused to praise Trump as a parent and said he wisely was not the type to give a kid a trophy for just showing up. If they did mediocre work, he told them.

Trump was not a big presence in the daily lives of his oldest three children from his first marriage until they started working at the Trump Organization, and he spent less time with his fourth child, Tiffany, as she was growing up. His fifth child, Barron, was born on March 20, 2006. As a toddler and young child, Barron was often formally dressed in suits, jackets, and elegant sweaters—just like his father. Melania made him her top priority and was a hands-on mother. *Redbook* quoted her as saying that she had let him write "Barron's Bakery" on the wall in crayons in his playroom—knowing it could be painted over.

But having a child also changed how present Melania was in Trump's public life. While they were dating, she had often sat on his lap at parties and was seen snuggling up against him, but after they married, spontaneous public affection became far more restrained. While Trump still calls her "baby," Melania is more formal in many ways and calls him "Donald." After Barron was born, some of Trump's friends thought that he was less interested in Melania. "He wasn't showing her off and they were not going out like before," said a friend of the couple. Tellingly, Trump had said to ABC's Nancy Collins in 1994, "I create stars. I love creating stars. And, to a certain extent, I've done that with Ivana. To a certain extent, I've done that with Marla . . . Unfortunately, after they're a star, the fun is over for me."

Two women have very publicly stated that they had affairs with Trump after Barron was born and while Trump was filming *The Apprentice* in Los Angeles. Another woman told me that around this time Trump was also trying to pursue her romantically, including offering rides in his jet to wherever she wanted and dinners with famous people. Until the 2016 campaign was underway, Melania did not realize the extent of his philandering, according to three people close to the couple. But she did attend

The Jutranka factory that made children's clothes was central to Melania's childhood. Her mother worked as a patternmaker there, and Melania and her older sister modeled in factory fashion shows. This photograph from the archives of the National Museum of Contemporary History in Slovenia shows unknown women working at Jutranka in November 1983, when Melania was thirteen.

When Melania attended elementary school in the 1970s, all students in Yugoslavia wore identical uniforms for a ceremony that took place around age seven, where they pledged to study hard, respect their parents, and love their socialist country. This photograph shows a Union of Pioneers event in November 1979 at a school in Ljubljana.

Melania grew up in Sevnica (pronounced SEH-oo-nee-tsa), a town of around five thousand people, about fifty miles from the Italian border city of Trieste. In a November 2016 campaign speech, the first lady described it as "a small town in Slovenia near a beautiful river and forest."

4

Photographer Stane Jerko holds a picture he took of sixteen-year-old Melania, then called Melanija Knavs. After Jerko spotted her one evening outside a festival hall, she agreed to a photo session. Jerko was struck by how analytical Melanija was, asking questions about camera angles and lighting.

5

Marina Masowietsky spotted Melania's photographs in a pile of two hundred applications for a modeling contest she organized. "Yes, she could be a model," Masowietsky thought. "There is something there." Melania ended up in second place in the contest, but that was enough to get her a contract with an agency in Milan. In this photo, Melania's picture is on the wall above and just to the left of Masowietsky's head.

Melania played the role of the first female U.S. president in a short video that aired on Slovenia TV in 1993. "It's the most extraordinary historical coincidence," said Jožica Brodaric, who wrote the script for the video directed by Andrej Košak.

Melania Trump at a campaign stop in a suburb of Philadelphia on November 3, 2016. She spoke of her early memories of the United States. "America was the word for freedom and opportunity. America meant if you could dream it, you could become it."

Melania Trump spoke for hours to journalists in Paris in 1998, talking about her modeling career and her aspirations to be an actress. "Luck is important because you have to be at the right place at the right time," she said.

Melania was aware of Trump's complicated family life right from the start. He had been married twice before and had children with each wife. Here at a November 28, 2000, party and benefit auction at Cipriani in New York City, Melania is pictured with Trump as well as his first wife, Ivana, and her boyfriend at the time, Roffredo Gaetani.

By the time Melanija Knavs arrived in the United States in 1996, she was known as Melania Knauss. The next year, she appeared in this Camel ad that ran on a billboard near Times Square, where a film director saw it and asked her to audition for a movie.

The April 2000 issue of *Tatler* magazine featured an eight-page spread of Melania posing in many different bikinis, including this one. She was dating Donald Trump, and appeared in several magazines around this time.

Donald Trump is flanked by Victoria Silvstedt and Melania at *Playboy* magazine's fiftieth anniversary celebration in 2003. Silvstedt, the 1997 Playmate of the Year, and Melania had been roommates in Paris when both modeled there in the 1990s.

Melania Knauss during a party for the 2000 *Sports Illustrated* Swimsuit Issue in New York City. She was one of the models featured in the magazine that had Daniela Peštová on the cover.

For the December 2000 issue of now-defunct men's magazine *FHM*, Melania poses in lingerie. "No one pays too much attention to Donald Trump anymore—they're too interested in his girlfriend," the magazine declared.

Creative director Scott Woodward works on the set of a shoot for a Concord watch ad campaign that ran in 1999. Melania Knauss is lying in a hotel bed where one of the ads in the "Be Late" campaign was shot.

16

Melania was the model in this 1999 award-winning "Be Late" ad campaign for luxury watches. Its message was that some things were worth being late for; the real luxury was not the watch but time.

17

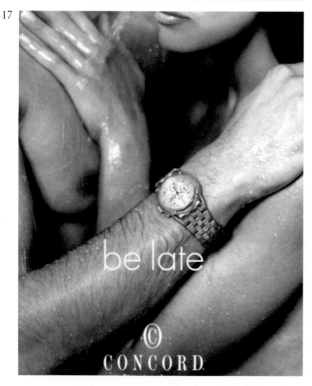

Trump dropped by the Mercer Hotel in SoHo just as this ad was being shot. "I got out of the shower and put a towel around my waist," male model Sascha Eiblmayr said. "He said, 'It looks like I have some stiff competition.'"

Donald Trump and Melania Knauss, along with her sister, Ines, raise their glasses for a New Year's toast at Mar-a-Lago in 2004, the year before they were married.

Donald, Melania, and Barron Trump with Melania's parents, Amalija and Viktor Knavs, and Santa Claus, on Christmas Day in 2008. Born in the former Yugoslavia, Melania's parents became American citizens in 2018.

Melania and Donald Trump arrive for a campaign rally in Wilmington, North Carolina, days before the November 2016 election. For most of the race, Melania kept a low profile on the campaign trail, explaining she wanted to stay home with her son.

Melania waves to the crowd at the 2016 Republican National Convention in Cleveland, Ohio. Coverage of her speech was dominated by news reports that some lines were nearly identical to ones spoken by Michelle Obama at the 2008 Democratic National Convention.

Melania visited the Giza pyramids in Egypt in 2018 during a week-long trip to Africa. After posing for photos widely seen around the world, she said to reporters, "I wish people would focus on what I do, not what I wear," an eyebrow-raising comment for a former model who wears such distinctive clothing.

Melania's jacket drew international attention in June 2018 because she is a careful dresser and the jacket had a confounding "I Really Don't Care. Do U?" message on the back as she headed to visit migrant children at a shelter in Texas. Melania explained months later that the message was meant "for the people and for the left-wing media who are criticizing me," but questions linger about why she wore it.

Melania sits in the Oval Office one day in February 2019. The first lady's office is in the East Wing of the White House, and the Oval Office is in the West Wing, where she sometimes attends official meetings.

Melania and her mother, Amalija Knavs, walk the grounds of the White House in June 2018. Her mother has been a huge support and influence, and she frequently stays at the White House, where she speaks Slovenian with her grandson, Barron.

Melania and Donald Trump met with Pope Francis at the Vatican in May 2017. Melania is Catholic and described the visit as "one I'll never forget."

Donald Trump, accompanied by Melania and son Barron, makes a brief stop to talk to reporters before departing for Palm Beach in February 2019. Throughout the presidency, Melania has frequently visited Mar-a-Lago.

Melania speaks to guests at a state dinner she planned at the White House for Australian Prime Minister Scott Morrison and his wife, Jenny, in September 2019.

Melania and her husband are similar in more ways than many people realize, and even their signatures look alike. Both Trumps signed a 2019 Christmas card delivered to members of Congress.

parties where she watched her husband rekindle his modelizer ways, gravitating to and putting his arm around young models. At one party at the *Playboy* Mansion, the guests included a former Playmate of the Year, Karen McDougal. She would later go public with claims that she had a lengthy affair with Trump that started shortly after Barron was born. A person at this party said that Melania was talking about her new son, Barron, and looking "extremely uncomfortable as she saw her husband grab women and hold them for photos."

Melania stayed at home more, spending her days inside Trump Tower or at Mar-a-Lago or Bedminster. Said one long-time friend, "I think her favorite place is Mar-a-Lago. She loves the weather. It's relaxed. I think she feels like she can be very private there. People don't bother her. She's not very approachable. She's not like him. He's around like, 'How's your drink? Did you like the lunch? Was it good? Was the club sandwich good?' Melania is sitting by the pool, reading a book. They don't bother her. I've watched it; they don't approach her."

To carve out some space inside their gold-plated home in New York, she had a personal spa constructed in a section of the top floor of the Trump Tower penthouse, where Marla and Tiffany had lived when she first started dating Trump. In 2008, she told *Allure* that she began the Trump Tower spa project because, "I wanted some privacy and comfort when I needed to get a massage, manicure or pedicure, or have my hair or makeup done."

Melania told the magazine that she was proud that the room-size spa reflected her own tastes. "It's 300 square feet, all white marble and silver fixtures with white towels and robes," she said. "Everything is from Italy, and it's all very modern—a very different look from the rest of the apartment, which is more . . . baroque."

Allure asked if she invited friends.

"No, it is private, more for myself."

"What about your husband?"

"NO [*laughs and laughs*], my husband never comes in! Of course he has seen it, but . . . well, he doesn't have time. Everybody has different hobbies and what they do for relaxation. He likes to play golf and be out—and that's fine with me."

Melania was once asked what advice she had received from older models when she started her career. Her response was that she never got advice from other models but did from her mother. "She was always taking care of herself. That was very important, and I guess she instilled that in me as well." She said that her mother told her that relaxation time was vital for the mind as well as the body, and that "when you take care of yourself, you can take care of others." And increasingly, Melania relied on her mother and father as she devoted herself to her son. The story of their presence in the United States is intensely tied to her own immigration story, which received new scrutiny after her husband began his run for president.

On July 28, 2006, the summer of the year Barron was born, Melania Trump officially became a U.S. citizen, five years after being granted a green card and slightly less than ten years after she first arrived in New York. Later, questions about her visa status were fueled largely by the couple's refusal to make her documentation public—just as Donald Trump had refused to make his tax returns public. Trump made opposition to immigration a cornerstone of his campaign. He insisted that his wife had come to America legally, but the lack of transparency led to suspicion that there was something improper about Melania's immigration story.

In August 2016, the *New York Post* published the nude photos that Melania had done for *Max* magazine, and incorrectly reported that they had been shot in 1995. That seemed to contradict Melania's assertions that she had first arrived in the United States in 1996. While the *Post*'s reporting turned out to be wrong (the newspaper later corrected it), it was picked up by other outlets and her immigration history caused a continuing distraction for the campaign.

On August 9, Trump promised that Melania would hold a news conference to set the record straight. "They said my wife, Melania, might have come in illegally. Can you believe that one?" Trump said during a campaign rally in North Carolina. "Let me tell you one thing. She has got it so documented, so she's going to have a little news conference over the next couple of weeks. That's good. I love it. I love it."

But that news conference never happened, and the Trumps have never publicly released Melania's immigration records—or even identified the attorney who originally represented her. Instead, on September 14, less than two months before the election,

Melania tweeted: "I am pleased to enclose a letter from my immigration attorney which states that, with 100% certainty, I correctly went through the legal process when arriving in the USA." The letter—displayed beside her tweet—was from Michael J. Wildes, an immigration lawyer who had done work for Trump, including helping with visas for foreign contestants in Trump's beauty pageants. Wildes is a Democrat and mayor of Englewood, New Jersey.

In the lobby of his sleek Manhattan offices, Wildes displays huge photographs of two celebrity clients: Melania and Jean-Georges Vongerichten, the French-born celebrity chef and namesake of Jean-Georges, the restaurant in the Trump International Hotel. Vongerichten helped cater Melania and Trump's wedding. Along with soccer legend Pelé, singer Boy George, and celebrity lawyer Alan Dershowitz, Melania provided a laudatory blurb for *Safe Haven in America: Battles to Open the Golden Door* (2018), a book by Wildes. She wrote, "I thank Michael Wildes for his counsel in reviewing my own path to the American Dream, for his knowledge and professional dedication, not to mention his warmth and concern. He has shown himself to be a scholar in this field."

Wildes is the son of immigration lawyer Leon Wildes, who became famous in the early 1970s for successfully defending John Lennon against the Nixon administration's efforts to deport him for overstaying a tourist visa. Now Wildes, the son, was speaking on behalf of the wife of a Republican presidential candidate. He had not handled Melania's original immigration matters but reviewed them and wrote, in the letter Melania posted: "Following a review of her relevant immigration paperwork, I can unequivocally state that these allegations are not supported by the record, and are therefore completely without merit."

Wildes laid out the timeline. He said that Melania first arrived in the United States on August 27, 1996, on a B-1/B-2 visitor visa. About six weeks later, on October 18, the American embassy in Slovenia issued her an H-1B visa that allowed her to work legally as a model in the United States. Wildes confirmed that Melania would have had to return to Slovenia to pick up that visa. Wildes said that the H-1B was good for one year, and that Melania was issued five in total over the next five years. He also noted that she "self-sponsored" in 2000 for her green card, which then allowed her to apply for citizenship in five years. In March 2001, she was issued that green card through the elite EB-1 program, which was designed for people "of extraordinary ability." Among the recipients were renowned academic researchers, multinational business executives, and others—including Olympic athletes and Oscar-winning actors—who demonstrated "sustained national and international acclaim."

When I wrote about Melania's visa for the *Washington Post*, Bruce Morrison, a former Democratic congressman, told me, "We called it the Einstein visa." Morrison was the chairman of the House subcommittee that wrote the Immigration Act of 1990, which defined this visa category. I found out that in 2001, more than one million green cards were issued to non–U.S. citizens, but only a fraction of 1 percent—just 3,376—were for EB-1 visas. To qualify for these, immigrants had to demonstrate "extraordinary ability" by meeting certain criteria, such as having won "recognized prizes and awards" and enjoyed "commercial successes."

The process of deciding who meets the "extraordinary ability" standard is subjective, and at the time many models were applying for visas under this category. It is not known what Melania put on her application. By 2000, she had a number of high-profile modeling credits—the Camel ad campaign, the cover of British *GQ*, a photo in the *Sports Illustrated* swimsuit edition. But did that add up to "extraordinary ability"? When I pressed Wildes about why Melania qualified, he insisted that she was more than eligible but would not discuss any details of her case. "There is no reason to adjudicate her petition publicly when her privacy is so important to her," he said. But others disagreed and said the wife of a candidate railing against people abusing the immigration system should be more forthcoming. "What did she submit?" asked David Leopold, an immigration lawyer and a past president of the American Immigration Lawyers Association. "There are a lot of questions about how she procured entry into the United States," he told me.

More questions about Melania's immigration path were raised on November 4, 2016, days before the U.S. presidential election, when the Associated Press reported that Melania was paid more than $20,000 for ten modeling jobs before she was granted a visa permitting her to work. The AP reported that detailed ledgers and other records showed she worked in the month before she received her visa in October 1996 for, among others, *Fitness* magazine and the Bergdorf Goodman department store.

Because of Trump's proposals to crack down on foreign

nationals illegally living and working in the United States, the story of Melania's visa process was of great interest to immigration advocates who said that Trump would not hesitate to deport a Mexican for the slightest immigration violation. "He has a double standard when it comes to immigration—one for his family and one for immigrants he doesn't like," said Morrison.

The Trumps have never directly addressed the issues the AP story raised about her first modeling jobs, but Wildes insists that that Melania "is meticulous about compliance." Melania herself explained to *Harper's Bazaar* that she was proud of following the immigration rules: "I came here for my career, and I did so well, I moved here. It never crossed my mind to stay here without papers. That is just the person you are. You follow the rules. You follow the law. Every few months you need to fly back to Europe and stamp your visa."

During the 2016 campaign, Melania also talked about how much her U.S. citizenship meant to her, calling it "the greatest privilege in the world." She said living and working in America was a blessing, "but I wanted something more. I wanted to be an American. After a ten-year process, which included many visas and a green card, in 2006, I studied for the test and became a U.S. citizen. . . . I'm an immigrant, and let me tell you, no one values the freedom and opportunity of America more than me, both as an independent woman, and as someone who immigrated to America."

Melania often talks about how proud she is of her American citizenship, but less well known is the fact that she has also kept her Slovenian citizenship. Not only is she a dual citizen, but she has also made sure that Barron is, too. According to multiple sources, Melania applied for and received Slovenian citizenship for Barron; he is entitled to it because his mother was born in the country. Both Melania and Barron Trump have renewed their Slovenian passports since they moved into the White House. The United States does not object to dual citizenship, but all U.S. citizens are required to use their American passport when they enter and leave the country. There are no statistics on how many Americans hold dual citizenship, but while it is not uncommon, it is very unusual for members of the first family to be citizens of another country. (Louisa Adams, wife of John Quincy Adams, is the only other first lady to have been born outside of the United States; she was born in London in 1775.) Slovenian citizenship makes it easier for a person to inherit property and buy land in Slovenia. It also makes it easier to get both a job and health care in all twenty-seven countries of the European Union. Some EU countries have a cumbersome work permit process for foreigners, similar to the process in the United States. Melania essentially has given her son the same options she had. As she told the Slovenian journalists gathered in Paris in 1998, additional citizenship means "more doors in the world might be open to you."

A key reason people keep dual citizenship is for its conveniences, but it can also be inconvenient. According to the State Department:

It is important to note the problems attendant to dual nationality. Claims of other countries upon U.S. dual-nationals often place them in situations where their obligations to one country are in conflict with the laws of the other. In addition, their dual nationality may hamper efforts of the U.S. Government to provide consular protection to them when they are abroad, especially when they are in the country of their second nationality.

After Melania received her U.S. citizenship, she focused her attention on her parents, and especially on her sister, who is Barron's godmother. One day in 2006 she summoned immigration lawyer Eric Bland to Trump Tower to seek his help, leaving word with security at the side entrance to the building on Fifty-Sixth Street to let Bland take the elevator up to the penthouse. He was told to wait for her in her sitting room. Bland had walked by Trump Tower a million times but had never entered—not even the lobby.

He arrived before her and sat down in what seemed to him to be a living room, mesmerized by what looked to him like Roman columns and all the marble and gold. There was a little red wagon sitting there, with "Barron" written on the side. A homey family touch, he thought, in what otherwise felt like how Louis XIV might have decorated the Taj Mahal. And then there she was, the elegant Mrs. Trump. Melania sat down on a couch. No small talk. She got right to it: "What are the options for my sister?"

"Your parents will be relatively easy," Bland said. "But your sister will be harder." Bland explained the realities of what Donald Trump would later deride as "chain migration." As a citizen, Melania could petition for her family members to join her in the

United States. But it's far easier for an immigrant who becomes a citizen to sponsor a child and parents than siblings. It could take twenty years or more of paperwork, persistence, and patience to get permanent residence for a sister.

Her parents and sister had been coming to visit her for years on visitor visas. That was fine for her parents, but her sister was in her late thirties. To work and to easily travel in and out of the country, she would need legal status—and not have to wait for two decades.

Ines and her parents have a special place in Melania's life. They were just about the only ones who really knew her. Arranging for them to be permanently and legally living in the United States would be the final step in Melania's immigrant journey. Bland had never met or spoken to her before, even though he had helped with the paperwork for her citizenship application. He was struck by how single-minded she was about her family's immigration options. He tried to lighten things up, but that went nowhere. "I like to joke a little; that's my personality, to be chatty. But she was very serious," he said. He left with the impression that she was quite innocent. He described her as "a nice, kind young woman" who seemed out of place in Trump Tower.

Her efforts to keep her family close have succeeded. After her husband became the president of the United States, her parents would join her as naturalized U.S. citizens. Without any public notice, her sister would also become a legal permanent resident.

• • •

"AND HOW about chain migration? How about that?"

Twenty-three minutes into an Ohio rally on August 4, 2018, President Trump was firing up the crowd. Call-and-response. A roar rose to jeer immigrants bringing family members into the country.

"BOOOOOOOOOO!!"

"Somebody comes in, he brings his mother, and his father, and his aunt and uncle, fifteen times removed."

"BOOOOOOOOO!!"

Five days later in Manhattan, Viktor and Amalija Knavs raised their right hands and recited the oath of citizenship that more than seven million people have spoken in the past decade:

> I hereby declare, on oath, that I absolutely and entirely renounce and abjure all allegiance and fidelity to any foreign prince, potentate, state, or sovereignty, of whom or which I have heretofore been a subject or citizen; that I will support and defend the Constitution and laws of the United States of America against all enemies, foreign and domestic; that I will bear true faith and allegiance to the same; that I will bear arms on behalf of the United States when required by the law; that I will perform noncombatant service in the Armed Forces of the United States when required by the law; that I will perform work of national importance under civilian direction when required by the law; and that I take this obligation freely, without any mental reservation or purpose of evasion; so help me God.

What Donald Trump was fuming about on August 4, his in-laws were celebrating on August 9. Viktor and Amalija's naturalization ceremony was held quietly in the Jacob K. Javits Federal Building in Manhattan. As Melania's parents, both in their seventies, exited the side door of the federal building, escorted by Department of Homeland Security police, one of the reporters waiting asked how it felt to finally be U.S. citizens.

"Thank you," Viktor said. Then his lawyer, Michael Wildes, interjected. "This is an example of it going right," Wildes said. He added that other than security arrangements, Melania's parents did not receive special treatment. "The application, the process, the interview was no different than anybody else's." The attorney said, "This golden experiment, these doors that are in America, remain hinged open to beautiful people as they have today."

Melania, who was staying in Bedminster, New Jersey, did not accompany her parents. Stephanie Grisham, Melania's spokeswoman, said the first lady's parents "are not part of the administration and deserve privacy."

But what was most interesting is that Wildes, identified as Melania's immigration lawyer, began publicly criticizing Trump's immigration rhetoric and policies. The day after Viktor and Amalija got their U.S. citizenship with the help of their daughter who sponsored them, Wildes appeared on CNN. He called Trump's opposition to family reunification "unconscionable" and accused the president of fearmongering at his Ohio rally. In an interview, Wildes said that he spoke to Melania beforehand and told her he had been asked to go on CNN: "She said, 'Make it clear that I need babysitting. If I am going to do the work for the nation, I want to make sure my son is in the hands of my parents and they have the right to be here permanently." Melania rarely talks directly about immigration, but she was allowing those close to her to criticize her husband's policy. Her spokeswoman has also praised U.S immigration policies that allow a naturalized citizen to sponsor family members. Wildes on CNN called family reunification "a beautiful bedrock of immigration law."

IN THE first years of the Trump administration, the number of new immigrants allowed into the United States has decreased dramatically. Denials of new applications for H-1B visas have quadrupled, while average processing time for all types of visas has increased by nearly 50 percent. In 2018, the United States added just 200,000 immigrants to the population, a remarkable 70 percent drop from the prior year. Wildes said that Trump's policy of family separations "reminds us of our past mistakes," including internment camps for Japanese Americans during World War II. "You can tell just by the language just being used, 'anchor babies, chain migration,' they are effectively changing the narrative away from the beautiful notion of family reunification," Wildes said.

When I asked Wildes about how long it would be until Melania's sister is granted her U.S. citizenship, he told me that he couldn't talk about client matters. But typically, people are eligible for U.S. citizenship five years after they get a green card.

Melania Trump launching her skin care line in 2013

CHAPTER 9

Jewelry and Caviar

TRUMP OFTEN included Melania in his business meetings when they were dating. Several New York businessmen as well as a former Trump business associate all recounted similar stories of how Trump would usher Melania into a room full of men while they were working on a deal. Sometimes there would be just a few men, sometimes a couple dozen, and occasionally one other woman who was often older and certainly not dressed like Melania. They all told the same story: Melania would arrive looking gorgeous and say next to nothing. It seemed to everyone in the room that there was no need for her to be there except Trump liked that men had a hard time keeping their eyes off her.

She was often theatrically introduced at his meetings, too. Michael Streck, then the U.S.-based correspondent for the German publication *Stern*, recalls an interview in his office in Trump Tower in November 2001. Trump unexpectedly invited him to the penthouse. Streck told me, "He called Melania. She was up-stairs preparing herself for a dinner later on. And she came down the, basically . . . the stairs . . . and he said, 'Isn't she stunning? Isn't she beautiful? Could you turn your back?'

"And he called her 'honey' all the time, which was kind of weird. It was kind of embarrassing, I have to say, because I could tell the way he treated her was not the way I would treat my wife, to be honest. We chatted briefly, and I really can't say what she told us. I think it was actually him who spoke all the time." Streck described the entire scene as "a bit like a cattle show, award-winning cows are presented to farmers or something like that. I do remember leaving his apartment later on. I called my wife. I said, 'You really won't believe what happened.' [Melania] was obviously comfortable and was used to it. It was weird."

Streck said that Melania wore "a very tight minidress, that's what I do vividly remember. And he was obviously very proud of her. It was an awkward moment." But Streck said that Melania seemed perfectly at ease: "Obviously she was used to this stuff."

All the same, Trump had made it clear that he did not want his third wife too involved in business dealings. His first wife, Ivana, held high-ranking positions in the Trump Organization and Trump told ABC's Nancy Collins that after that experience, "I will never again give a wife responsibility within my business." Trump said when he got home at night, Ivana just wanted to talk business and not the "softer subjects in life." For years Melania focused on being a full-time mother, but in 2009 she applied for a trademark for her planned jewelry collection and notably called it *Melania*, without using her famous last name. (Two years earlier, Ivanka had launched Ivanka Trump jewelry, capitalizing on the family name.) Melania said that now that Barron was a little older, she wanted to design luxurious-looking rings, bracelets, and watches that everyone could afford. Many of the pieces retailed for under fifty dollars, and she sold them on the QVC shopping network.

But as she went on TV to promote her jewelry, she was also being asked about her husband's politics. On the Fox Business Network in 2011, Gerri Willis asked Melania about watches and brooches in her fast-selling collections, and then about the possibility of a Donald Trump presidential candidacy. Comedian and talk show personality Joy Behar introduced Melania and her jewelry on *The Joy Behar Show* under a sign proclaiming her "The Melania," a play on her husband's nickname "The Donald." Then Behar asked, "Is he really running for the presidency, or is this a big publicity stunt? The wife knows the truth, what is it?"

"Look, he doesn't need the publicity stunt," Melania replied.

Behar, who had attended Trump's wedding to Marla Maples, listened as Melania talked about how Trump was "very passionate about the country," a "brilliant negotiator" with a "genius's mind."

"I don't know what skeletons he has in the closet. But everybody gets vetted when they're going to be president," Behar said. "You know what that means, vetted?"

Melania said she did.

"They're going to look into everything. He's had a few wives, he's had financial difficulties. All of that's going to come out. How do you feel about that?"

"Well, that's part of it. If he decided to run, he knows that's part of it."

Behar paused for a second, then asked a political question. "But what is this with the birth certificate obsession? Did he ask to see yours when you met him?"

Behar was referring to Trump's history as a primary driver behind the "birther" attacks on President Barack Obama. As early as 2011, Trump had been peddling the conspiracy theory that Obama had not been born in the United States. Despite producing his official birth records, proving that he had been born in Hawaii to an American mother and a Kenyan father, Obama was unable to persuade the "birthers." What followed on the air was a back-and-forth in which Melania sounded just like her husband, charging ahead with a bogus claim without any evidence.

"Well," said Melania, "I needed to put mine anyway because if you want to become an American citizen you need to put the birth certificate. I have a birth certificate from Slovenia, and do you want to see President Obama birth certificate or not?"

"I've seen it, I've seen it," Behar said.

"It's not a birth certificate," Melania replied.

"Well, it's a certificate of live birth, which they give [in Hawaii]. But, Melania, if he insists on what he's saying, then no one in Hawaii can ever run for president. Because they all get the same live-birth certificate."

"Well, but they need to have—"

"Bette Midler is finished, for example!" (The singer and actress was born in Honolulu.)

The audience laughed. Melania didn't appear amused.

"They need to have, and, in one way, it would be very easy if President Obama just show it. It's not only Donald who wants to see it. It's American people, who voted for him, and who didn't voted for him, they want to see that!"

"But it's on display in Chicago. We've seen it on the internet. We've seen it. It's not the same as yours, but it's a certificate of live birth."

"We feel it's different than birth certificate," Melania said, seeming to speak for both herself and her husband.

"Well, I think you should give it up at this point," Behar said. Neither of the Trumps took her advice. Michelle Obama would later write in her memoir, *Becoming*, "The whole thing was crazy and mean-spirited, of course, its underlying bigotry and xenophobia hardly concealed. But it was also dangerous, deliberately meant to stir up the wingnuts and kooks . . . What if someone with an unstable mind loaded a gun and drove to Washington? What if that person went looking for our girls? Donald Trump, with his loud and reckless innuendos, was putting my family's safety at risk. And for this I'd never forgive him." It was an unusually strong statement from the former first lady, whose only mention of Melania in her book was to say that they had ridden together to Trump's inauguration.

Melania and Joy Behar's exchange in many ways foreshadowed what was to come. After her husband entered politics, the easy questions posed by the lifestyle magazines seemed to be from a long-ago era. In a 2006 article in *Glamour*, Melania was asked to tell readers five things they did not know about her. She replied by saying that she had studied architecture and design and, "If I ever had another job, I'd go in that direction." She also said that she loved opera, found swimming relaxing, and that "I'd wear nothing but white every day if I could." But given the "Lock her up" chants that Trump and his rallygoers would yell about Hillary during the 2016 campaign, the most surprising thing Melania listed in that 2006 article was: "Bill and Hillary Clinton came to my wedding. My husband and I are close to both of them."

BUOYED BY the success of her Melania jewelry, two years later she announced a new skin care line. Melania spoke of these business efforts as hers and took pride in doing them independently from the family business. But Trump did devote an entire episode of *The Celebrity Apprentice* to the launch of the caviar-infused products. Because of the way the show was produced, however, Melania seemed to unwittingly become the punch line of a joke.

Standing in the lobby of Trump Tower, in front of contestants including NBA wild man Dennis Rodman, actor Gary Busey, and former Playmate of the Year Brande Roderick, Melania announced, "After ten years of researching, I'm thrilled to launch my debut skin care collection: Melania Caviar Complexe C6."

Two teams of celebrities would compete to produce a marketing plan to introduce the new line of skin care products. Earlier in the day, Melania, operating under the company name Melania Marks Skincare, had signed a five-year, $1 million license agreement with an Indianapolis-based company to manufacture, promote, and sell her products. That company, New Sunshine, which owned several tanning businesses, belonged in part to Steve Hilbert, a friend and business partner of Donald Trump.

Caviar Complexe was the centerpiece and chief selling point of Melania's line. Her website boasted that her products were developed in "intense collaboration with Melania's research laboratory" and described them in a dazzling string of trademarked buzzwords: "Melania Trump's Caviar Complexe C6™ with Lipid Matrix Receptor™ Technology is Melania's revolutionary approach to skin care that addresses the most advanced signs of aging," with caviar harvested from a cultured sturgeon farm in the South of France. It would cost $150 an ounce, and she told reporters at the time that she slathered it on Barron, then seven, "from head to toe."

On the *Celebrity Apprentice* episode, she met first with the team headed by Rodman, the eccentric NBA Hall of Famer. He asked her, "Did you start this?" Melania answered that she had "worked and researched for ten years" and had created "everything." Rodman then asked if he might be allowed upstairs to see her private bathroom in Trump Tower, to get a sense of what kind of cosmetics she uses. His teammate on the show, country singer Trace Adkins, told Rodman that this was a bad idea and an inappropriate question for Melania. "Luckily she doesn't speak English," Adkins quipped in his sandpaper baritone. The cameras cut to actor Gary Busey, who offered this assessment of Melania's looks: "Have you ever had your genitalia so excited that it spins like a Ferris wheel in a carnival ride? That's how beautiful she is."

The two *Celebrity Apprentice* teams competing against each other then began their task of developing promotional posters for Melania's new skin care line. They chose gold trays, plates, and crystal cups from the NBC prop shop and bought $2,000 worth of caviar. During their presentation, Rodman's team revealed a poster that read "Simply . . . Milania." Ivanka and Eric Trump, acting as judges, noticed the misspelling immediately. "It's shocking," Ivanka said to Melania after the team left the room. "I'm surprised you were even able to hold your tongue." The other team, led by magician and entertainer Penn Jillette, produced materials that referred to Melania as the "spokesperson" for the product, not the entrepreneur who had launched it. "She has given ten years of her life," Ivanka Trump said, putting the contestants in their place. "She has contributed years of her life to developing this formula."

When the two teams appeared in the show's famous dark-paneled boardroom and Donald Trump entered, *Apprentice* fans knew: somebody would win, and somebody would be "fired." Trump pronounced the teams' errors "not good." But before rendering his verdict, he had a question for actress Marilu Henner, a member of Jillette's team: "Marilu, how was Melania different from what you thought?" Henner replied, "She is so stunningly beautiful you almost don't hear what she's saying at first, because you're looking at flawless skin and a flawless face. But then you realize how warm she is. Her warmth just comes radiating off her. She's lovely."

That was clearly the answer Trump was looking for. "Very nice," he said. Then he fired Rodman.

The skin care line never got off the ground, through no fault of Melania's. At the time she signed her deal, New Sunshine was being ripped apart in a brutal dispute between Steve Hilbert and his business partner, John Menard Jr., a billionaire hardware store mogul. Melania hosted fashion and beauty journalists at an event at Jean-Georges in Manhattan, appeared on *The View,* and had signed up with Lord & Taylor as a "launch partner." Macy's, Bloomingdale's, and other big stores were set to join afterward. But New Sunshine was unraveling. *The Celebrity Apprentice* segment that had taped the previous November aired on April 7, 2013, when the product was supposed to be in stores, but wasn't.

In March 2013, Melania received notice from Menard's lawyers that they believed the contract was void. They would later argue that Trump's friend Hilbert had cut Melania a "grossly favorable" sweetheart deal because of their personal relationship. Hilbert and his wife, Tomisue, were longtime friends and business associates of the Trumps. In 1998, Hilbert and Trump had purchased the famed fifty-story General Motors Building near Trump Tower in Manhattan for more than $800 million. The

Hilberts had also attended the Trumps' wedding, and in 2011 they appeared on *The Celebrity Apprentice* to promote their Australian Gold sunscreen. That same year, Hilbert approached Melania about joining forces on her skin care line. Now, Hilbert's partner sought an injunction to void their licensing agreement with Melania. The legal action questioned Melania's credentials and suggested she was "pretty much nothing other than Mrs. Donald Trump."

The case was heard in U.S. District Court in Indianapolis in November, and according to a copy of the courtroom transcripts, Melania unleashed a cool fury from the witness stand. Journalist Peter Moskowitz, who wrote about the case in 2016, noted, "It's hard to find emotion in court transcripts, but Melania's anger jumps off the page." She testified that she was involved "from A to Z" with developing her line, which she had been working on for over a decade—everything from researching the chemical makeup of the creams, lotions, and other products to selecting their logo and packaging. She discussed how she had promoted the line on her social media, including Facebook, her website, and Twitter, adding that she had received "a lot of bad responses" from fans who were trying to buy the products and couldn't.

At one point, she said, "This is not how the business is done, and they were blaming me. They were blaming my brand, and I had nothing to do with it . . . the product was nowhere to be found." She essentially said she was the victim of a feud between two partners, and the result was that by the time the product arrived in the stores, "it was too late. The damage was done. They didn't honor the contract. I didn't get paid. I did everything, and I would do much, much more," but the other parties to the deal did not "honor the contract."

Judge Jane Magnus-Stinson, the Obama appointee who heard the case, ruled in Melania's favor, rejecting the allegation that she received unfair special treatment and finding that Menard's company had improperly voided the contract. She ordered the company and Melania to work out a settlement in arbitration. Melania sought $50 million in damages, what her attorneys argued she would have made if the line had been properly launched. The parties later settled out of court, and terms were not made public. Trump continued to maintain a relationship with the Hilberts, who contributed to his presidential campaign; Tomisue Hilbert is listed as a $100,000 donor to Trump's 2017 inauguration. In an interview with me in 2016, Hilbert said that he was sorry that the Melania skin care line never happened. "This was a passion of Melania's," he said. "She has so much depth, creativity, an eye for detail, and dedication to the project." But there were no second chances, and she dropped the whole business venture.

Moskowitz's 2016 piece, "What Happened to Melania Trump's Caviar Skincare Line?," also contained, in parentheses, a footnote to the whole failed enterprise: "If the media reports about her never receiving a degree from a university in Slovenia are true, the court transcripts also reveal Melania lied under oath about her degree when she told the court she'd graduated with a bachelor's in architecture." A copy of the transcript I obtained shows this exchange:

Q: "Would you please explain to the Judge your formal education including what schools you attended and from which you graduated?"

A: "I attended and graduated from design school, from Fashion and Industrial Design School and also attended, graduated from architecture degree, bachelor degree."

In fact, this was not true. Melania dropped out of college during her first year, at age nineteen. As late as July 2016, her biography on her website, melaniatrump.com, also said that she had a degree from the University of Ljubljana. That website was taken down, but Melania never acknowledged the inaccurate characterization of her formal education.

IF HIGH-PROFILE interviews and celebrity product launches were the public face of Melania, the private one was far harder to find. Often, the people who saw it were either family or staff who were all but invisible in the room. Jose Gabriel Juarez worked for Melania and Donald Trump for a decade, from 2008 to 2018, at the Trump National Golf Club in Westchester, New York, where he became the head waiter. In ten years, he saw Trump many times, but he said that he never witnessed a significant conversation between Trump and Melania. That may very well be because they made sure staff like Juarez didn't, but the only one he ever heard took place when Melania was not even present—she was on television.

In April 2010, Melania was on QVC promoting her new line of jewelry. Watching on TV from the Westchester golf club restaurant, Trump picked up his cell phone and called in to the show. Juarez said that he watched Trump and Melania have a public conversation, he on his phone and she on the big screen. The restaurant was full of people, so they turned the volume up loud. Patrons in the restaurant were impressed that Trump could just dial directly into the show. "He was sweet with her," Juarez said. "But that was on TV. In person, I never saw them talk like that."

Juarez and two housekeepers at Trump National Golf Club in Bedminster whom I interviewed had unusually intimate access to the Trumps' daily lives. Their accounts were remarkably consistent and painted a portrait of a marriage that seems to thrive on husband and wife maintaining parallel lives that barely intersect. From their meals—Trump's well-done cheeseburgers and Melania's healthier food prepared by her mother—to their daily activities, the Trumps do things their own way, on their own time. When necessary, they could present a cuddly, unified public front for club members. But in private, they preferred separate spaces and routines. During their interviews, housekeepers and others who worked at Trump properties all said that they noticed how little time the couple spent together.

The Bedminster club, about an hour west of New York City, is a family favorite, the place where they spend the most time after the White House and Mar-a-Lago. Bedminster has special importance to Melania and Trump. He bought the property in

2002, when he was with Melania. (He was married to Ivana when he bought Mar-a-Lago, and he was married to Marla when he bought the Trump National Golf Club in Westchester.) At Bedminster, he built two eighteen-hole golf courses and installed gardens modeled after those in Versailles (just as the interior of his Trump Tower penthouse is modeled after the famous chateau of French kings).

Trump has said that he likes Bedminster so much that he has even talked about being buried there. He spent nearly one hundred days there as president by early 2020. Some summers, Melania and Barron, and often her parents, have lived on the premises for nearly two months. Trump and Melania have a mansion on the property. Several employees at Bedminster said that Trump's bedroom is on the first floor, while Melania and Barron have bedroom suites on the second.

Housekeepers on staff said that Trump's room was mainly decorated with photos of himself with Michael Jackson and other celebrities, while Melania's room was mainly decorated with photos of Barron, with a photo of her and Barron on her nightstand. During the day, Trump would usually be up at dawn, reading many newspapers and watching TV, and then out of the house by 7:00 to play golf, while Melania would wake later and spend much of the day inside and often on her computer. Many days at Bedminster, Melania got a massage in a room that former housekeeper Victorina Morales prepared. "I got it all ready," Morales said, explaining that Melania liked candles and music with nature sounds—birds and running water. Trump typically did not eat with Melania and Barron; he usually had lunch and dinner at the clubhouse. He sometimes ate with Ivanka and Jared when they were staying at a separate mansion on the property—they were married at the club in 2009.

In recent years, Melania has tended to eat in the house, where she and her parents and Barron speak Slovenian. (Trump has complained to others that he has no idea what they are saying.) Amalija and Viktor have stayed in a cottage near the clubhouse pool, but her parents spend a lot of time in Melania's residence. Her mother not only cooks but does the dishes afterward. "I never saw them have dinner together," Morales said of Melania and Trump. Speaking in Spanish, she said, "She didn't go to the club because she didn't like the food. She always ate at home." Morales said she has seen Trump sit on a couch in the residence in the evening, watching TV with his feet up on a coffee table. Barron would be sitting on the floor watching the TV or play-ing a video game and Melania would be on the computer. "It's a strange marriage," Morales said, through a translator. "I never saw them like a normal family, sitting together at a table, eat-ing together, talking. Never, never, never. They spend time in the same place, but they don't interact." At the White House, the Trumps also sleep in separate bedrooms. Trump has gone golfing so many times since becoming president that a site called Trump Golf Count tracks his outings—two hundred forty-nine visits to his golf clubs while president, and evidence of playing golf at least one hundred seventeen times as of mid-March 2020. While he golfs, Melania is almost always somewhere else, out of sight.

Morales said Melania often seemed sad. "She would talk to us, but never a smile," she said. "She seems burdened." Sandra Diaz, another housekeeper, as well as other staff, said that Melania led an insulated life at Bedminster. A handful of times, some "elegant ladies" came for lunch. But mainly she was there with just her parents and Barron. Morales said that in the five years she worked there, she never met Melania's sister, Ines.

Diaz said that Melania would sometimes get dressed up to accompany Trump to the main Bedminster clubhouse to attend a wedding or some other public event. But after greeting the crowd, she would quickly retreat to her private space. Diaz recalled one night when Trump came into the house and asked Melania to come greet Ivanka and other guests around the pool. Melania said, "I can't go now." But Trump insisted and Melania reluctantly went with him, staying for only about ten minutes before she returned. "Melania is always very apart," Diaz said. "I always saw Melania living in a completely different world than his. I never saw them share as a couple. I never saw them holding hands." Diaz and Morales said that Melania seemed happiest when she was with Barron.

Morales worked at Bedminster from 2013 until 2018. After Trump became president, the Secret Service gave her a flag lapel pin with a Secret Service insignia to wear when she was on the property. Morales would spend long days at the club, especially in the summer, when the Trumps visited most. She wore a uniform, in later years beige, as she made beds, washed clothes, and cleaned the family's bathrooms. Diaz said Trump was very specific about

214

what he wanted in his bedroom suite, from his bathroom to his closet, where she was to make sure he always had ready six white polo shirts, six pairs of beige pants, and six ironed pairs of boxer shorts.

One of the worst jobs was cleaning up the residue from Melania's regular applications of tanning spray to make sure any traces were removed from all the white surfaces in the bathroom. The bronzer washed off in the shower, and Melania used it nearly every time she left the house, the housekeeper said. Diaz also said that she was told to make sure Trump always had two bottles of liquid face makeup. She would test the open bottles by pouring a little liquid on her hand to make sure there was still plenty inside. Morales said that Melania always treated her with respect and seemed to value and appreciate the work she did. Diaz said she and other housekeepers entering the Trumps' residence had to put on latex gloves and blue cloth shoe covers like those worn by doctors and nurses. Melania wanted white and pink roses on her table and certain candles in her massage room. The maids were instructed to leave perfect vacuum tracks in her white carpet and not to touch the six cinnamon-scented candles she kept near her computer.

The housekeepers described an often tense dynamic outside the immediate family. Both said that Melania and Ivanka had strained relations and seemed to be competitive with each other. Diaz recalled Ivanka telling her to come clean her house at exactly the same time Melania wanted her house cleaned. She said it seemed like a deliberate power play. Both housekeepers said they preferred working for Melania, who, despite the language gap and her strict demands, always treated them with more respect. They also liked Amalija, who would often slip them a $10 or $20 tip, whispering not to let Melania know.

The housekeepers said that Trump and Viktor Knavs weren't close. They recalled Trump blowing up at Viktor over a cap. Trump had a reputation at the club for being very generous; he would hand out $100 bills when he was happy with the service. But he was also known to be incredibly frugal. Trump had a specific place in his bedroom suite where he put clothes or other things he no longer wanted. Maids were instructed not to toss out even the tiniest thing, if it wasn't in that discard pile—not even the last little sliver of his bar of Irish Spring soap.

Viktor sometimes ended up with Trump's cast-off clothing. "They're the same size and everything," Morales said. One day in 2013, Amalija found a red hat in a pile where Trump had placed some items that he no longer wanted to wear. She thought Viktor could use it, so she picked it up and gave it to her husband. Viktor put it on one morning and wore it to the golf course, where he ran into Trump.

Employees knew that Trump had an unwritten rule that only he could wear his distinctive red caps—making him unmistakable anywhere on the property. When he saw Melania's father in the cap, he became furious and demanded that he take it off and leave. The caddies and housekeepers who saw this scene unfold said it was an unforgettable moment. "Nobody could wear the red hat but [Trump]," Diaz said. "The whole

THE ART OF HER DEAL

world saw what Trump had done to his father-in-law," Morales added. Viktor "was very embarrassed." Diaz said that Viktor came back to the house and screamed about "that fucking guy." Diaz said Melania's mother tried to calm her husband down, but recalled that Melania remained silent.

The Trumps would occasionally travel to the Trump club in Westchester, about eighty miles northeast of Bedminster, on summer Sundays, Jose Gabriel Juarez recalled. Juarez said that they would arrive in two cars—Trump in one and Melania, Barron, and Viktor in another. Trump would play golf while his family had lunch in the club. Juarez said that on weekends when there was a golf tournament, Trump would sometimes stay overnight at the club. Melania and Barron never did. "I never saw them together," Juarez said of Melania and Trump.

When they came for lunch, he said Melania would have a salad, and Barron would usually have a grilled cheese sandwich and fries. He said that Viktor always seemed to be in a good mood and would often slip him a $20 tip. After lunch, Melania and Viktor would walk Barron over to the driving range so he could hit balls. Viktor would sometimes hit with him while Melania watched.

Juarez, Morales, and Diaz were at one point all undocumented workers employed at Trump properties, a fact that has brought more scrutiny to Trump's immigration policies as president. Juarez came from Mexico. Morales came to the United States from Guatemala in 1999 and was an undocumented immigrant for her entire time at Bedminster. Diaz was an undocumented worker from Costa Rica who was employed at Bedminster from 2010 until 2013, using a fake Social Security card she had bought for fifty dollars.

Trump's talk of Mexican criminals and "rapists," his promise to wall off the U.S.-Mexico border, and his administration's policy of separating immigrant children from their families created tension among the undocumented workers at his properties. Juarez recalled Trump's wealthy club members taking a cue from Trump and making rough comments and jokes once he was elected president. "You're still here? How come we can't get rid of you? I'm going to call Trump, you [expletive] Mexican," Juarez said a member told him. By the end of 2018, Morales and Diaz had had enough. They gave interviews to the *Washington Post*, the *New York Times*, and other publications, hoping to highlight what they considered Trump's hypocrisy and unfairness to immigrants. Two months later, Democrats in Congress hosted Morales and Diaz as their guests at Trump's State of the Union address. Neither Diaz nor Morales works for the Trump Organization today, and after they spoke out, the Trump Organization announced a crackdown on undocumented workers, firing many of them.

After leaving her job at Bedminster, Diaz became a permanent U.S. resident; as Melania Trump had done for her mother, Diaz's daughter, a U.S. citizen, petitioned on her behalf. As of early 2020, Morales had filed for asylum and Juarez was still trying to get legal status. "I don't understand why the first lady, who's an immigrant, doesn't help us," Diaz said. "She does speak out sometimes. Why doesn't she speak out to help us?" Melania has made it clear to those around her that she sees her path as being very different from the paths of those crossing the U.S.-Mexico border, and that she believes immigrants should enter the United States legally, as she did.

Many immigration activists have criticized both Trumps—Melania for not speaking up, and the president for making-tougher immigration laws a centerpiece of his agenda while he is surrounded by immigrants: his wife, his in-laws, and even the people caring for one of his homes. On June 16, 2015, when Donald Trump announced his candidacy with promises to "build a great wall" and clamp down on immigration, he began his run by taking the escalator down to the lobby of Trump Tower. This time—a rare time—Trump ushered Melania ahead of him. A woman who had been an American citizen for less than nine years led the way.

The president and first lady

The Trumps holding hands

CHAPTER 10

"We give a space to each other"

DURING THE 2016 campaign, it was far easier to interview Donald Trump than Melania, and that is true to this day. When I put in a request to speak with Mrs. Trump, I had to meet with her husband before I received the green light to speak to her. I took the train from Washington to New York to meet him at Trump Tower.

My first view inside his office was of piles of magazines with Trump's face on the cover and framed pictures of him leaning against the wall. It appeared so cluttered that I asked him if he was moving. No, he said, adding that I should not trust CEOs with tidy desks. As we talked about Trump the husband, he glanced at times at the small TV on his desk; the Masters Tournament, one of professional golf's signature events, was on. I tried to keep him on the subject, but he darted in different directions. How would he describe Melania, I asked, reminding him that he had described Ivana as "a hard worker" and Marla Maples as "a performer."

"Melania was a very, very successful person before I met her. She was a model, but she was tremendously successful. There's a solidity in her that's amazing. I mean she's a beautiful woman and all, but she's very solid—very solid, tremendously smart person." I said that I had heard that he exaggerated his love life because it was good for his image. Trump replied that there might be something to that, and that people might be surprised because "my life is much less glamorous than they thought, including with all the stories about every supermodel that ever lived."

After talking to the presidential candidate, I got word that I could interview Melania Trump.

"Not a lot of people know me," Melania told me when we finally spoke. She declined to meet me, a correspondent for the *Washington Post* writing about the campaign. She preferred to talk on the phone. Since the start of her husband's run for president, she had read articles about herself and heard people on TV talking about her. She said they had gotten her all wrong. "I am not shy," she said. "I'm not reserved." She continued, "Only I know my story, and I see people who want to have maybe five, fifteen minutes of fame, and they say, 'Oh, I met her for five minutes. I know her,' and describing me. And they don't really know me."

I had already been warned by Hope Hicks, the twenty-six-year-old spokesperson for the Trump campaign, that Melania did not like being called "shy." So, I asked her, "What is the correct description of you?"

"I know what I want, and I don't need to talk, and to, you know, be an attention seeker. I'm not that way. And, because I know who I am. I'm very comfortable in my body, and I get involved and I talk when I want to do that, not when somebody else want it."

"What do you want?" This question caused her to hesitate.

"I live meaningful life," Melania said in her accented English, a reminder that she had grown up four thousand miles from Trump Tower. She didn't really answer the question about what she wants in life and chose instead to return to her previous statement: "I know that talking every time, blabbing something around isn't good. That's not my style."

I wished I could have seen the look in her eyes when she said this, but perhaps that's why she preferred that we not meet in person. She told me that she would not spend much time on the campaign trail. Barron Trump was ten years old, and, as Melania put it, "My son is my priority."

In the end, Melania would make few campaign appearances and speeches. Friends have noted that she doesn't like crowds. Her stepdaughter Ivanka would be the go-to surrogate. The campaign wanted Melania to be more visible, but she alone decided her level of involvement. That came through during our forty-four-minute conversation. Several times, Melania stressed that she is independent. Of her marriage, she said, "We like to do what we like to do, and we give ourselves and each other space. I allowed him to do, to have his passion and his dreams come true, and he let me do the same." She added, "I'm not a yeller. I'm not a screamer. I'm calm person."

Her message was that while she is married to Donald Trump, she is not Donald Trump. She called herself his "close partner" and said that they talk "several times a day" by phone when he is away. She watched his rallies on TV and how the public reacted, and she "tells him the truth." She said, "I am very opinionated. I'm very strong. I have 'yes' or 'no.' I'm not a 'maybe' person. I don't say 'maybe.' I know what I like."

I asked for an example of advice she has given her husband, but she demurred. I asked her to tell voters something that might surprise them about her. "I'm compassionate," she said. "I am kind when people are kind." I had thought that she might say something like she played the piano. Now I thought how sad it must be to believe others didn't think she cared. "I love the truth," she continued. "I'm telling the truth. I like fairness. I don't like people when they say lies." She said that she pays attention to details and is a perfectionist.

I asked her what she and her husband did together as a couple for fun. She said they watched movies at home or on their private jet. Her favorites? *Gone with the Wind*. *Sunset Boulevard*. *An Affair to Remember*. All classic movies about complicated love. (In 2020, as Trump complained that *Parasite*, a South Korean film, had won the Academy Award for Best Picture, he singled out two movies as great ones: *Gone with the Wind* and *Sunset Boulevard*.)

Melania described her husband by saying that he was "very kind and a great heart. He is always there." Both Trumps have always maintained that they "had a great chemistry" from the moment they met. I asked about his days as a playboy bachelor.

"I guess he now settled down," she replied. "He found the person that he's compatible, comfortable, has a trust. We have a trust in each other. We are loyal to each other. We respect each other. We give a space to each other. We don't control each other. So I think it's very important. You know, to find each other it's very special. It's a very special thing."

She continued, "We are not fighting. We have, of course, disagreements. That's very normal in the relationship, but we accept each other the way we are, and we love each other the way we are." When I pressed her for details, her reply was, "You are so into details." She laughed, flashing a sense of humor. Melania was easy to talk to, and yet it also seemed that she was thinking far more than she was willing to say.

I would later realize that she has built a wall around herself to keep people at a distance. Backstage at an event, she will smile easily, be warm, and make small talk, but once she steps into the public arena, it is as if she is stepping onto a fashion runway, where she projects icy control or aloofness. Melania is not the only woman who has been criticized for appearing rigid. Hillary Clinton, too, is famous for being funny, warm, and gregarious in private while coming across as more stiff in public. That contrast has long frustrated Hillary supporters, who have pleaded for her to put her private side on display. People who know Melania are also frustrated that few see her as they do. They note that Melania is fun, clever, and interesting, and believe that those who say otherwise don't really know her.

Part of this divide may be due to Melania's suspicion of others.

She is less trusting than her husband, but also sometimes more insightful than he is about the people around him. Chris Christie, the former New Jersey governor and Trump supporter, explained, "She knew Bannon was no good; she knew it right from the beginning. She was not a Paul Manafort fan, right from the beginning. She's very loyal. She's only cold to you if she doesn't trust you." And, he added, she is "extraordinarily self-confident."

Many people on the campaign, including Corey Lewandowski and Christie, said that the first call Trump made after a rally was to Melania. "He'd get on the plane, he'd get settled, and he'd call her and say, 'Sweetheart, were you watching? Were you watching on TV? What did you think?' And she would say to him, 'I liked this, I didn't like that.'" Christie explained. "She would just give it to him. It was almost without exception always his first call when he would get back on the plane after a rally that he knew had been televised. 'Were you watching it? If you were watching, what did you think?' She always had commentary to give him, and I think that tells a lot about what he thinks of her. You know, he's famous for calling dozens of people, myself included, to get opinions sometimes, but she's the first one."

Lewandowski recalled being in the car with Trump on the campaign trail as different issues arose—such as something about Hillary Clinton or Republican presidential primary rival Marco Rubio, a U.S. senator from Florida. "Trump would get on the phone with Melania, and say, 'Hey, I'm about to go on, and I'm going to say this. Do you think I should say that?'" Lewandowski said. "She would sometimes say, 'Don't mention that. Nobody cares about that anymore,' and he would say, 'OK,' and he would leave that component out of his speech." When he called Melania to run ideas by her before giving a speech, Lewandowski said, "She would give him such good, solid, concrete advice. I would say 95 percent of the time, he took that advice . . . She has amazing political instincts. She is exceptionally smart, and people misread her because she is quiet."

During the campaign and later in the White House, several people working with Trump said that far from trying to rein him in, as some of his aides attempted to do, Melania advises him, "Be yourself, let Trump be Trump." A person who has spent years with both Trumps, separately and together, noted, "This is much more of a conventional marriage than people are willing to accept. Conventional in the sense that these are people who have different opinions, they interact, they're influenced by each other, they push each other, they test each other's limits— like every good marriage does." Melania believes marriage is something you stick with, that there will be ups and downs, and her mother will remind her that she made her wedding vows for life, said one family friend. As for those who think that the Trump's marriage is "some sort of phony, make-believe thing, it just isn't." Those who know Melania say her independent streak has helped her survive, and at times thrive, next to Trump. Her modeling career and her efforts to have her own projects after they started dating and later after they married "was her way of saying 'I don't need a man to support me. I don't need a man to define my sense of self-worth. I'm special. I'm my own person.'

I think that's what gives her the confidence to be with someone like the president."

One area where she does try to rein in her husband is in his use of rough language. In a CNN interview with Anderson Cooper during the presidential primaries, Melania publicly said that she disagreed with her husband on "many things—some language, of course." Trump had just called his Republican primary rival Senator Ted Cruz of Texas a "pussy," repeating the word that an attendee at one of his rallies in New Hampshire had shouted out. Melania recounted being at the event with him. When she heard that "inappropriate word," she'd hoped her husband wouldn't re-peat it: "I'm thinking like, 'Don't repeat it,' in my head, for him, 'Don't repeat it. Just don't say it because the next day, media, all they will talk is about that.' But he repeated it." But she added that she can't change him, because "he's with the momentum, he goes with the flow, he goes with the people. They're having fun, everybody was cheering." The underlying message being that she is not her husband's keeper; she can't change him.

The inconsistent Trump political machine did not always look out for Melania. Her debut at the Republican National Convention was marred by an embarrassing mistake. Melania's speech contained plagiarized lines from Michelle Obama's Dem-ocratic National Convention keynote address in 2008. Although a Trump Organization employee, Meredith McIver, took the blame, several insiders say the person most responsible was Rick Gates, deputy chairman of the campaign. But Melania was the one who was left humiliated in public. (Gates has said he is not to blame for the speech. He was later sentenced to forty-five days in jail for making false statements to the FBI and conspiracy to commit financial fraud.)

Trump was furious. He felt his campaign had let Melania down and was heard angrily saying, "She got screwed. Who did this to her?" Corey Lewandowski told me that the speech blunder was especially terrible because Melania is a perfectionist.

The most difficult moments by far for Melania have come around Donald Trump's alleged infidelities, particularly Karen McDougal's and porn star Stormy Daniels's claims that they had sexual encounters with Trump. Both women alleged that sex with Trump took place during the long weekend of July 13–16, 2006, at a golf tournament at Lake Tahoe in Nevada. McDougal also alleged that she met Trump at a party a month before and began a longer-term sexual relationship with him that included a tryst at the Tahoe tournament. Friends say that Melania did not know of at least some of Trump's past relationships or these allegations until his presidential run. At one point, according to someone who worked on the Trump campaign, she checked into a hotel to get away from her husband.

Melania reads to children in 2019

CHAPTER 11

Be Best

AT TIMES, pundits' efforts to read the Trumps' relationship are reminiscent of Western experts' attempts to analyze the government of the old Soviet Union. "Kremlinologists" pored over images of military parade reviewing stands, identifying who stood where to determine which Soviet officials had more power or who might be falling out of favor. Melania-watchers similarly study the Trumps' joint public appearances—or the lack of them—and try to glean larger meanings.

Occasionally, Melania and Donald Trump (or "Muse" and "Mogul," as the Secret Service calls them) travel down the road from the White House to dine together at the Trump International Hotel. But they are rarely seen just casually enjoying a laugh or quiet moment together. The White House chooses which official photos to release to the public, but unlike with many past presidencies, the images shared are rarely candid snippets of their lives—such as a family movie night or a stroll on the South Lawn.

On June 4, 2017, a week before Melania moved into the White House, the Trumps attended the annual gala for Ford's Theatre. The historic building where Abraham Lincoln was shot is administered by the National Park Service. Trump told people in the administration that he would attend because Obama had declined the invitation in the past—Trump loves to draw distinctions between himself and his predecessor. The theater's seats were filled with members of Congress, top executives, and other patrons, and some present said that they perceived friction between Trump and Melania. At one point, Trump attempted to grab Melania's hand, but she rebuffed him. One of the attendees noted that it was memorable because of the recent viral video of Melania slapping away her husband's hand on the Ben Gurion airport tarmac in Israel during an official visit. A White House official later insisted that she was just trying to follow protocol on that trip, and that the incident should not be mistaken as demonstrating a lack of affection.

The next year, Melania attended the Ford's Theatre event alone, but the president and first lady appeared together again in 2019 and sat in the front row. I was also in the theater that night and saw them frequently whisper to each other. Melania smiled and laughed a few times at what Trump said. Guests who had been present two years before said that the couple's dynamic seemed to have shifted from frosty to warm.

Melania's onetime confidante Stephanie Winston Wolkoff told me that Melania "will never show you her emotion in public—that's just not who she is." Others have seen that when she is upset or angry, she just walks away. In Trump's first three years in office, there have certainly been plenty of times when Melania has walked away. In January 2018, after the *Wall Street Journal* published details of the $130,000 hush-money payment made by Trump's personal attorney to Stormy Daniels and *In Touch* magazine published Daniels's first-person account of her alleged affair with Trump, Melania abruptly canceled plans to join her husband at the World Economic Forum in Davos, Switzerland. She also broke with tradition and rode separately from her husband to his State of the Union speech before Congress at the end of the month. At that point, she had not been seen in public with her husband since the Stormy Daniels news broke.

In February, hours after the *New Yorker* published a detailed account of Trump's alleged affair, with Karen McDougal, and included McDougal's handwritten notes—"We got naked + had sex"—both Trumps headed to a planned weekend at Mar-a-Lago. But instead of making the very public, familiar walk across the White House lawn with her husband to Marine One, the presidential helicopter, Melania traveled separately to Andrews Air Force Base, the Maryland military airport, to catch Air Force One. Her spokeswoman explained the unusual arrangement at the time by saying that it was due to the first lady's schedule. But then when Melania's motorcade arrived on the tarmac, journalists were shooed off the plane until after she had boarded, and no photos were allowed of her arrival. She never said anything publicly. But she clearly put physical distance between herself and her husband.

In the most crucial moments, however, Melania has publicly

backed Trump even when friends recall her privately fuming. Her televised interviews supporting him after his *Access Hollywood* comments may well have saved his presidential candidacy. She has also publicly downplayed the reports of his serial infidelity and allegations from the roughly two dozen women who have accused him of sexual impropriety or abuse. In an October 2018 interview with ABC News reporter Tom Llamas, she waved off a question about her husband's infidelity. "It is not a concern and focus of mine. I am a mother and first lady, and I have much more important things to think about and to do." While hardly a ringing endorsement of her husband or her marriage, it offered Trump cover. When Trump is in trouble, Melania is in a unique position to embarrass him or save him, and she has consistently chosen to remain publicly on his side.

That has been of great value to Trump—and Melania knew it. She turned out to be a sharp negotiator, even when dealing with the man who boasts that no one can make a better deal than he can. There were several factors behind why Melania seemed visibly happier by mid-2018, which is something many in the White House had noticed. According to three people close to Trump, a key reason was that she had finally reached a new and significantly improved financial agreement with Trump, which had left her in a notably better financial position. Those sources did not know precisely what she sought but it was not simply more money. She wanted proof in writing that when it came to financial opportunities and inheritance, Barron would be treated as more of an equal to Trump's oldest three children. Among the items under discussion was involvement in the family business, the Trump Organization, and ownership of Trump property. One person aware of the negotiations noted that Barron has Slovenian citizenship, so he could be especially well-positioned if the young teenager ever wanted to be involved in a Trump business in Europe. Melania wanted—and got—options for him.

Trump was experienced at crafting prenups and obsessed with keeping his fortune intact. After Ivana successfully renegotiated her prenup, Trump had lawyers insert every conceivable clause into his prenup with Marla to try to make it unbreakable. If she contested it, Marla would even have to pay his legal fees, according to a lawyer directly involved. By the time Trump married Melania in 2005, he already had four children. Melania convinced Trump to have one more child, according to a close friend of Trump's: "That's where she used her power—her nonnegotiable back then was that she wanted to have a baby. But did she get some great prenup deal? No way."

Especially after *Access Hollywood* and Stormy Daniels and Karen McDougal spoke publicly about their affairs with Trump right after Barron was born, Melania's nonnegotiable was that her son would be treated more like Trump's oldest children. Trump's oldest, Don Jr., was twenty-nine when Barron was born, one year after Melania and Trump married. The number of heirs in line for a share of the Trump fortune has kept growing: Don Jr. now has five children, Ivanka has three, and Eric has two. Melania did not want Barron treated as somehow a "lesser Trump." In a press briefing in the White House in 2019 about efforts to curb e-cigarettes, Trump famously referred to Barron as Melania's son: "She's got a son," he said, then awkwardly adding, "together, that's a beautiful young man."

Melania, a long-game player, could not have picked a better time to push for an improved financial agreement. The fact that Trump was in the White House instead of Trump Tower, and needed her to play a particularly public role, strengthened her hand. In 1996, the year Melania arrived in the United States, Ivana Trump appeared in the hit movie *The First Wives Club* and gave this long-remembered advice: "Ladies, we have to be strong and independent. And remember: Don't get mad—get everything!" Melania, a third wife, appears to have come closest to getting out of Trump what she wanted.

AS ONE of her official duties as first lady, Melania Trump is the honorary chair of the Kennedy Center for the Performing Arts, best known for its annual honors program, which recognizes leading American artists who have made significant contributions to the nation's cultural life. But many in the arts community refuse to have any association with Donald Trump or to be present in the same room. They reject his divisive rhetoric and social policies and were angered by his proposals to eliminate funding for both the National Endowment for the Arts and the National Endowment for the Humanities, two federal agencies created to support the arts, education, and culture. (Congress voted to continue their funding.) Trump's positions put Melania in a tough spot. Many of her friends and acquaintances in the New York arts and fashion worlds had initially urged her to use her visibility to showcase culture, arts, and fashion. Instead, she has largely avoided those topics, perhaps well aware that if she invited cultural icons to the White House, they would likely turn her down.

Some Kennedy Center honorees have been particularly pointed in their rejection of Trump. In 2017, TV producer Norman Lear, being recognized for his outstanding contribution to American culture, and dancer Carmen de Lavallade announced that they would boycott the usual White House reception before the televised event. The White House event was canceled for the first time in the awards' history, and the president and Melania stayed away from the big ceremony at the Kennedy Center. The next year, *Hamilton* musical creator Lin-Manuel Miranda was selected to be honored. Miranda, of Puerto Rican descent, had already stated that Trump was "going straight to hell" for his tepid relief response following Hurricane Maria, which devastated Puerto Rico. Trump and Melania ignored the honors again.

So it was noteworthy when Melania appeared at the Kennedy Center for the first time in July 2019, to participate in a music program for disabled children. She had her picture taken with the young musicians; they were being recognized by the Jean Kennedy Smith Arts and Disabilities Program. Melania had been reassured that she would not face a hostile reception. The Kennedy Center has thirty-six presidentially appointed trustees on its governing board. During his eight years in office, President Obama had selected all of them. But a few months before Melania's first visit, Trump had begun to fill vacant openings with some of his supporters and friends, including actor Jon Voight, former Arkansas governor Mike Huckabee, and Karen Tucker LeFrak, an author and composer married to the New York real estate developer Richard LeFrak. Karen LeFrak is a friend of Melania's.

In September, Melania returned to the Kennedy Center to speak at the opening of the new REACH annex. The event was closed to the press. According to several invited guests, she was warmly received and applauded, and looked happy and relaxed in front of a crowd that included Supreme Court Chief Justice John Roberts. The next day, she tweeted: "Honored to join the Kennedy Center @Kencen last night in celebration of the grand opening of the REACH. This is an amazing investment in the/ arts and our next generation."

THE WHITE HOUSE has given Melania many opportunities, including introductions to world leaders from the president of France to Pope Francis. But these events have also subjected to scrutiny one of the most often repeated parts of her life story: that she speaks five languages. In October 1999, the *Daily News* reported, "Knauss would have little trouble talking to VIPs. She speaks French, German, Italian, English and Slovene." In 2016, MSNBC's Mika Brzezinski asked her directly: "How many languages do you speak?"

"I speak a few languages," Melania replied.

"A few?"

"English, Italian, French, German," Melania said.

She told me the same in our 2016 interview, and she and

Trump have repeatedly told interviewers that over the years. But her language expertise was not on display when she and the president visited the Vatican in May 2017 as part of his first official overseas trip. At the start of their audience, Pope Francis extended a hand to Melania, a Roman Catholic, as she approached him wearing a black lace veil covering her hair.

"Thank you. Nice to meet you," she said, almost in a whisper. They were still shaking hands when the pope spoke to her in Italian, asking lightheartedly if she fed her husband potica, a traditional Slovenian pastry. She looked at him and said nothing. Francis motioned to his interpreter, who stepped forward and translated the pope's words into English: "What do you give him to eat—is it potica?"

"Potica, yes!" Melania laughed. A papal aide handed her a rosary for the pope to bless. "Oh, I would love it, thank you. Grazie," she said to the pope, as he held his hand over hers and blessed the beads. "Thank you. Thank you," she said. A few minutes later, as the first couple were leaving, Francis locked eyes with Melania again. "Thank you very much," he said, expressing gratitude for her visit. She shook his hand and told him about her next stop. "I'm going to visit a hospital, for bambinos. Thank you so much."

Perhaps Melania was starstruck or being polite. Or maybe she has taken a page out of Trump's playbook: There's nothing wrong with exaggerating if it builds the brand and polishes the image. The narrative of Melania's language skills also fits with another Trump storyline: that she is the new Jacqueline Kennedy Onassis. Trump told *Fox & Friends* in 2019: "We have our own Jackie O, it's called Melania, Melania T." But in 1962, when First Lady Jackie Kennedy met with Pope John XXIII in the Vatican, he greeted her with open arms and said, "Ah, Jacqueline!" They proceeded to have a conversation entirely in French for thirty-two minutes.

I tried to independently confirm the extent of Melania's language abilities, but I couldn't find any videos showing her fluency in anything other than Slovenian and English. I asked the White House if they could point to any evidence, and they did not respond. The videos that do exist of her speaking to children in France and Italy show her using only a few basic and universally known words, like "bonjour" and "ciao," before switching quickly to English.

In 1993, when she arrived in Vienna, where the main language is German, modeling agent Wolfgang Schwarz recalled that she knew so little German that they spoke English together. Photographers and others who have worked with her over the years—including native speakers of Italian, French, and German—told me that they never heard her use more than a few words in those languages.

During that same May 2017 trip, Melania joined other G7 leaders' spouses to tour the elegant Palazzo degli Elefanti in Catania, Sicily. At lunch, Melania was seated beside then-mayor Enzo Bianco. She spoke entirely in English, communicating to the mayor through her Italian interpreter. Bianco said that he thought it proper etiquette to converse in English with the first lady. But others involved in the planning of the trip said it would have been a nice gesture if Melania had spoken even a few words in Italian. Two months later, Melania and Trump visited Paris. Melania walked into a children's hospital and brightly greeted the children with a cheerful,

"Bonjour! Bonjour!" Then she sat down with the French kids and started chatting to them in English through an interpreter. "How are you? Nice to meet you," she said to one little girl. Although she placed her hand over her heart and offered a "Je m'appelle Melania. Et toi?," she then switched back to English. In August 2019, at a G7 summit in Biarritz, France, Melania picked up translation headphones to listen to a speech by French president Emmanuel Macron. CNN commentator Keith Boykin spotted the problem: "Wait. I thought Melania Trump spoke French fluently."

FIRST LADIES have often said that living in the White House is like living in a fishbowl. Melania's way of dealing with life in a public building visited by thousands of people each week is to spend large amounts of her day cocooned in the White House's private quarters. The first lady is officially in charge of a White House staff of one hundred people, from the chefs to the housekeepers and butlers. Melania involves herself in the minute details of running the house, but often from her residence rooms rather than the formal first lady's East Wing office.

In her first three years, Melania oversaw multiple restoration projects in the White House public rooms, plus a redo of the basement bowling alley, originally installed by Richard Nixon. The first lady also designed a new rug for the Diplomatic Reception Room. Too much heavy use had left the prior rug worn down. The new rug's border is ornamented with the flowers of each state, a design element Melania added.

Similar to what she did at Trump Tower with her spa, Melania overhauled the small area in the White House where first ladies have their hair done, making it mostly white. Laura Bush, after watching the heavy criticism Hillary Clinton endured for her hair, paid to have hers professionally styled, as did Michelle Obama. Melania spends less time in the West Wing and more time in the private residence than past first ladies. Her parents often stay in the family residence, too, and have their own bedroom, as did Michelle Obama's mother. Melania, her parents, and Barron often speak Slovenian to one another when they're together. This gives them in essence a private language, so they can continue to speak freely even in front of residence staff or the Secret Service agents standing watch at the door.

In her East Wing offices, Melania maintains a small and loyal staff. Many of them have less experience in government, policy, and speechwriting than those who worked for previous first ladies. Michelle Obama hired two power lawyers to run her office: Susan Sher, the top lawyer under Chicago mayor Richard Daley, followed in her second term by Tina Tchen, who had previously led the White House Office of Public Engagement and been a special assistant to President Obama. Laura Bush hired Andi Ball, who had worked for her in the governor's office, and then Anita McBride, whose White House experience spanned two decades. Melania's first chief of staff, Lindsay Reynolds, was associate director of the White House Visitors Center under George W. Bush and then led an event planning business in Ohio. During her tenure, she returned home most weekends to be with her husband and small children. Stephanie Grisham, Melania's spokeswoman, got her start in national politics in 2012 as a press aide to Mitt Romney's campaign. Rickie Niceta Lloyd, her social secretary, was a well-liked executive at Design Cuisine, a high-end caterer for many Washington events. At the White House, both Trumps prized a person's loyalty to them above anything on their resume. Lewandowski noted, "There are no leaks that come out of [Melania's] staff," adding, "Her staff is small and tight-lipped, and they have 100 percent loyalty to her."

In April 2020, with the reelection campaign looming, Melania made big changes to her staff. Reynolds left the White House and Grisham, who had been promoted to White House communications director, joined Melania's staff as chief of staff and spokesperson. Most significantly, Melania named Marcia Lee Kelly, the CEO of the 2020 Republican National Convention with an impressive track record of government service and organizing huge events, as her senior adviser. The first lady also brought over from the West Wing Emma Doyle to work on policy for her. Many saw the addition of Kelly, known for making things happen, as a sign that Melania wanted to raise her profile.

Melania's approach to the first lady's job has been different from that of her predecessors. She was invisible at first, then ducked out of public view for weeks at a time. She has stayed silent on big issues many hoped she would address and surprised people when she did decide to speak up. She has limited her public speaking but offers polished short videos of what she's doing in the White House. The Melania effect may be to allow the spouse of the next president to feel less bound by tradition and public expectations. "She really relieved a burden for any future occupant, male or female, that they do not have to feel compelled to follow the way that we were, as Americans, used to seeing things done," said Anita McBride, who serves on the board of directors of the White House Historical Association.

Lauren A. Wright, an associate research scholar at Princeton University, noted that Melania Trump made eight speeches in 2017, while Michelle Obama made seventy-four and Laura Bush gave forty-two during their husbands' first year in office. In her first three years as first lady, she did only a small number of television interviews, including with CNN White House correspondent Kate Bennett on a trip to China in 2017, and the next year with ABC News's Tom Llamas during her Africa trip, and with Fox News personality and Trump booster Sean Hannity aboard the aircraft carrier USS *George H. W. Bush*. Phillip Bloch, who had worked on Trump's beauty pageants, said that Melania knows to "stay in her lane." Bloch said he believes that one of the reasons she is not very active as a first lady is that she knows the White House is really the Donald Trump Show.

Melania has a compelling personal story to tell, and it confounds some who have worked with her that she is not more willing to tell it. One person who worked for Melania said that it was unusually difficult to help her prepare her public remarks. Personal stories help connect speakers with their audiences and help create a more memorable voice. But in meetings to prepare for her speeches, she was often reluctant to share personal anecdotes. Even getting her to describe her motivation to focus on children's issues had proven difficult. "She just felt more comfortable talking in platitudes, such as, 'Cyberbullying is not a good thing. We need to stop it,'" the aide said. She felt pressure to look good in public, he said, and that often seemed to take priority over the substance and delivery of the speech. "If she had ten hours to spend getting ready for an event, nine of them would be devoted to her appearance. That left no time to practice with the teleprompter, to say the words out loud, to have her input into the remarks she was making."

She gave a speech about children at a luncheon she hosted for spouses of world leaders in 2017 during the United Nations General Assembly in New York. As she spoke, Melania appeared nervous and her voice quivered. "The most important and joyous role I've ever had is to be a mother to my young son," she said. "Together we must acknowledge that all too often it is the weakest, most innocent and vulnerable among us, our children, who ultimately suffer the most from the challenges that plague our societies." She spoke of the "moral imperative" to take responsibility for the "bullying" and content that children "are exposed to on a daily basis through social media . . . and in person." The message she wanted to relay was strong but it was largely lost because of her poor delivery. Several people in the room thought that if she had wowed the audience with her speech, and even lingered afterward to talk to the guests, she would have gotten more attention for her initiative. Instead, her appearance ended up in style pages and tabloids, mentioned more because of what she wore than what she said. "She's electric!" wrote the British tabloid *Daily Mail*, describing her "eye-catching $3,000 neon pink" Delpozo coat dress with huge puffy sleeves and matching "hot pink" stilettos. It would become a constant dilemma. She loved dressing well and wanted to make a statement with her clothes. But she also wanted to be taken seriously, for people to listen to her.

MELANIA'S SIGNATURE program, an initiative known as Be Best, was unveiled in the Rose Garden on May 7, 2018, in front of the full press corps and a crowd of invited guests. Everyone turned their heads as Melania walked toward the podium, her high heels clicking with each careful step. She didn't rush. Shoulders back, she swept past photographers, Secret Service agents, and staffers. She wore a tan leather jacket the color of sand. It took a full forty-four seconds for her to reach the podium. Her appearance came only four days after Trump had been forced to acknowledge that, despite prior denials, he was aware of a hush-money payment to Stormy Daniels—and that he had repaid the money to his personal lawyer. Now, in a powerful display of support, Team Trump was out in force. Vice President Mike Pence and his wife, Karen, five cabinet secretaries, and many top advisers and officials, including Kellyanne Conway, were seated in the baking sun waiting for Melania to speak. Treasury Secretary Steven Mnuchin wore sunglasses. Commerce Secretary Wilbur Ross's bald head pinkened in the heat.

"As a mother and as First Lady, it concerns me that in today's fast-paced and ever-connected world, children can be less prepared to express or manage their emotions and oftentimes turn to forums of destructive or addictive behavior, such as bullying, drug addiction or even suicide," Melania said. "I feel strongly that, as adults, we can and should be best at educating our children about the importance of a healthy and balanced life. So today, I'm very excited to announce BE BEST." Its three main pillars were child well-being, social media use, and the consequences of the opioid epidemic.

As was the case with her UN speech, it was not the substance of her remarks that attracted attention. Instead, it was the name of her new initiative, Be Best, that drew the most notice. Although Michelle Obama had great success with her two-word health and exercise initiative Let's Move, Be Best didn't have the same ring, and it provided fodder for late-night comics. Stephanie Winston Wolkoff, who was working with Melania at the time, said that they had considered other names. These included Children First, which Melania had discarded, saying it sounded too much like her husband's America First slogan. Some wondered why Melania hadn't called the program Be the Best or Be Your Best. But Melania had made up her mind, saying: "At least they won't say I plagiarized it!"

Now she was telling the country that she would focus on children, whom she called "the most valuable and fragile among us." When she invited her husband to join her at the podium, she referred to him as "Mr. President" and then stood stiffly as Trump kissed her right cheek, left cheek, and right cheek again, in the European style. "That's the way she feels—very strongly!" Trump said, praising his wife. He said that everywhere she went, "Americans have been touched by her sincerity, moved by her grace and lifted by her love."

Melania has made a number of Be Best appearances since launching the initiative. One that came as a surprise, given her husband's penchant for attacking people on Twitter, was a March 2018 White House conference to stop what she called the "evil" of cyberbullying. "I am well aware that people are skeptical of me discussing this topic," she told top executives from Twitter, Facebook, and other tech companies. "I have been criticized for my commitment to tackling this issue, and I know that will continue. But it will not stop me for doing what I know is right." She added, "We have to find a better way to talk to each other, to disagree with each other, to respect each other." Seated at the table with the first lady was Stephen Balkam, founder and CEO of the Family Online Safety Institute, who recalled, "It was a pretty remarkable opening. I was pleased that she addressed the elephant in the room."

Melania had told others that she recognized that her husband had contributed to the combative tone online, but she wanted to talk about the issue even though West Wing advisers urged her to pick another topic. But after the cyberbullying event, Melania seemed to focus Be Best more on its other two pillars: child well-being and the consequences of the opioid epidemic.

One of Melania's Be Best appearances that drew significant attention was on November 26, 2019, in Baltimore, a city that Donald Trump had previously derided as a "disgusting, rat- and rodent-infested mess." Approximately one thousand middle and high school students were in the audience for the B'More Youth Summit to raise awareness about the opioid crisis. A mix of boos and cheers started when Melania strode onto the stage in a pricey caramel-colored suede trench coat and matching knee-high suede boots. "It is my pleasure to introduce to you the first lady of the

United States of America," said Jim Wahlberg, representing the Mark Wahlberg Youth Foundation, run by his actor brother. "Thank you, Jim, for the warm introduction," Melania said, reading from a teleprompter, "and for inviting me to join you today for such an important event centered on opioid awareness." As she spoke, the crowd remained loud, talking and jeering.

Realizing what was happening, Melania looked amused and did not get flustered. She turned her attention from the teleprompter and gazed at the students. "Hello, everyone," she said with a big smile. Melania then spoke for about five minutes on the dangers of drug use and about how Be Best was working to highlight efforts to fight online abuse and opioid addiction. "Since its launch, I have used Be Best to shine a light on programs like these that show what it means to Be Best," she said. When she had finished, she said, "Thank you." There were cheers, but a loud chorus of boos grew as she walked off the stage, waving and giving a big smile. Later, she responded to the behavior with a public statement, "We live in a democracy and everyone is entitled to their opinion, but the fact is we have a serious crisis in our country and I remain committed to educating children on the dangers and deadly consequences of drug abuse."

The Baltimore incident underscored the challenge of being married to a president who is seen as exceptionally divisive. Melania has the highest poll numbers of anyone in the first family. But while being in politics has given her new opportunities, it has also closed off other avenues. Magazine editors who featured Michelle Obama and other first ladies on their covers have bypassed Melania. Her friends blame biased liberals in the fashion and magazine world and point to *Vogue* editor in chief Anna Wintour's response to a question posed by CNN's Christiane Amanpour in 2019. "We profile women in the magazine that we believe in," Wintour said. "We believe that women should have a leadership position and we intend to support them." The editor named both Michelle Obama and Hillary Clinton, but conspicuously never mentioned Melania Trump. Two decades ago, an association with Donald Trump would be a potential selling point for a glossy magazine cover; today he is seen as so polarizing that anything connected to him—including his wife—risks alienating many readers.

A few days later, spokeswoman Stephanie Grisham addressed the controversy by telling Fox News, "To be on the cover of *Vogue* doesn't define Mrs. Trump, she's been there, done that long before she was first lady. Her role as first lady of the United States and all that she does is much more important than some superficial photo shoot and cover." The put-down struck many as odd since Melania spent years doing photo shoots. Grisham went on to sharply criticize Wintour, whose relationship with Melania in the White House stood in stark contrast to the chummy coverage *Vogue* had given to her in the past. It also illustrated how personal the divide had become. "This just further demonstrates how biased the fashion magazine industry is and shows how insecure and small-minded Anna Wintour really is. Unfortunately, Mrs. Trump is used to this kind of divisive behavior." Grisham's tough and personal statement was seen as yet another reminder that Melania, like her husband, often hits back when she feels attacked.

But statements like this also stand out because of how generally tight-lipped the first lady's office is. Her staff has been directed not to answer even basic media questions. Aside from limited events and periodic photo ops, very little is known about the most basic details of the first lady's schedule, including whether she is in Washington or traveling. Many days are a blank, with no official engagements. That unusual information vacuum about the first lady of the United States has led to a cottage industry of speculation about Melania. At one point she was not seen publicly for twenty-four days. In her absence, rumors flew that her marriage was faltering, and that she was staying with Barron and her parents in a house in the Washington suburb of Potomac, Maryland, near her son's school. "It's 1,000 percent false. We laugh at it all the time," Grisham said in 2018, when asked about the speculation that Melania sometimes escaped to another house. Rickie Niceta Lloyd, the White House social secretary, called it "an urban legend."

Melania has returned to New York and visited Mar-a-Lago quietly at times without her husband—for a while, reporters staked out the Palm Beach airport looking for signs of a government plane to track her travels—but she is often where Barron is, and he is in the White House. Many people in the White House have a special affection for Melania and describe her as "drama-free" and "not demanding." One added that she is a rare person around Trump who doesn't cause any problems. "Trump loves her cool," said Winston Wolkoff. "She knows exactly what he does not want, which makes her exactly what he wants."

The Trumps after his impeachment acquittal in February 2020

CHAPTER 12

"The Protector"

THE LONGER Melania Trump has been in Washington, the more she has embraced her role as first lady. Says a longtime friend of both Trumps, "She loves Washington for her son, she loves the school where Barron goes, he's excelled at sports there and has made friends. When he's happy, she's happy." Melania visibly brightens when talking about her son and when talking about children in general. I have seen it many times, as have others who follow or cover her. She consistently visits children's hospitals and has made it an annual tradition to spend Valentine's Day at the Children's Inn, a residential home for children being treated for rare or complex diseases at the National Institutes of Health in Bethesda, Maryland. At Children's National Hospital in Washington, D.C., she befriended a girl undergoing care for leukemia, Caoilinn McLane. "She took the time to listen and made me feel important," said McLane, in an interview. Since she met Melania three years ago at the hospital when she was fifteen, she has seen the first lady two more times and also talked to her on the phone. McLane was in an ambulance when a cell phone rang, and she was told the first lady wanted to talk to her. "She was very generous with her time and seems very genuine—and relatable. I told her I play soccer and she said her son plays soccer, too." McLane joined Melania for the ribbon-cutting ceremony for the hospital's rooftop Bunny Mellon Healing Garden, dedicated to U.S. first ladies and designed to be used by patients and their families. McLane said Melania sat on the ledge and helped young patients plant some seeds in the garden. Melania seems most at ease and happy when she is with children, and she is often photographed sitting in a small chair at a low table with youngsters.

Parents and children at St. Andrew's Episcopal School, the private school that Barron attends in suburban Washington, have seen Melania at the school, but say Donald Trump has stayed away. Melania has spoken to other parents at St. Andrew's about the teen vaping epidemic and has heard from them about how common it is to open a middle schooler's backpack and find nicotine pods. They have told her that they appreciated that she spoke up and used her influence to help convince her husband to ban fruit-flavored e-cigarettes, which are particularly attractive to kids.

When Barron arrived in Washington, he joined a soccer league affiliated with the local professional soccer team, D.C. United, and Melania would go to watch him play. After her presence was noted on the sidelines, she was seen at least once watching the game at a distance from inside a Secret Service car with tinted windows. Mindful of how disruptive his family's presence can be, Barron has told other kids that he does not want his father to come to games or to his school because it causes such a commotion. Melania also had a soccer coach come to the White House to kick the ball around with Barron—she added a net to the grounds outside the Oval Office.

Even before Barron officially moved into the White House, for his first Easter Egg Roll, Melania invited D.C. United players and their children and set up goals on the White House lawn. Patrick Mullins and Marcelo Sarvas were invited inside, where they talked to Barron and gave him a signed soccer ball. Sarvas brought his son, who joined Barron on the grass with a ball. Mullins told the *Washington Post* that Barron had a passion for the game and at eleven was able to hold a good conversation. "He was very knowledgeable about soccer, knew about D.C. United and was interested to know more."

In the intervening years, Barron has added to his soccer ball collection, even receiving a World Cup final ball from Vladimir Putin. Putin handed it to Donald Trump at a joint press conference in Helsinki in 2018, prompting Trump to say that he would give it to Barron; he then tossed it to Melania, who was sitting near the podium. She missed it, but Secretary of State Mike Pompeo caught the ball and handed it to her. The gift didn't arrive politics-free. Republican senator Lindsey Graham, a Trump ally, tweeted, "If it were me, I'd check the soccer ball for listening devices and never allow it in the White House."

Like many kids his age, Barron plays video games and likes to compete with other kids playing popular online games. He also invites friends to the White House. Barron occasionally appears in the news, primarily in media photos taken when he is walking with both parents to or from a plane or helicopter. At one such appearance, in early 2020, Barron caused a stir: at age thirteen, he towered over both his parents—the *Daily Mail* had already cheekily headlined a photo of Barron "Trump Tower." In Slovenia, people were chatting about whether he could soon be taller than Luka Dončić, the hugely popular Slovenian-born Dallas Mavericks basketball star, who is six foot seven. (Dončić is featured far more than Melania in the Slovenian news.)

Barron's grandparents are central to his life as well as Melania's. Amalija is a constant support. Winston Wolkoff, who has seen Melania with her mother, said of Amalija: "She is her left hand and her right hand, and she enables her to be who she is."

In recent years, Melania has helped her mother through a serious illness, making sure she received the best care. Melania has also faced her own health issues while in the White House; she has a kidney condition that required surgery, and over the years also suffered from painful kidney stones. In 2018, she was admitted to Walter Reed National Military Medical Center, and according to her office, "underwent an embolization procedure to treat a benign kidney condition," with no further details except to say the procedure was successful and there were no complications. One person who has observed Melania with her mother said, "It's more like they're sisters than they're mother and daughter."

While Trump has called Melania his "rock," those close to the family say Melania's rock is her mother.

The grandparents have taught Barron songs in Slovenian. Friends of Viktor's recalled him sitting in a café in Sevnica in early 2018, happy to be home and among a group of men he has known for decades, when his phone rang. It was Barron, calling from the White House and wanting to tell his grandfather about his day. "Viktor was so proud. He put him on speakerphone. Barron spoke 100 percent Slovenian!" said one man who listened in. I met with several of Viktor's friends a few months after that phone call, and they said that Viktor had told them not to talk publicly, so they did not want to give their names. But they were proud, too, of this boy who liked Slovenian food and knew the language and was so close to his grandparents. The men said that Viktor loves to talk about Barron but mostly avoids talk of his son-in-law. Viktor does not agree with Trump's "anti-immigration talk," his friends said. On his trips back to his hometown, Viktor walks a couple miles a day along the Sava River, enjoying the far simpler life.

One family member who has not been visible in the White House or at related events, and who was not seen publicly during the inauguration, is Melania's sister, Ines, the maid of honor at her wedding. Ines Knauss (she also changed Knavs to Knauss) has an apartment a couple blocks from Trump Tower. Very little is known about how she spends her time. As of early 2020, she had received her green card, or permanent U.S. residence status, according to immigration attorney Michael Wildes. Those who know her describe her as creative. She has posted on her social media accounts lovely old pictures of growing up in Slovenia. She noted that Stane Jerko, the photographer who took pictures of Melania, took pictures of Ines herself several years before, when she was thirteen, for a Jutranka clothing catalog.

Periodically Ines has made puzzling or unexpected comments in response to things said about her famous sister. Just after the 2016 election, a childhood friend of Melania's was quoted as saying nice things about Melania and recalling that as teenagers they listened to Duran Duran and Queen and drank "Coca-Cola by taking really small sips, as it was considered a rare luxury." Ines tweeted: "What kind of nonsense is that—talking about Coca Cola." There have been news reports that Ines offers her sister style advice. In 2018, the *New York Post* wrote that "once or twice a month, the first lady quietly comes to New York, and has her sister come over to give advice as she tries on outfits." It was unclear why Melania felt the need to address that, but her spokeswoman responded, "Mrs. Trump and her sister are very close, but she is not who helps her with styling her wardrobe. At the end of the day, it is Mrs. Trump who decides what she will wear."

Perhaps it was inevitable, with all the focus on Melania's clothes, that her most memorable misstep as first lady involved one of her fashion choices. In June 2018, she appeared to publicly split with her husband over the administration's policy of separating families and children at the U.S.-Mexico border. When images of the conditions first appeared, the *Washington Post* published a devastating op-ed by former first lady Laura Bush, who broke her usual silence on policy matters and wrote that "this zero-tolerance policy is cruel. It is immoral. And it breaks my heart," adding, "These images are eerily reminiscent of the internment camps for U.S. citizens and noncitizens of Japanese descent during World War II, now considered to have been one of the most shameful episodes in U.S. history." Through a spokesperson, Melania weighed in with her own criticism: "Mrs. Trump hates to see children separated from their families and hopes both sides of the aisle can finally come together to achieve successful immigration reform," Stephanie Grisham told CNN. "She believes we need to be a country that follows all laws, but also a country that governs with heart." Within a day, all first ladies had called for an end to family separation, including Michelle Obama, Hillary Clinton, and Rosalynn Carter. Inside the White House, Ivanka was making it clear that she, too, opposed the policy. To some it appeared that both Ivanka and Melania were angling to get public credit for getting the policy changed.

In a later interview with ABC News, Melania addressed the border issue directly. "It was unacceptable for me to see children and parents separated. It was heartbreaking. And I reacted with my own voice," she said. "Yes [I disagree], and I let him know. I didn't know that that policy would come out. I was blindsided by it. I told him at home, and I said to him that I feel that's unacceptable, and he felt the same." Days after Melania's public rebuke, the president issued an executive order ending the "zero tolerance" policy that had separated more than four thousand children from their parents or guardians. Trump explained his decision:

"Ivanka feels very strongly. My wife feels very strongly about it." Melania had told him it was terrible, for the children, for the country, for him, and that she wanted to go to the border.

But while Melania's repudiation of the child separation policy is often seen as her standing up to her husband, some inside the White House say her response was coordinated with her husband, who realized that he had made a mistake and was happy for Melania to help him fix it. The criticism generated by the TV images from the border had upset him. Even his Republican Party allies labeled the situation unacceptable. Trump blamed his aides for not realizing the damage. He had wanted to project strength at the border, but instead he had created a a humanitarian crisis and a public mess.

Melania made an unannounced trip to McAllen, Texas, and toured a shelter for migrant children, some of whom had been separated from their parents. Her visit, coming the day after Trump made a rare reversal of policy and signed the executive order, was a way to project a softer side of the administration, and Trump wanted Melania—not his critics—to receive credit for it. It was good cop, bad cop, Trump-style.

Then came the jacket. As she boarded the government jet at Andrews Air Force Base, on her way to Texas, photographers took note of her olive green $39 Zara jacket, with big white graffiti-style letters on the back that read "I REALLY DON'T CARE. DO U?" Melania did not wear the coat while she toured the facility on the border, but she did wear it again on her return to Maryland. The choice seemed deliberate: It was eighty degrees and humid, and the jacket had been a topic of controversy for hours.

What was the first lady trying to say? She clearly cared about the children—she was going to visit them. But curiosity was quickly overtaken by outrage on social media. Stephanie Grisham said that it was just a jacket, with "no hidden message." But both Trumps would later say that it actually did have a message. First, Donald Trump tweeted: "'I REALLY DON'T CARE, DO U?' written on the back of Melania's jacket, refers to the Fake News Media. Melania has learned how dishonest they are, and she truly no longer cares!" A few months later, Melania offered her own explanation: "It's obvious I didn't wear that jacket for the children . . . It was for the people and for the left-wing media who are criticizing me. I want to show them that I don't care. You could criticize whatever you want to say. But it will not stop me to do what feels right." Melania's real message with the jacket appears to have been more broadly directed at many of her critics, not just the media. Several people in the White House said that also included Ivanka.

Melania's first—and, so far, only—solo trip abroad also generated controversy. The trip, in October 2018, brought her to Ghana, Malawi, Kenya, and Egypt. Near the end of the trip, she stood before the Great Sphinx in Giza, Egypt. Her skinny black necktie was blown over her shoulder by the hot desert breeze, and a white fedora with a black band shielded her eyes from the heavy sun. Her snow-white Chanel blouse was buttoned to the top, and she had draped a sand-colored Ralph Lauren jacket over her shoulders. She used one of the world's greatest historical landmarks as the dramatic background for what looked like a fashion photo shoot.

Melania then stood before reporters and answered questions, a rarity from a first lady who has been so sparing with her public statements. A reporter started to ask about the white pith helmet that she wore on safari in Kenya, which for many on the African continent symbolizes a brutal and painful colonial past. Melania responded with a faint puff of irritation: "I wish people would focus on what I do, not what I wear." To many in the press pool, the reply, coming from a longtime model, seemed like LeBron James complaining about people asking him about basketball.

Melania crisscrossed Africa. She bottle-fed baby elephants in Kenya and visited Cape Coast Castle in Ghana, where Africans were held captive in dungeons before they were shipped in chains abroad. She seemed most relaxed and natural visiting with children at orphanages, hospitals, and schools. She exuded an easy warmth as she read with them, embraced them, and spoke with the people caring for them, becoming Melania, the Mom-in-Chief. "Thank you for educating them to be best," she told staff at a school in Malawi, "and to grow up into educated adults for generations to come." Like other first ladies before her, especially Laura Bush and Michelle Obama, she charmed Africans at every stop.

"Many Ghanaians are saying that she is the nicer of the Trumps," Samuel Okudzeto Ablakwa, an opposition party leader in Ghana's parliament, told the *Washington Post*. "Melania is an immigrant, too. She is from a humble background . . . There's a soft spot. She can become an ally, she can give her husband fresher perspectives about Africa. We need someone to tell him now that Africa is not a basket case as he thinks." Throughout the trip, Melania highlighted programs run by the U.S. Agency for International Development (USAID), and she was accompanied on the trip by USAID administrator Mark Green. In Ghana, Melania visited a hospital that received USAID funding for programs to help mothers and newborns. She visited a school in Malawi that relied on USAID funding for literacy programs, and she donated 1.4 million books to that effort. "I wanted to be here to see the successful programs that the United States is providing the children," she said at the Malawi school. Before she departed for her trip, she had remarked at the UN General Assembly, "I am so proud of the work this Administration is doing through USAID."

What made Melania's focus on USAID particularly noteworthy was that her husband's administration was seeking to cut USAID's funding to Africa by up to 30 percent. (When Laura Bush made a solo visit to South Africa, Tanzania, and Rwanda in 2005, it came at a time when her husband was working to double U.S. aid to Africa. And he had made addressing Africa's HIV/AIDS pandemic a cornerstone of his administration.) Critics pointed out that such deep cuts would devastate development and health programs, especially initiatives to treat and prevent AIDS and malaria. Congress ultimately rejected the Trump administration cuts and restored the aid. In Egypt, Melania skated right past a question about her husband's funding cuts. She said that the message of her trip was "that we care, and we want to show the world that we care."

The Africa trip continued to make headlines a month later and would play a prominent role in a high-profile firing inside the White House. On November 13, 2018, a Tuesday afternoon, Melania's spokeswoman Stephanie Grisham issued a statement about Mira Ricardel, the deputy national security adviser and one of the highest-ranking women in the White House: "It is the position of the Office of the First Lady that she no longer deserves the honor of serving in this White House." First ladies, including Melania, have privately urged their husbands to fire people, but no historian could recall one publicly calling for the ouster of a top West Wing official. Katherine Jellison, a professor at Ohio University who studies first ladies, said it was a moment that made people realize that Melania is not "just the striking-looking former international model standing silently next to her husband."

Ricardel, then fifty-eight, of Croatian descent—her father had emigrated from Yugoslavia in 1954—had a top security clearance, and her portfolio included North Korean sanctions and protecting U.S. elections from foreign, specifically Russian, interference. A Washington veteran who had worked in George W. Bush's Department of Defense, Ricardel had a long career in international affairs and was not reluctant to assert herself. A former White House official who attended sensitive briefings alongside Ricardel in the Situation Room, said, "Mira knew more than anyone in the room and had an opinion." Ricardel felt that the Trump administration at times handed out credentials like candy to policy rookies more interested in taking a selfie in the Oval Office than in serving their country.

The conflict between Ricardel and Melania's staff dated back to an advance planning visit to Africa. During that trip, the team overnighted on the Mediterranean island of Cyprus, and according to five people familiar with the trip, at least one of the first lady's staffers got publicly drunk. Word had passed from Secret Service agents to others in the White House that at least one young staffer was so inebriated that she climbed up on the bar and, according to some accounts, performed a somersault. Excessive drinking on overseas advance trips is not new, and the Secret Service was an agency already familiar with its own alcohol-fueled scandals overseas during the Obama administration.

Ricardel weighed in and told people that Cyprus, located near Syria and Lebanon, was a particularly bad place for U.S. officials to get hammered. As word traveled through the White House, some thought that Ricardel was making too much of the event. She and her Africa experts also irritated members of the first lady's staff. They viewed her as condescending, and they did not appreciate her letting it be known that she thought they should focus less on photo ops for Melania in Africa and more on U.S. foreign policy objectives. Ricardel was worried about the trip and felt it should be used to reassure African leaders upset at Trump's "shithole countries" remark about African nations. "These are not sightseeing trips," Ricardel said. The personality clashes continued, and members of the first lady's staff increasingly saw Ricardel as a problem.

Ricardel's team felt that Melania's staff didn't understand the importance of certain gestures in the host countries. For example, Grisham had tried to cancel an airport welcoming ceremony with Ghana's first lady, proposing instead a brief greeting on the tarmac.

Right before the trip, the growing animosity between Melania's staff and Ricardel and her national security team resulted in a spat over the seemingly small issue of a seat on the first lady's plane. Reynolds emailed Ricardel that an Africa expert from Ricardel's team no longer could travel with the first lady. Although the White House later told the media that this decision was made to create more space for security personnel and reporters, Reynolds's email made no mention of the press. "The needs of the Office of the First Lady, the US Secret Service and White House Military Office are greater than anticipated," Reynolds wrote. She added that the National Security Council Africa expert was welcome to join at any of the stops, but that she would have to find her own commercial flights. Ricardel knew that made no sense: matching the first lady's itinerary would be all but impossible and she could send someone to only one stop. Some national security staffers said that perhaps if the country expert from Ricardel's team had gotten a seat, the controversial pith helmet would have remained in the first lady's luggage.

With Melania back home in Washington, Ricardel thought that the issues had blown over. But then Stephanie Grisham issued the stinging statement about Ricardel. It led the news. The White House spin at the time was that Melania did not like it when other people bullied her staff and had made a dramatic move. While this may have been true, there was much more to the story.

Melania and Ricardel had never met. Ricardel was stunned. After the release of the "no longer deserves the honor" statement, Ricardel had awakened her boss, national security adviser John Bolton, at 2:00 a.m. He was in Singapore and outraged that his number two had been summarily dismissed: "They can't do that. You work for me." As Ricardel watched her face appear on TV screens in her office, she asked to see the president, but when she entered the Oval Office, Grisham and Reynolds from Melania's staff, and John Kelly, Trump's chief of staff, were waiting. Ricardel took the empty seat between Grisham and Reynolds in front of the president's desk. "It's terrible," Trump said about the statement, and acted as though it had caught him off guard. Ricardel requested that the statement be withdrawn, saying, "It's not just humiliating to me. It's going to make the White House look bad, the First Lady look bad, the presidency look bad." Trump shook his head, repeating, "This is terrible."

During the meeting, Grisham went on the offensive and accused Ricardel of leaking to the media, a mortal sin in Trump's eyes. Ricardel defended herself, telling Trump that she did not talk to the press. Reynolds then accused Ricardel of having "investigated" Melania's staff. Ricardel said that she had only raised justifiable concern about unprofessional behavior overseas on the advance trip. As the back-and-forth played out in front of Trump, he turned to Grisham and asked, "Who told you to do this?"

"I was told," she replied, an oddly vague answer.

In the end, Ricardel was forced out.

Melania has not spoken publicly about the firing, but in interviews, multiple White House officials have indicated that, at least in part, West Wing presidential staff used the first lady's influence to push their own agenda. Three officials said that John Kelly wanted to remove Ricardel, and they said his fingerprints were all over her ouster. "John Kelly orchestrated the whole thing," one said. He had never liked "that awful woman," as he called her when she started to clash with Defense Secretary James Mattis. The fact that she was also Bolton's deputy was another strike against her, in Kelly's eyes. Hours before the bombshell statement, Zach Fuentes, Kelly's deputy, had stopped by Ricardel's office to say that the first lady was upset about press coverage of her Africa trip. Others noted that Kelly's first attempt to get Ricardel fired had failed, and that his Plan B was to enlist Melania's team, because, as a White House official said, "He knew Grisham and Lindsay were killers if anyone crossed Melania."

Several West Wing staffers also said that Trump knew in advance about Melania's statement on Ricardel, but that after a string of high-profile firings, including of Attorney General Jeff Sessions, he didn't want more discussion of rapid turnover. He also had plans to remove Homeland Security Secretary Kirstjen Nielsen, and especially didn't want to be seen firing another of the few top women in the administration. It was easier if Melania did it. "I thought it was outrageous Mira was treated that way," John Bolton wrote in an email to me in 2020. "She behaved throughout with dignity and professionalism and it was a big loss to the Trump administration and to our national security." How much

Melania was told about all the guns out for Ricardel before she signed off on axing her is unclear. But that unprecedented firing illustrates key things about the Trump White House: top administration officials sometimes try to use Melania's power for their own agenda, and Melania is not afraid of owning a bold move even in the West Wing. And sometimes when it appears Melania is acting independently from her husband, she is actually working with him.

Trump often consults Melania on personnel matters, and she is not shy about sharing her views. When it comes to decisions in the White House, a Trump confidant says, "My guess is that she wins more than she loses."

MELANIA INCREASINGLY made her voice heard in 2019. On September 9, she spoke out about one of the biggest health concerns in the country, using her official Twitter account to take a pointed position against vaping: "I am deeply concerned about the growing epidemic of e-cigarette use in our children. We need to do all we can to protect the public from tobacco-related disease and death, and prevent e-cigarettes from becoming an on-ramp to nicotine addiction for a generation of youth." Her tweet tagged the Department of Health and Human Services. It was the first public expression of a campaign that Melania had quietly been waging behind the scenes for weeks as she urged her husband to respond to the nationwide spread of a mysterious vaping-related illness that had already caused multiple hospitalizations and dozens of deaths. The vaping issue was also personal to Melania, the mother of a teenager. At Barron's school, St. Andrew's Episcopal, she knew that many parents were worried about the sudden rise in "juuling," a term derived from a brand of e-cigarette that resembles a small computer flash drive.

While one of Melania's first big career breaks came as a model in an advertising campaign for Camel cigarettes, she was not a smoker. Aides said that she viewed the issue as one of child safety, which dovetailed well with her Be Best campaign. Two days later, Trump announced, to the surprise of many fellow Republicans, that his administration would pull certain e-cigarettes, whose flavors had names such as "grape slushie" and "strawberry cotton candy," from the market. The next month, Melania hosted a listening session at the White House where nine teens from across the country shared stories of vape-related panic attacks, chest pain, and even stints in e-cigarette rehab. Melania was engaged, asking questions about how the teens acquired their e-cigarettes and praising retailers for halting sales of the product.

But ultimately, Melania's influence did not entirely hold sway. The powerful tobacco lobby mounted a counterpush, and Trump backed away from signing the decision memo, which would have ordered candy, fruit, and mint e-cigarette flavors off the market within thirty days. "He didn't know much about the issue and was just doing it for Melania and Ivanka," one senior official told the *Washington Post* in November. By January 2, 2020, his administration ultimately settled on a ban on single-use cartridges with fruit flavors, but not on menthol or tobacco pods or tank-style e-cigarettes sold in vape shops.

When it comes to her own child, Melania is known at the White House as "The Protector" because of how much effort she devotes to Barron, especially to keep him separated from the intense political fray.

On December 4, testifying before the House Judiciary Committee in a high-profile televised hearing in the impeachment proceedings against Trump, Pamela S. Karlan, a Stanford University constitutional law professor, mentioned Barron's name. "The Constitution says there can be no titles of nobility, so while the president can name his son Barron, he can't make him a baron," she said. Karlan was trying to make a joke, but shortly after she apologized to the committee: "It was wrong of me to do that. I wish the president would apologize, obviously, for the things that he's done that's wrong, but I do regret having said that."

Trump's campaign and his allies called Karlan's words "mean" and "disgusting." Melania tweeted to her millions of followers: "A minor child deserves privacy and should be kept out of politics. Pamela Karlan, you should be ashamed of your very angry and obviously biased public pandering, and using a child to do it." With one tough tweet, Melania had defended her child and helped her husband change the subject from impeachment. But the first lady had a different response a week later when her husband took to Twitter to dismiss passionate climate change activist Greta Thunberg, who at age sixteen had been selected by *Time* magazine as its Person of the Year. "So ridiculous," Trump wrote on December 12. "Greta must work on her Anger Management problem, then go to a good old fashioned movie with a friend! Chill Greta, Chill!"

Many commentators criticized the president's decision to pick on a teenager, who has been diagnosed as being on the autism spectrum. And when Melania supported him, she took heat, too. When others asked how she could weigh in on what Karlan had said about Barron but ignore what her husband had said about Greta Thunberg, Melania's office issued a statement: "Be Best is the First Lady's initiative, and she will continue to use it to do all she can to help children. It is no secret that the President and First Lady often communicate differently—as most married couples do. Their son is not an activist who travels the globe giving speeches. He is a 13-year-old who wants and deserves privacy."

ONE REASON why Melania's influence is not well known is that she avoids the West Wing, where her every move would be visible. She appears only for ceremonial events, preferring to offer Trump advice in private, when it is just the two of them. In late 2017, Melania told her husband that he should be more concerned about the investigation being led by special counsel Robert S. Mueller III. Muller was appointed by Deputy Attorney General Rod Rosenstein in May 2017 to explore allegations of Russian interference in the 2016 U.S. presidential election and whether Trump's campaign coordinated with Moscow. She also said that she didn't believe his legal team was doing enough to protect him, according to a person who was present when she expressed her views. Trump at the time paid less attention. Later, he would say she was right. Months after Melania had warned him about his attorneys, he also reshuffled his legal team.

Though her presence is often unseen, Melania has been at his side at key public moments. In November 2018, on the sidelines of the G20 meeting in Argentina, Melania and Trump held an extraordinary fifteen-minute meeting with Russian leader Vladimir Putin. Putin was accompanied by a translator, but, in a highly unusual move, there was no one with Trump besides Melania, not even a notetaker or translator.

In the White House, Melania has joined Trump in meetings with candidates for key jobs. When Chris Christie was summoned to meet with Trump in December 2018 to discuss the chief of staff job, Melania sat in on the conversation. The three met alone in the private residence, and Christie said that Melania asked the key question: How would he deal with Jared Kushner? When Christie was the U.S. Attorney for New Jersey (and while he and his wife were Donald Trump and Melania's regular dinner companions), he led a federal criminal investigation into Kushner's father. Charles Kushner ultimately pleaded guilty to eighteen counts of making illegal campaign contributions, tax evasion, and witness tampering, shortly before Donald and Melania Trump were married, and was sentenced to two years in federal prison. As Philip Rucker and Carol Leonnig would report in their 2020 book, *A Very Stable Genius*, after Christie left the White House, Trump personally leaked to Axios reporter Jonathan Swan that he had just met Christie and was considering him to replace John Kelly. The scoop was attributed to "a source familiar with the president's thinking." There was no mention of Melania's being in the meeting. But while Trump leaks, Melania is known as the vault. She is the best keeper of secrets in the White House.

Trump is very concerned about his appearance, and Melania has tried to help improve how he looks. She has shared modeling tips: when someone is taking his photo, he can tighten and define his facial muscles by placing his tongue on the roof of his mouth, and if he stands slightly back in a group photo, he will appear thinner than if he is standing in front of others. Whether he heeds her advice that she has offered over the years, is, as she has said, "up to him." However, before a photo shoot, she has been heard telling Trump to slightly lift and extend his chin. At the 2018 state dinner she organized for the French president Emmanuel Macron and his wife, Brigitte, she was overheard "stage managing" Trump's movements, as one person described it. Melania also installed professional lights in a White House room where the Trumps take many of their official photos.

THE 2020 election year may well put Melania center stage.

Three days before the 2018 midterm election, Melania gave permission for an email to go out to Republican voters under her name. The Republican National Committee knew that she didn't want to campaign but asked for help, and she agreed. "Democrats and the opposition media are doing everything they possibly can to discredit Donald with false accusations by spreading their fake news," Melania said in the fundraising email. "This is a battle we must win together. I'm asking you and other Americans across the country to personally register your support and help prove that the Democrats and media are wrong."

Republicans lost their majority in the House of Representatives on Election Day. The new Democratic Speaker of the House, Nancy Pelosi, started impeachment proceedings against Trump the next year. The House voted to put him on trial for abuse of power and obstruction of Congress over allegations that he withheld U.S. military aid to pressure Ukraine to conduct investigations that would benefit Trump politically. He became only the third president in history to be impeached, although the Senate ultimately voted not to remove him from office. Trump called the impeachment process "a witch hunt" and called Pelosi "very evil and sick." While Trump was going through "hell," as he called impeachment, Melania said little about it. She continued her low-key activities and tweeted a video of her East Room redecoration project and pictures of her reading to sick children. But behind the scenes, she was angry. She felt unfairly criticized, like her husband. She has called herself "one of the most bullied" people in the world and chided anonymous people who take hurtful shots at her online. She has also said that she has thick skin and prides herself on never appearing upset, even if she is.

At first she laughed about the FREE MELANIA signs that people carried in front of the White House, and the late-night comedy skits in which she was portrayed as being trapped. But it also bothered her that anyone thought that she was helpless or a hostage. Harder to laugh off are the critics of her husband's politics who call her a Trump accomplice. They say she is complicit for not speaking out, not even about Trump policies that now make it harder for many foreigners to get into the United States. She has said repeatedly that she is independent and follows her own compass and has stressed that while she offers her husband advice, he makes his own decisions. But she also recognizes that the way people see her is often colored by the way they view her husband. She knows, too, that as she becomes a more visible campaigner in 2020, she will likely become more of a target. Still, she has told people she wants to win reelection, and, now that Barron is older, she is in a position to be more actively involved. It would be further vindication after the impeachment trial.

She has other reasons, too, for wanting to stay in Washington. In 2020, Barron was fourteen, and after a second term, he would be college age, a perfect time to move. An election defeat would require a disruptive change in the middle of the school year. A second term would also give her more time to make her own mark. "She is very happy being first lady," said Paolo Zampolli. According to Zampolli, all those people who said she couldn't wait to go back to her old life, that she hated politics, were just wrong. "I am telling you she is happy in the White House."

Melania agreed to be the marquee name on two 2020 fundraisers, one in Beverly Hills and another at Mar-a-Lago. Concern about the spread of the coronavirus would cancel these events, but she was becoming a more active and visible campaigner. In

2016, that was unthinkable. "Neither of them wants a one-term presidency," said a person who knows the couple. "She sees this as *their* legacy. She wants to win." "It's the bunker mentality," added a White House official. Another used similar words: "They both feel under constant attack. They feel everyone is out to get anyone named Trump. That is a bond."

On February 4, 2020, Melania looked more at ease than usual as she sat in the gallery of the House of Representatives, listening to her husband's third State of the Union address. For the first time, she had ridden with him for the two-mile, ten-minute trip from the White House to the Capitol. In previous years, she had asked for a separate car, but this year she even agreed to be part of one of the speech's dramatic, made-for-TV moments. Trump announced that he was giving the Presidential Medal of Freedom to Rush Limbaugh, the conservative radio host, and that Melania would present it to him. Limbaugh, recently diagnosed with advanced lung cancer, was seated in the gallery next to Melania. The TV cameras zoomed in on Limbaugh and Melania to capture the announcement and his emotion.

As Melania draped the medal around his neck, many of the Democrats in the room were outraged. The Trumps were giving Limbaugh an honor reserved for the most admirable, inspirational, and accomplished people in American life. While Limbaugh is extraordinarily popular with many Americans, he has a long history of offending women, black Americans, Latinos, the LGBTQ community, and others, with comments such as, "Feminism was established so that unattractive ugly broads could have easy access to the mainstream." But in the House chamber and in front of all those watching, Trump praised Limbaugh for "decades of tireless devotion to our country," and Melania, who once might have stayed in the shadows at such a politically divisive moment, was front and center. A visual echo of her husband, she too wore a dark navy designer suit, a clear contrast to the sea of white worn by Pelosi and Democratic congresswomen in the chamber.

Two days later, Trump filled the East Room of the White House with those closest to him to celebrate the Senate vote to acquit him of impeachment charges. Melania sat in the front row and listened to his hour-long speech, in which he trashed FBI officials as "top scum" and Pelosi as a "horrible person." He called the investigations against him "bullshit," a word not normally heard at the microphone in the ornate East Room. Melania clapped along with Trump's most fervent supporters. "I want to apologize to my family for having them have to go through a phony, rotten deal," Trump said. "This was not part of the deal. They stuck with me." He even mentioned Barron publicly. Trump called Ivanka up to the podium and they hugged. Then Trump looked at Melania, sitting in the front row, gazing up at him admiringly, as she has for more than two decades. "Come on, baby," he said, motioning her up to the stage, where they received a long, standing ovation from their supporters. They had weathered impeachment, and now Donald and Melania Trump left the room to walk the White House's red-carpeted hallway, holding hands, smiling, and together.

Within weeks, impeachment would fade from the national

conversation as the coronavirus killing people in China escalated to become a global pandemic. On February 5, the day that Trump was acquitted by the Senate, the United States had twelve recorded cases of the novel coronavirus, and the World Health Organization reported that 99 percent of all confirmed cases were still inside China. But for weeks U.S. intelligence officials had warned the White House that the virus could pose a grave threat to the United States. Still, the president continued to downplay the threat into early March, even when it began taking its toll in the United States.

On March 5, Melania, too, seemed unconcerned, and posted to her 13 million followers about a very different subject, a renovation project: "I am excited to share the progress of the Tennis Pavillion at @WhiteHouse." She tweeted pictures of herself wearing a white hard hat, studying blueprints on a plywood table near the White House tennis court. Many people criticized her of being tone-deaf, even comparing her to Marie Antoinette, the wife of the French King Louis XVI, who continued to spend lavishly while the country's citizens suffered. Melania responded to her critics: "I encourage everyone who chooses to be negative & question my work at the @WhiteHouse to take time and contribute something good & productive in their own communities. #BeBest." Defiantly, she reposted the original message.

But in the following days, as the White House and U.S. Capitol shut to outside visitors and COVID-19 became the worst pandemic in a century, Melania's online messaging completely changed. On TV, her husband talked about the country "opened up and just raring to go" by Easter, April 12, but Melania cancelled the White House's annual Easter Egg Roll and donated its 25,000 commemorative wooden eggs to children's hospitals and frontline workers. Over the next few weeks, as daily life in the United States ground to a halt and restaurants, stores, businesses, beaches, sports stadiums, and churches all shut down, she recorded public service announcements with practical information, including about social distancing. She talked about resilience and unity, saying, "Stay safe and remember, while many of us are apart, we are all in this together." She thanked "doctors, nurses, and first responders," and shared online resources, including how to listen to astronauts reading books in space. "Our great country is fighting hard against the #Coronavirus. This nation is strong & ready & we will overcome," she wrote on Twitter. She also said, "If we support one another through this challenging time, America will come out stronger in the end."

Her husband would frequently tweet more in one day than she would all month, but during the crisis Melania ramped up her use of Twitter to amplify advice from public health officials. Her messaging was often exactly the opposite of her husband's. After the Centers for Disease Control and Prevention recommended that everyone wear a mask in public places, Trump announced he would not be: "I just don't want to be doing, I don't know, somehow, sitting in the Oval Office behind that beautiful Resolute Desk, the great Resolute Desk—I think wearing a face mask as I greet presidents, prime ministers, dictators, kings, queens, I don't know, I don't see it for myself." He also emphasized the guidance was "voluntary." But Melania posted a photograph of herself wearing a mask over her nose and mouth, reminding people that it was the safe thing to do at a time when thousands of Americans were dying. She added, "Remember, this does NOT replace the importance of social distancing."

Those who know the couple say Melania fills in Trump's blind spots. Unlike her husband, she was warning that daily life could be different for quite some time, thanking health officials treating the sick, and publicly talking of working with other nations to defeat the disease. She began making calls to first ladies around the world, first checking in with Sophie Gregoire Trudeau, the wife of the Canadian prime minister who was herself recovering from the virus. Melania reached out to the daughter of the Italian president, a widower, and the wives of the leaders of Japan, France, and Germany. She offered condolences for the lives lost in their countries, and pledged unity in the shared crisis. According to an April 14 statement released by the Office of the First Lady, Melania and Elke Büdenbender, the wife of the president of Germany, "noted shared concern over some of the disinformation that has emerged, and committed to encouraging Americans and Germans to be cautious."

Melania had first started talking about what type of first lady she would be more than twenty years ago, when her new boyfriend started flirting with a run for president. When she first arrived at the White House, she seemed halting, uncertain, and uncomfortable. But three years later, after a bruising impeachment process and in the midst of a devastating global health crisis, she seemed to be finding her footing and enjoy being a player on the global stage. Her message was realistic yet optimistic. As long as she was married to Trump, she would be associated with his deeply polarizing behavior that some loved and others despised. But the #FreeMelania signs were gone. She was increasingly seen as her own person. Melania had struck a complicated deal with a complicated man and taken on a complicated job. She wasn't Jackie Kennedy, Hillary Clinton, or anyone else who had held that role. She was Melania, and she would make this deal her own.

Acknowledgments

MELANIA TRUMP arrived at age twenty-six to the United States and at forty-six she was first lady of the United States, and I am grateful to the many people who helped me understand her remarkable journey. A daughter of Irish immigrants, I was particularly interested in her roots and motivations and I especially thank those who knew Melania before she met Donald Trump, as well as all those who agreed to on-the-record interviews for the first time. A big thank-you, too, to those in Slovenia, Italy, and elsewhere who found old newspapers, documents, and photos—sometimes in attics and garages—that shed light on the often-seen but little-known Melania.

Isabelle Taft, a star young journalist who assisted in every possible way, was crucial to getting this project finished. The resourceful Alice Crites helped me find contacts for people in many parts of the world, beginning in 2015 when I first began writing about Melania for the *Washington Post*. The talented Bronwen Latimer found vital photos and a way to have fun on deadline. I am grateful to Rachel Hazan, who dug up key information, as well as Patrick Mulholland and Susan Ortiz for their invaluable help at clutch moments—there is nothing that these three enterprising young people cannot do.

In Rome, Sabrina Righi was not just a translator but a sleuth, and she helped tremendously while delivering a baby and a PhD. Thank you also to Pierluigi Erbaggio for his important research help. A big thanks to wonderful Stefano Pitrelli who came through in so many ways and times in Italy. At Stanford University, Dr. Robert Jackler, who studies the impact advertising has on tobacco use, combed through his archives and found a 1997 cigarette ad that featured Melania. Axel Gietz in Hamburg, Germany, provided key understanding of tobacco marketing in Europe in the 1990s. Some catalogs and articles in fashion, lifestyle, and men's publications that Melania appeared in are now defunct or not kept in searchable databases, and I am grateful to librarians and other kind people who helped me track them down. A special shout-out to Sylvia Espinoza, research manager at Condé Nast, and Gerardo Reyes at Univision.

Igor Omerza, a former member of parliament in Slovenia and coauthor of *Melania Trump: The Inside Story*, was a generous guide to Melania's family history. Thank you Nino Milahek, a photographer who took Melania's picture when she was twenty-one, for allowing me to publish one of them, which is also seen in *First Lady Melania Trump: As She Once Was*. I so appreciate

Nejc Trušnovec for his translation work. I am lucky to know and grateful to Victor Jackovich, Tamara Vodopivec, Andrej Stopar, and Luka Zibelnik for their translations and Slovenian history and culture tutorials—each of them are yet another reason I love Slovenia, a beautiful country. And, a very special thanks to Lin Delaney, one of the smartest divorce lawyers in the country.

I first started writing about Melania Trump as a correspondent for the *Washington Post* and I am grateful for the support of Marty Baron, Cameron Barr, Tracy Grant, Steven Ginsberg, Lori Montgomery, and the rest of the best team of newsroom leaders in the business, including Peter Wallsten, Dan Eggen, Matea Gold, Cathleen Decker, and Donna Cassata. I'm also lucky to have generous colleagues always ready to pitch in: Karen Tumulty, David Finkel, Lynda Robinson, Josh Dawsey, Phil Rucker, Ashley Parker, Dan Balz, Krissah Thompson, Emily Heil, Robin Givhan, Karen Heller, Roxanne Roberts, Frances Sellers, David Fahrenthold, Rosalind Helderman, Marc Fisher, Michael Kranish, and Tom Hamburger. Thank you, too, to those I cannot name here because they prefer that the Trumps do not know they helped a member of the media.

This book was the idea of Priscilla Painton, a gifted editor and manager. I am grateful to the aces at Simon & Schuster: Jonathan Karp, Julia Prosser, Hana Park, Janet Byrne, and for Eric Rayman's help. Bob Barnett is far more than a top agent and lawyer; he is wise, enthusiastic, and fun. Katharine Weymouth, Molly Elkin, Ivan Wasserman, Linda Potter, and Christie Jorge are simply the best—each one helped. Nora Jordan and Allen Reiser turned over their New York apartment to me for much of 2019, and special thanks to others in my big family: Julie Jordan and Jim Cummings, Maggie and John Keaney, Tom Jordan, Kathleen Jordan, Paul Machle, Sharon Sobol Jordan, and Dave Wallace. I'm inspired every day by the memories of my brother, Patrick, and my parents, Nora and Tom Jordan. I know how lucky I am to have two amazing children—thank you, Kate, for helping constantly in big ways and small, and thank you, Tom, for all your help and coming up with the book's title, too. Most of all, thank you, Kevin Sullivan. Without you, my husband and writing partner, there would be no book. You are my wingman, always.

Notes

PROLOGUE: "I HAVE AN OPINION"

1 *"I moved on her, actually"*: David A. Fahrenthold, "Trump Recorded Having Extremely Lewd Conversation About Women in 2005," *Washington Post*, October 8, 2016, https://www.washingtonpost .com/politics/trump-recorded-having-extremely-lewd-conversation -about-women-in-2005/2016/10/07/3b9ce776-8cb4-11e6-bf8a 3d26847eeed4_story.html.

3 *"She was the elephant"*: Chris Christie, interview with author, New Jersey, April 8, 2019.

5 *"The words my husband used"*: Jenna Johnson, "Melania Trump Hopes Voters Will Accept Her Husband's Apology for His 'Unacceptable and Offensive' Comments About Women," *Washington Post*, October 8, 2016, https://www.washingtonpost.com/news/post-politics/wp /2016/10/08/melania-trump-hopes-voters-will-accept-her-husbands -apology-for-his-unacceptable-and-offensive-comments-about -women/.

5 *"I WILL NEVER DROP"*: Donald J. Trump (@realDonaldTrump), Twitter, October 8, 2016, 3:40 p.m., https://twitter.com/realDonald Trump/status/784840992734064641.

6 *"This is not some wallflower"*: Chris Christie interview.

6 *"I said it, I was wrong"*: Jenna Johnson, "Trump Apologizes for 'Foolish' Comments About Women, Then Attacks the Clintons," *Washington Post*, October 8, 2016, https://www.washingtonpost.com/news /post-politics/wp/2016/10/08/trump-apologizes-for-foolish-com ments-about-women-then-attacks-the-clintons/.

7 *"locker-room talk"*: Robert Costa and Philip Rucker, "Second Presidential Debate Takes the Low Road as Attacks and Slurs Dominate," *Washington Post*, October 9, 2016, https://www .washingtonpost.com/politics/second-presidential-debate-takes-the -low-road-as-attacks-and-slurs-dominate/2016/10/09/d0ad5c3a-8e29 -11e6-9c85-ac42097b8cc0_story.html.

7 *"She makes good choices"*: Marina Masowietsky, interview with author, Los Angeles, February 18, 2019.

8 *"She's very deliberative"*: Corey Lewandowksi, interview with author, Las Vegas, May 9, 2019.

8 *"This has obviously been"*: Melania Trump interviewed by Anderson Cooper, *Anderson Cooper 360*, CNN, October 16–17, 2016.

11 *In sworn testimony before Congress*: Hearing with Michael Cohen, former attorney to President Donald Trump, before the House Committee on Oversight and Reform, February 27, 2019, https://docs.house .gov/meetings/GO/GO00/20190227/108969/HHRG-116-GO00 -20190227-SD003.pdf.

11 *Melania promised the crowd*: Julia Zorthian, "Read Melania Trump's Campaign Speech Addressing Cyberbullying," *Time*, November 3, 2016, https://time.com/4557033/transcript-melania-trump-campaign -speech/.

CHAPTER 1: OLIVE BRANCH?

15 *After his 2005 wedding:* Donald J. Trump interviewed by Larry King, "Donald and Melania Trump as Newlyweds," *Larry King Live*, CNN, May 17, 2005, https://www.youtube.com/watch?v=q4XfyYFa9yo.

16 *"feel more at home":* Daphne Barak, *To Plea or Not to Plea: The Story of Rick Gates and the Mueller Investigation* (New York: Center Street/ Hatchette, 2019), 127.

18 *"classic and sophisticated":* Robin Givhan, "Melania Trump Picks Patriotism and International Glamour for Her Debut as First Lady," *Washington Post*, January 20, 2017, https://www.washingtonpost.com /news/arts-and-entertainment/wp/2017/01/20/ralph-lauren-the -most-bipartisan-of-designers-dresses-first-lady-melania-trump -and-hillary-clinton-for-inauguration/.

18 *"protect our borders":* "The Inaugural Address," White House release, January 20, 2017, https://www.whitehouse.gov/briefings-statements /the-inaugural-address/.

19 *"seemed like a bit of an olive branch":* Givhan, "Melania Trump Picks Patriotism and International Glamour for Her Debut as First Lady."

21 *"People say, 'Oh, she's a model' ":* Roger Stone, interview with author and Tom Hamburger, New York City, May 11, 2016.

22 *"my best pollster":* Amy Davidson Sorkin, "Iowa Meets the Trump Family," *New Yorker*, February 1, 2016, https://www.newyorker .com/news/amy-davidson/iowa-meets-the-trump-family.

CHAPTER 2: CHASING MELANIA

25 *"She is like a ghost":* Jarl Alé de Basseville, interviews with author. An interview was conducted in person in Paris, France, in August 2018, and there were several phone interviews over the following year.

28 *"If I weren't beautiful":* Sara James, "Memo Pad: Martha Speaks," *Women's Wear Daily,* May 6, 2005, 11, https://pmcwwd.files.wordpress .com/2005/05/issue-815841.pdf.

29 *"I don't try to change him":* Eric Bradner and Theodore Schleifer,

"Melania Trump: I Don't Always Agree with Donald, and That's OK," CNN, Feb. 26, 2016, https://www.cnn.com/2016/02/29/politics /melania-trump-donald-trumps-language/index.html.

30 *"Melania is very smart":* Anthony Scaramucci, interview with author, Washington, D.C., April 29, 2019.

30 *"At this moment, she's really":* Liz Smith, "At Lunch with Liz: Donald Trump," *Good Housekeeping,* October 2004, 130–34.

31 *"I've wanted to be a model":* Marcus Casey, "Daddy's Girl," *Sunday Telegraph*, October 20, 1996.

34 *"The best thing you can do":* Donald J. Trump with Tony Schwartz, *Trump: The Art of the Deal* (New York: Ballantine Books, 1987), 53.

35 *"this administration is running":* "Remarks by President Trump in Press Conference," White House release, February 16, 2017, https:// www.whitehouse.gov/briefings-statements/remarks-president -trump-press-conference/.

37 *the senior adviser helping:* Darlene Superville, "Melania Trump says she'll keep predecessor's produce garden," AP, February 14, 2017, https://apnews.com/0dc8ea83de6245e0a554306234a66b55/Melania -Trump-says-she'll-keep-predecessor's-produce-garden.

38 *"a moderating force in an administration":* Jodi Kantor, Rachel Abrams, and Maggie Haberman, "Ivanka Trump Has the President's Ear. Here's Her Agenda*," New York Times,* May 2, 2017, https://www.ny times.com/2017/05/02/us/politics/ivanka-trump.html.

40 *"sometimes" he listens:* Emily Heil, Sudarsan Raghavan, and Mary Jordan, "Melania Trump Wraps First Solo International Trip in Egypt with Comments on Kavanaugh and Ford," *Washington Post*, October 6, 2018, https://www.washingtonpost.com/lifestyle /melania-trump-wraps-first-solo-international-trip-in-egypt-with -comments-on-kavanaugh-and-ford/2018/10/06/f98e5fd8-c8d7-11e8 -9b1c-a90f1daae309_story.html.

40 *"Melania is very behind-the-scenes":* Sean Spicer, phone interview with author, April 15, 2019.

44   *"The idea that she is* not": Chris Christie, interview with author, April 8, 2019.

CHAPTER 3: FACE OF THE YEAR

47   *"I grew up in a small town":* Julia Zorthian, "Read Melania's Campaign Speech Addressing Cyberbullying," *Time*, November 3, 2016, https://time.com/4557033/enums/.

47   *Viktor was born in a territory:* Some details of Melania Trump's family history are drawn from a book by Bojan Požar and Igor Omerza, *Melania Trump—The Inside Story: From a Slovenian Communist Village to the White House* (Ljubljana, Slovenia: Založba Ombo d.o.o, 2016).

48   *"She had the skill to make":* Estera Savić, interview with author, Sevnica, Slovenia, August 2018.

49   *"I think it was opportunism":* Igor Omerza, interviews with author, in person in Slovenia on August 23, 2018, and subsequently on the phone.

49   *"Everybody smuggled":* Urska Faller, interview with author, Slovenia, August 2018.

50   *Journalist Julia Ioffe found:* Julia Ioffe, "Melania Trump on Her Rise, Her Family Secrets, and Her True Political Views: 'Nobody Will Ever Know,'" *GQ*, April 27, 2016, https://www.gq.com/story/melania-trump-gq-interview.

50   *"Melanija has elegance in the blood":* Meri Kelemina, interview with author, Sevnica, Slovenia, August 29, 2018.

51   *"The light in Amalija's window":* Urska Faller interview.

51   *Every morning before going:* Ines Knauss (@inesknauss), Twitter, March 10, 2020. Ines Knauss has a "protected" Twitter account, which means only followers she approves see her posts, but she has several hundred followers and one of them showed me her tweets. Twitter tells users with these accounts: "Please keep in mind, your followers may still capture images of your Tweets and share them."

52   *"It was just something fun to do":* Nena Bedek, interview with author, Sevnica, Slovenia, August 28, 2018.

53 *"For the homeland"*: For the text of the pledge and formal greetings of members of the Union of Pioneers of Yugoslavia, see: Štefka Batinić, Igor Radeka, and Snježana Šušnjara, "Today, as I Become a Pioneer: Education in the Spirit of Socialism," *Historia Scholastica* 2, no. 1 (2016): 29–41; see p. 32.

54 *"It was an honor"*: Vladimira Tomšič, interview with author, Sevnica, Slovenia, August 2018.

54 *"The match is canceled"*: Jože Pirjevec, "Titova Smrt" ("Tito's Death"), *Dnevnik,* August 29, 2011, https://www.dnevnik.si/1042468597.

54 *"Comrade Tito has died"*: Michael Dobbs, "President Tito Dies," *Washington Post*, May 5, 1980, https://www.washingtonpost.com/archive/politics/1980/05/05/president-tito-dies/0df00f64-f525-4783-8a0c-2af1b92b2f9a/.

55 *"This is a difficult and dangerous world"*: John F. Kennedy, "Remarks of Welcome at the White House to President Tito of Yugoslavia," October 17, 1963, published in *John F. Kennedy: Containing the Public Messages, Speeches, and Statements of the President* (Washington, D.C.: U.S. Government Printing Office, 1964), 788–89.

55 *"President Reagan's Morning in America"*: Julia Zorthian, "Read Melania's Campaign Speech Addressing Cyberbullying."

56 *"She was a very quiet girl"*: Tomi Lombar, phone with author, April 2019.

57 *The British rocker, dressed up*: David Bodoh, "Elton John 1984 Concerts," Eltonography.com, http://eltonography.com/tours/1984.html.

57 *Melania's sister said the first time*: Ines Knauss (@inesknauss), Twitter, January 22, 2020.

57 *"any channel she wants"*: Kate Bennett, "Melania Trump Will Watch 'Any Channel She Wants,' Spokeswoman Says," CNN, July 25, 2018, https://www.cnn.com/2018/07/25/politics/melania-trump-channel/index.html.

58 *"They were endless"*: Stane Jerko, interview with author, Ljubljana, Slovenia, August 24, 2018.

61 *"I think she realized there was another path"*: Blaž Matija Vogelnik, interview with author, Ljubljana, Slovenia, August 24, 2018.

62 *"Seeing her and falling in love with her"*: Riccardo Colao, interview with author, December 14, 2019.

62 *"Melania Knaus . . . has not turned"*: "Melania Knaus," *Hollywood*, the magazine of Cinecittà, December 1989.

63 *"She told the producer"*: Riccardo Colao, interview.

63 *Mihalek hit the brakes:* Nino Mihalek, phone interview with author, February 2020.

64 *"We don't wake up for less"*: Arielle Tsoukatos, "Your Definitive Guide To The Most Famous Supermodels Of The '90s," *InStyle*, February 12, 2019.

65 *"Some of these girls I stopped"*: Marina Masowietsky, interview with author, Los Angeles, February 18, 2019.

65 *"Young Beauties Marching on Europe!"*: Issues of *Jana* from 1992 before the June contest, including the March 1992 issue.

66 *"Yes, she could be"*: Marina Masowietsky interview.

66 *"She had the eyes of a tigress"*: Bernarda Jeklin, interviews with author, 2016 and 2018, phone and in Ljubljana, Slovenia.

67 *"very special face"*: Petar Radović, interview and email exchange with author, March–April 2019.

68 *"Dejan was key"*: Vesna Zarkov, interview with author, Milan, June 2019.

69 *"There were issues of that kind"*: Dejan Markovic, phone interview with author, February 2020.

69 *"Fashion is a business of glamour"*: Zorthian, "Read Melania's Campaign Speech Addressing Cyberbullying."

70 *"The girls have to stand"*: Interview with Amalija Knavs, *Jana*, July 1992.

70 *"She was just one of the thousands of models"*: Sergio Salerni, interview with author, Milan, Italy, June 2019.

70 *"Nobody asked about tax or anything"*: Čedo Komljenović, interview with author, Milan, Italy, June 2019.

71   *"If you had your wits about you"*: Lauren Gott, phone interview with author, July 2019.

71   *"It was very decadent"*: Anna Momigliano, phone interview with author, December 12, 2019.

71   *"Many of these girls destroyed"*: PierCarlo Borgogelli, interview with author, Milan, Italy, June 2019.

72   *"It's the most extraordinary"*: Jožica Brodarič, interviews with author and email exchange, January 2020.

74   *"She was a beautiful, professional lady"*: Riccardo Gay, phone interview with author, April 2019.

74   *"Melania to me is"*: Sergio Salerni interview.

75   *"She was not a big model"*: PierCarlo Borgogelli interview.

76   *"amazing smile"*: Wolfgang Schwarz, interview with author, Vienna, Austria, August 31, 2018, and email exchanges 2018–19.

76   *"This was the time before cell phones"*: Rosemary Feitelberg, "Melania Trump's Modeling Days in Paris: Lessons in Determination," *Women's Wear Daily,* November 11, 2016, https://wwd.com/eye/people/melania -trumps-mode-paris-donald-trump-10704025/.

76–77 *"I don't think I could have"*: Inside Edition Staff, "Melania Trump's Ex-Roommate Victoria Silvstedt Reveals First Lady Wanted to Be Like Sophia Loren," *Inside Edition*, January 26, 2018, https://www .aol.com/article/lifestyle/2018/01/26/melania-trumps-ex-roommate -victoria-silvstedt-reveals-first-lady-wanted-to-be-like-sophia-loren /23343904/.

77   *"Come on, we'll run down"*: Marc Fourny, "Quand Melania Trump Vivait en Colocation à Paris" ["When Melania Trump Lived in a Shared Flat in Paris"], *Le Point*, June 29, 2018, https://www .lepoint.fr/people/quand-melania-trump-vivait-en-colocation-a -paris-29-06-2018-2231737_2116.php.

77   *"never wanted the attention"*: Richard Johnson, "Former Roommate: Melania Doesn't Socialize Enough," *Page Six*, December 12, 2017,

https://pagesix.com/2017/12/12/former-roommate-melania-doesnt -socialize-enough/.

77 *"She was motivated by"*: Fourny, "Quand Melania Trump Vivait en Colocation à Paris."

77 *"Obviously, she was her style icon"*: Interview with Victoria Silvstedt, "Arriva Victoria Silvstedt," *Domenica Live,* September 24, 2017, https://www.mediasetplay.mediaset.it/video/domenicalive/arriva -victoria-silvstedt_F308459101002C05.

77 *"When you spend time around Melania"*: Eve MacSweeney, "Golden Girl: At Seven Months Pregnant, Melania Trump Can Still Knock 'em Dead in Her Strapless Party Dress—and in a Teeny Bikini, for that Matter," *Vogue*, April 2006.

78 *claimed the actress bought a place*: Sophia Loren was asked whether she owned a place in Trump Tower by an Italian newspaper in 2017. "It is not true!" she said. "Mr. Trump invented it." Elvira Serra, "Sophia Loren: "Sapevo che ero innocente ma rifarei quei giorni in cella. Io e Mastroianni, che coppia!" ["Sophia Loren: "I knew I was innocent but I would (happily) spend those days in jail. Mastroianni and I, what a pair!"] *Corriere Della Sera,* September 20, 2017, https://www .corriere.it/cronache/17_settembre_20/sophia-loren-quando-sto-bene -preparo-sugo-il-carcere-lo-rifarei-2d51379c-9e26-11e7-a6ea-ab d1a52d72e1.shtml.

78 *"Melania Trump is simply the most"*: Newt Gingrich (@newtgingrich), Twitter, January 1, 2017, 6:11 a.m., https://twitter.com/newtgingrich /status/822763642588372992.

78 *"It's kind of surreal"*: *Inside Edition* Staff, "Melania Trump's Ex-Roommate Victoria Silvstedt Reveals First Lady Wanted to Be Like Sophia Loren."

79 *"stable and focused"*: Paolo Zampolli, interviews with author from 2015 to 2020.

CHAPTER 4: MAKING HER WAY IN MANHATTAN

81 *"Hello, my name is Paolo":* Matthew Atanian, interview with author, October 12, 2018.

83 *Zampolli told me that he paid for Melania:* Paolo Zampolli interview.

83 *She initially arrived:* Michael J. Wildes, letter on Melania Trump's immigration history, September 14, 2016; published in tweet by Melania Trump on September 14, 2016, https://twitter.com /MELANIATRUMP/status/776050512772886529.

84 *"Mary u know i love my President":* Email exchange with Paolo Zampolli, June 22, 2019.

85 *"Now he is a politician":* Matthew Atanian interview.

86 *"she looked like she had just walked off a set":* Ibid.

89 *"I always loved women together":* Isabel Vincent, "Melania Trump's Girl-on-Girl Photos from Racy Shoot Revealed," *New York Post*, August 1, 2016. The *Post* originally reported that the shoot had taken place in 1995. A few weeks later, *Politico* obtained a copy of the magazine that showed it was published in February 1997. Ben Schreckinger, *"New York Post* Corrects Timeline of Melania Trump Photo Shoot," *Politico*, September 16, 2016, https://www.politico.com /story/2016/09/melania-trump-photos-visa-immigration-228295.

90 *on the day of the shoot:* Jarl Alé de Basseville, interviews with author, in person in Paris, France, in August 2018 and subsequently over the phone.

90 *Emma Eriksson later described:* Linnea Järkstig, "Svenska Emma i Trumps Nakenskandal" ["Swedish Emma in Trump's Nude Scandal"], *Aftonbladet,* August 1, 2016, https://www.aftonbladet.se /nyheter/a/oRez3a/svenska-emma-i-trumps-nakenskandal.

91 *"Sitting on the edge of the bed":* Ann Scott, "Emma and Melania Are on the Roof . . . ," *Max*, February 1997.

92 *"Melania Trump had an impressive body":* "Menage A Trump," cover page of the *New York Post*, August 1, 2016.

93 *"the very first day she landed":* Federico Pignatelli, interview with Slovenian TV channel RTV 4, aired August 2019.

93 *"She was not one of these models":* Federico Pignatelli, interview with author in New York City, February 2019.

93 *In a sworn affidavit, one of Zampolli's:* Affidavit of Michele August, *Paolo Zampolli v. Metropolitan International Management, LLC,* in the Supreme Court of the State of New York, County of New York, Index No. 605599/97, affidavit filed November 13, 1997.

94 *Zampolli told me:* Paolo Zampolli interview.

94 *In 1998,* Playboy *magazine named Trump:* "*Playboy* Picks Princes of the City," *New York Post,* November 26, 1998.

95 *"Camel is embracing night life":* William L. Hamilton, "Style Noir," *New York Times,* September 14, 1997, https://www.nytimes.com/1997/09/14/style/style-noir.html.

95 *By law, models had to be at least:* "Text of Cigarette Industry's New Code," *New York Times,* April 28, 1964. Dr. Robert Jackler, a Stanford professor who founded and is chief investigator of Stanford Research into the Impact of Tobacco Advertising (SRITA), located an image of the Camel ad that Melania posed in more than twenty years ago and pinpointed the location of the billboard near Times Square where the ad ran. Dr. Jackler and Laurie Jackler, the curator at SRITA, provided analysis of the ad, as well as helpful information about the history of tobacco advertising regulations. SRITA, an interdisciplinary research group, maintains an online collection of tobacco ads for scholars, nonprofits, and the general public: http://tobacco.stanford.edu/tobacco_main/mission.php.

96 *In April 2010, Regine Mahaux:* Photograph by Regine Mahaux, Getty Images, shot April 10, 2010, https://www.gettyimages.de/detail/nachrichtenfoto/general-view-during-a-portrait-session-with-donald-nachrichtenfoto/103174263.

97 *"I didn't make any changes":* Julia Ioffe, "Melania Trump on Her Rise,

Her Family Secrets, and Her True Political Views: 'Nobody Will Ever Know,' " *GQ*, April 27, 2016, https://www.gq.com/story/melania -trump-gq-interview.

CHAPTER 5: "HE WANTED MY NUMBER, BUT . . . I DIDN'T GIVE IT TO HIM"

100 *"No photography, please"*: Sebastian Kopušar, "One Beautiful Day: What Does She Have in Common with Donald Trump?" *MAG*, 1999, translated from the Slovenian. This account of Melania's Paris press event is based on multiple contemporaneous reports by the half-dozen Slovenian journalists who attended the press conference, as well as recent interviews with nearly all those who attended, and a video of Melania Trump taken by one reporter that day.

100 *"She went from normal"*: Sebastian Kopušar, phone interview with author, August 2019.

101 *"Since no one in Slovenia"*: Dušan Nograšek, "The Slovenian Language Is Like a Song," *Nedeljski Dnevnik* (*Sunday Daily* newspaper), September 20, 1998, translated from the Slovenian.

101 *"among the top 50" internationally:* Nograšek, "The Slovenian Language Is Like a Song."

101 *"other big agencies"*: Boštjan Videmšek, "A Day with Melania Knauss," *Glamur*, 1998.

101 *"People all over the world"*: Hermina Kovačič, "The Model Who Says She Has No Faults—In Paris with Melania Knaus," *Plus*, September 11, 1998.

101 *A reporter, incredulous:* Tape of Slovenian journalists' interview with Melania Knauss; a short segment of the tape aired on the show *Trend*, on TV SLO (TV Slovenija) in 1998.

102 *"It's all been agreed to"*: Journalists' interview with Melania Knauss, *Trend*, TV SLO.

102 *"I am really excited"*: Videmšek, "A Day with Melania Knauss."

102 *"Slowly, slowly"*: Journalists' interview with Melania Knauss, *Trend*, TV SLO.

102 *"It's paradise"*: Videmšek, "A Day with Melania Knauss."

102 *"Would I be happy to have"*: Nograšek, "The Slovenian Language Is Like a Song."

103 *"Were you ever asked to be"*: Journalists' interview with Melania Knauss, *Trend*, TV SLO.

103 *"Yes, I have posed nude"*: Nograšek, "The Slovenian Language Is Like a Song."

103 *"finds time for love"*: Kovačič, "The Model Who Says She Has No Faults—In Paris with Melania Knaus."

103 *"Who is the most famous person"*: Videmšek, "A Day with Melania Knauss."

104 *"I always say what I mean"*: Nograšek, "The Slovenian Language Is Like a Song."

104 *"Luck is important"*: Journalists' interview with Melania Knauss, *Trend*, TV SLO.

104 *"must be yawning"*: Kopušar, "One Beautiful Day: What Does She Have in Common with Donald Trump?"

104 *"In a way it's like acting"*: Journalists' interview with Melania Knauss, *Trend*, TV SLO.

105 *"but she was not a girl with"*: Wolfgang Schwarz, interview with author, August 31, 2018.

105 *"stunning"*: Craig Singer, interview with author, August 2019.

105 *"She stepped through the doorway"*: Kopušar, "One Beautiful Day: What Does She Have in Common with Donald Trump?"

106 *"She told us something about"*: Kovačič, "The Model Who Says She Has No Faults—In Paris with Melania Knaus."

106 *"meant to give the journalists"*: Tamara Deu, series of interviews and email exchanges with author, September–December 2019.

107 *France had such strict laws*: In 1991, France passed strict regulations

on alcohol and tobacco advertising, called the Loi Évin, named for Claude Évin, the health minister who proposed the law. Axel Gietz, who was chief spokesman for R. J. Reynolds International in the 1990s, provided valuable information about the trajectory of European tobacco regulations and how they would have shaped the planned Boss advertising campaign. Gietz is now based in Germany and runs his own consulting firm, Headwind Communications, and writes the *I've Been Thinkin'* . . . blog.

107 *"She didn't want to talk about Trump":* Tamara Deu interview.

108 *"the way I promote is bravado":* Donald J. Trump with Tony Schwartz, *Trump: The Art of the Deal* (New York: Ballantine Books, 1987), 58.

108 *"Gossip travels quickly":* Wolfgang Schwarz interview.

109 *"I went crazy!":* Donald J. Trump interviewed by Larry King, "Donald and Melania Trump as Newlyweds," *Larry King Live*, CNN, May 17, 2005, https://www.youtube.com/watch?v=q4XfyYFa9yo.

109 *"He wanted my number, but he was":* Alex Kuczynski, "Melania Trump's American Dream," *Harper's Bazaar,* January 6, 2016, https://www.harpersbazaar.com/culture/features/a13529/melania-trump-interview-0216/.

109 *"If I give him my number":* Julia Ioffe, "Melania Trump on Her Rise, Her Family Secrets, and Her True Political Views: 'Nobody Will Ever Know,'" *GQ*, April 27, 2016, https://www.gq.com/story/melania-trump-gq-interview.

109 *Zampolli has said:* Paolo Zampolli interview.

110 *"You don't fuck around":* Edit Molnar, interview with author, September 2015.

111 *With Bax on his arm:* "If It's September, It Must Be Fashion Week. Sort of.: New York Confidential," *Independent* (London), September 25, 1998.

112 *"I had my life":* Ioffe, "Melania Trump on Her Rise."

112 *"a very rich man":* Federico Pignatelli interview.

114 *"some delicious-looking arm candy":* George Rush and Joanna Molloy

with Marcus Baram and K.C. Baker, "John-John & Wife Are Train-Spotted Together," *New York Daily News*, October 7, 1998. The article spells Melania's last name "Knaus."

114   *"a slinky brunette":* Jeannie Williams, "Grand Central Gala Remembers Jackie," *USA Today*, October 7, 1998.

114   *"DONALD Trump just scored big":* No headline, *New York Post,* October 8, 1998.

115   *Melania flew on Trump's private jet:* Jose Lambiet, "So, Where's Paradise? In the Bahamas, Baby!" *Fort Lauderdale Sun-Sentinel*, December 15, 1998.

115   *party said to cost $7 million:* Cheryl Blackerby, "The $7 Million Party," Cox News Service, December 15, 1998.

115   *"sort of eligible":* Roxanne Roberts, "His Heart Will Go On; Larry King, Celine Dion Team Up for Benefit Gala," *Washington Post*, November 21, 1998.

115   *"He's the greatest man":* Kitty Bean Yancey, "Father-to-Be King Takes a Ribbing at Cardiac Fund-raiser," *USA Today*, November 23, 1998. The article called her a "twentysomething Austrian."

115   *Just before he met Melania:* John Blosser, "Trump's New Jackpot," *National Enquirer,* September 1998, reprinted by *Mother Jones*: Natalie Schreyer, "The Trump Files: When Donald Won an Election . . . of Sexy Billionaires," *Mother Jones,* November 2, 2016, https://www.motherjones.com/politics/2016/11/trump-files-donald-election-sexy-billionaires/.

116   *"There was a group of us":* Kylie Bax, phone interview and email exchanges with author, July 2019–February 2020.

116   *"I love your husband":* Ivana Trump interviewed by Barbara Walters on *20/20*, ABC News, May 10, 1991.

116–117 *"I couldn't turn on the television":* Ivana Trump, *Raising Trump: Family Values from America's First Mother* (New York: Gallery Books, 2017), Kindle edition, location 1863 of 3385.

117   *"I was standing in the middle of these two":* Donald Trump interviewed

on *The Howard Stern Show*, April 11, 2002, transcript published by Factba.se, https://factba.se/transcript/donald-trump-interview-how ard-stern-show-april-11-2002.

117 *"Two world-class beauties":* John Blosser, "Trump's New Jackpot," re-printed in Schreyer, "The Trump Files: When Donald Won an Elec-tion . . . of Sexy Billionaires."

118 *"He doesn't check his pulse":* Lloyd Grove, "Best Press He's Ever Had," *Columbia Journalism Review,* Fall 2017, https://www.cjr.org/special _report/trump-tabloids-daily-news-new-york-post-press.php.

119 *chatted with Supreme Court Justice:* Historical Motorsports Stories, "Memories of Donald Trump and NASCAR," March 3, 2016, https:// www.racing-reference.info/showblog?id=2446.

119 *"For Melania Knauss":* "Lady Luxe: The Season's Haute Couture Is as Stunning as the Worldly Young Women Who Wear It," photo-graphs by Oberto Gili, styled by Lucy Sykes, *Town & Country,* May 1999.

120 *"Donald Trump didn't have to look far":* George Rush and Joanna Mol-loy with Marcus Baram and Marc S. Malkin, "Joe D. Balked at Sit-down with Clinton," New York *Daily News*, April 25, 1999.

121 *Melania's modeling day rate doubled:* Christopher Byron, "Behind Trump's Political Fling," *George*, February/March 2000.

121 *In April 1999, Melania appeared:* Sandi Powers, "Beauty and the Buzz: Meet Donald Trump's New Girlfriend, Melania Knauss," *Ocean Drive*, April 1999.

121 *Binn described Trump and Melania:* Jason Binn, phone interview with author, July 2019.

122 *"We were in a casting meeting":* Scott Woodward, interview with au-thor, New York, August 13, 2019, and subsequent phone interviews.

124 *The actor joked to a reporter that to keep:* George Rush and Joanna Mol-loy with Marcus Baram and Marc S. Malkin, "Trump on Stump with New Book?" *New York Daily News*, September 16, 1999.

124 *"the really great judgment to cast":* Richard Linnett, "The Gospel of

Peter: Arnell on a Mission," *AdAge,* November 18, 2002, https://adage
.com/article/news/gospel-peter-arnell-a-mission/50827.

124 *Manfred Gestrich, a photographer:* Manfred Gestrich, phone interview
with author, August 29, 2019.

125 *Melania's former roommate, Matthew Atanian:* Matthew Atanian interview.

125 *the Trump White House financial disclosure form:* Donald J. Trump Executive Branch Personnel Public Financial Disclosure Report, May 15,
2018, United States Office of Government Ethics, page 33, published
by *Open Secrets,* http://pfds.opensecrets.org/N00023864_2018.pdf.

CHAPTER 6: FIRST WHITE HOUSE RUN

127 *"My record of accomplishment in business":* Tom Squitteri and Jessica
Lee, "Trump on the Stump for 2000? Reform Party Talk Swirls,"
USA Today, July 13, 1999.

127 *"Is this a joke?":* "Trump Ready for Call from Reform Party," *Washington Post,* July 13, 1999.

128 *"I would imagine perhaps":* Donald Trump interviewed by Robert
O'Harrow, Shawn Boburg, Drew Harwell, Amy Goldstein, and Jerry
Markon, *Washington Post Live,* May 18, 2016.

128 *"You see the reaction":* Jeannie Williams, "Trump's Girlfriend Strikes
a First-Lady-like Pose," *USA Today*, October 13, 1990.

128 *"I think every woman":* Ibid.

129 *attended a Dominick Dunne book party:* Jeannie Williams, "'Name
Dropper' Pulls Back the Curtain on Hollywood," *USA Today,* October 7, 1999.

129 *"She was a different type":* Antoine Verglas, interviews with author,
New York City, 2015 and 2018.

131 *"Did it go well":* Bill Colson, phone interview with author, December
4, 2019.

131 *"I knew what he wanted":* Ibid.

132 *"Of course, I could have found":* Antoine Verglas interview.

132–133 *"It was huge because she"*: Dylan Jones, phone interview with author, July 17, 2019.

133 *"They seemed like they"*: Antoine Verglas interview.

134 *"But she wasn't doing it"*: Dylan Jones interview.

134 *"We wanted to do something"*: Antoine Verglas interview.

135 *"Naked supermodel special!"*: Cover of British *GQ*, January 2000, republished with photographs and excerpts November 7, 2016, https://www.gq-magazine.co.uk/article/donald-trump-melania-trump-knauss-first-lady-erections.

136 *"We were just trying"*: Antoine Verglas interview.

136 Donald Trump *"was very enthusiastic"*: Dylan Jones interview.

137 *At the Bay of Pigs Museum:* Maureen Dowd, "Liberties; Living la Vida Trumpa," *New York Times*, November 17, 1999.

137 *"We're having a good time"*: Joel Siegel, "Donald Does Miami as Prez Possibility," New York *Daily News,* November 16, 1999.

137 *"They were just falling"*: Phil Madsen, phone interview with author, July 2019.

138 *"To be blunt, people would vote for me"*: Maureen Dowd, "Liberties; Trump L'oeil Tease," *New York Times*, September 19, 1999, https://www.nytimes.com/1999/09/19/opinion/liberties-trump-l-oeil-tease.html.

139 *On the same day,* Time: Michael Duffy and Matthew Cooper, "Take My Party, Please," *Time*, September 19, 1999, http://content.time.com/time/magazine/article/0,9171,31139,00.html.

139 *"She was six feet tall"*: Donald Trump interviewed on *The Howard Stern Show*, February 12, 2007, transcript published by the website Factba.se, https://factba.se/transcript/donald-trump-interview-howard-stern-show-february-12-2007.

139 *"They were so flawless"*: Dave Shiflett, interview with author, July 2019.

140 *"Could We Next Have a Supermodel"*: K. C. Baker, "A Model First Lady for New Century?," New York *Daily News,* October 8, 1999.

140 *"I have my career"*: Williams, "Trump's Girlfriend Strikes a First-Lady-like Pose."

141 *"Let me talk to that broad"*: Donald Trump and Melania Knauss, interviewed by Howard Stern, Robin Quivers, and Gary Dell'Abate on *The Howard Stern Show*, November 9, 1999, transcript published by the website Factba.se, https://factba.se/transcript/donald-trump-interview-howard-stern-show-november-9-1999.

143 *By early December, the* New York Times: Joyce Wadler, "A Model as First Lady? Think Traditional," *New York Times*, December 1, 1999.

145 Good Morning America *aired:* Melania Knauss interviewed by Don Dahler, "Donald Trump's Girlfriend Melanie [*sic*] Knauss Talks About Her Relationship with Trump and His Possible Run for the Presidency," *Good Morning America*, ABC News, December 7, 1999.

147 *"Does being captured"*: Donald Trump and Melania Knauss interviewed by Dan Rather, "New York City Developer Donald Trump Wants to Be President of the United States," *60 Minutes*, CBS News, January 11, 2000.

147 *"He's a great leader"*: John Santucci, "Melania Trump Stumps for Her Husband in Wisconsin Amid Flagging Support Among Women," ABC News, April 4, 2016, https://abcnews.go.com/Politics/melania-trump-stumps-husband-wisconsin-amid-flagging-support/story?id=38151155.

148 *"As a person, as a man"*: Donald Trump and Melania Knauss interviewed by Dan Rather.

148 *"Donald is intensely loyal"*: Nick Gass, "Melania Trump: 'Donald Is Intensely Loyal,'" *Politico*, July 18, 2016, https://www.politico.com/story/2016/07/rnc-2016-melania-trump-225786.

148 *"what's the worst thing"*: Donald Trump and Melania Knauss interviewed by Dan Rather.

148 *"Trump's Bare Force One"*: George Rush and Joanna Molloy with Marcus Baram and Marc S. Malkin, "Flying Trump's Bare Force One," New York *Daily News*, December 22, 1999.

149 *"I think America needs":* Robin Givhan, "On a Different Plane; Money Bought Donald Trump an Unreal Life. Is His Presidential Bid Another Fantasy?," *Washington Post*, December 23, 1999.

CHAPTER 7: MELANIA OR KARA?

151 *"Trump Knixes Knauss":* Richard Johnson and Bill Hoffmann, "Trump Knixes Knauss: Donald-Dumped Supermodel Is 'Heartbroken,'" *New York Post*, January 11, 2001.

151 *A different Post writer filed a story:* Jared Paul Stern, *New York Post*, January 13, 2001; the article is described in a book by Allen Salkin and Aaron Short, *The Method to the Madness: Donald Trump's Ascent as Told by Those Who Were Hired, Fired, Inspired—and Inaugurated* (New York: All Points Books, 2019).

152 *"Melania is an amazing woman":* James Barron, "Public Lives: Ladies and Germs? The Germs Win," *New York Times*, January 13, 2000, https://www.nytimes.com/2000/01/13/nyregion/public-lives .html.

152 *"Most of the construction workers":* Simon Houpt, "He's Baaack! TRUMPED UP Conspicuous Consumption Is Here Again, and Real-Estate Magnus Donald J. Trump Is in the Thick of It, with New Deals, New Dalliances, Even Rumours of a Presidential Bid. It's the Return of Eighties Excess, but Is Anybody Really Buying It?," *Globe and Mail*, February 5, 2000.

153 *"This vision, emerging from nowhere":* Christopher Byron, "The Secret Behind Trump's Political Fling," *George*, February/March 2000, 115.

153 *"Even the beautiful":* Byron, "The Secret Behind Trump's Political Fling," 60.

153 *"Meet the First Babe":* Sean Neary, "Meet the First Babe," *George* magazine draft layout for February/March 2000, unpublished. A former *George* employee shared the draft with the author.

154 *"Meet the First Babes":* Sean Neary, "Meet the First Babes," *George*, February/March 2000, 62.

154 *"possible wife number three"*: Neary, "Meet the First Babe," *George* draft layout.

155 *"Just two weeks later"*: Neary, "Meet the First Babes," *George*, February/March 2000, 62.

155 *referred to her boyfriend as "Mr. Trump"*: Sean Neary, interview with author, August 8, 2019.

156 *"You play a role"*: Amy Brill, "A Model First Lady: Melania Knauss Gets Ready for the White House," *Talk*, February 2000, 76–77.

157 *"smart, polite, and savvy"*: Amy Brill, phone interview with author, July 18, 2019.

159 *"Melania . . . the curvaceous Slovenian model"*: Toby Young, "Lithe Damn Lithe," *Tatler*, April 2000, 198–205.

160 *Even the sober* New York Times *wondered*: Barron, "Public Lives: Ladies and Germs? The Germs Win."

160 *In January, Maples announced*: Mitchell Fink with Lauren Rubin, "Marla's Cooking Up Some Donald Dish," New York *Daily News*, January 14, 2000.

161 *"by mutual consent"*: Joseph P. Fried, "Following Up," *New York Times*, February 24, 2002, https://www.nytimes.com/2002/02/24/nyregion/following-up.html.

161 *"I noticed in the relationship"*: Jay Goldberg, interview with author, New York City, December 2018.

162 *"With Kara dating him"*: Jason Binn, interview with author, July 2019.

164 *"There is high maintenance"*: Donald J. Trump with Kate Bohner, *Trump: The Art of the Comeback* (New York: Times Books, 1997), 141.

164 *"The same assets"*: Donald J. Trump with Charles Leerhsen, *Trump: Surviving at the Top* (New York: Random House, 1990), 6.

165 *"Knauss' past is as mysterious"*: Verena Dobnik, "Trump's Presidential Ammunition Includes—a Model First Lady?," Associated Press, November 19, 1999.

166 *"How's it going with Trump?"*: Matthew Atanian interview.

167 *"She's glamorous and presents":* Philip Bloch, interview with author, Los Angeles, February 2019.

167 *"I had been very successful with your girlfriend":* A. J. Benza and Donald Trump interviewed by Howard Stern on *The Howard Stern Show*, May 10, 2001, transcript published by the website Factba.se, https://factba.se/transcript/donald-trump-interview-howard-stern-show-may-10-2001.

CHAPTER 8: "AREN'T I LUCKY?"

169 *"extra beautiful":* Jure Zorcic, interview with author, Slovenia, August 2018.

171 *"I left 15 years ago":* Camilla Long, "Melania Is the Unofficial Queen of New York," *Tatler,* May 2005.

172 *"devastating":* Stephanie Winston Wolkoff, interviews with author, 2019 and 2020.

173 *"Matthew, this is Donald Trump":* Matthew Atanian, interview with author, October 2019.

174 *"Melania was the only one":* Chris Christie, interview with author, April 8, 2019.

177 *a lot of media celebrities:* Michael Callahan, "Flashback: When Hillary and Bill Hit the Wedding of Donald and Melania," *Hollywood Reporter*, April 7, 2016.

177 *Marco Glaviano and Patrick Demarchelier:* "Fashion Behind the Scenes," *MF Fashion*, December 9, 2004. Other information drawn from interviews.

178 *Trump told people the wedding:* Karen S. Schneider, "A Magical Merger," *People*, February 7, 2005, https://people.com/archive/a-magical-merger-vol-63-no-5/.

178 *"I arranged everything":* Schneider, "A Magical Merger."

179 *She says with a laugh:* Sally Singer, "How to Marry a Billionaire," *Vogue*, February 2005, 166–79.

179 *"7 most spectacular"*: Jessica Siegel, "The 7 Most Spectacular Weddings of All Time," *Glamour*, March 2009, 172.

180 *"Donald Trump's name"*: Don Dahler, interview with Melania Knauss, "Donald Trump's Girlfriend Melanie [*sic*] Knauss Talks About Her Relationship with Trump and His Possible Run for Presidency," *Good Morning America*, ABC News, December 7, 1999.

181 *"too weird to go there"*: Ivana Trump, *Raising Trump: Family Values from America's First Mother* (New York: Gallery Books, 2017), Kindle edition, location 2188 of 3385.

181 *In a June 2019* Vanity Fair: Gabriel Sherman, "'Marla Was Under Duress': Revealed in His Marla Maples Prenup, Donald Trump's Draconian Art of the Marriage Deal," *Vanity Fair*, June 4, 2019, https://www.vanityfair.com/news/2019/06/marla-maple-prenup-donald-trump-marriage.

182 *"He kept questioning me"*: Jay Goldberg, interview with author, 2018.

182 *"After giving Donald two years"*: Salvatore Arena and K. C. Baker, "Marla Caves on Prenup: Gives up Battle over Pact and Takes $2M in Divorce," New York *Daily News*, June 9, 1999.

182 *"And had I not had"*: Liz Smith, "At Lunch with Liz: Donald Trump," *Good Housekeeping*, October 2004, 130–43.

184 *Redbook quoted her as saying*: Kaitlin Menza and Adam Schubak, "24 Things You Didn't Know About Melania Trump as a Mom," *Redbook*, May 8, 2018, https://www.redbookmag.com/life/news/g4270/melania-trump-parenting-style/?slide=6.

184 *"I create stars"*: Nancy Collins interview with Donald J. Trump on "'Baby Anna'—An Update on Baby Jessica," *Primetime Live*, ABC News, March 10, 1994.

184 *Two women have very publicly stated*: Karen McDougal and Stephanie Clifford have said they had affairs with Trump, beginning in the summer of 2006. McDougal says her affair with Trump lasted nine months, while Clifford met Trump just twice, in July 2006 and

again in July 2007. For details of McDougal's account: Ronan Farrow, "Donald Trump, A *Playboy* Model, and a System for Concealing Infidelity," *New Yorker*, February 16, 2018. For details of Clifford's account: Anderson Cooper, "Stormy Daniels Describes Her Alleged Affair with Donald Trump," *60 Minutes,* August 22, 2018.

185 *"I wanted some privacy":* Elizabeth Einstein, "Trump That," *Allure* spa issue, 2008, 27.

186 *"She was always taking care":* Kate Sullivan, "Melania Trump Will Never Get Botox, Has a Spa in Her Apartment," *Allure*, July 27, 2011, https://www.allure.com/story/melania-trump-will-never-get-b.

187 *"They said my wife":* Jeremy Diamond, "Melania Trump Will Address Immigration Controversy, Donald Trump Says," CNN, August 9, 2016, https://www.cnn.com/2016/08/09/politics/donald-trump-melania-immigration-controversy/index.html.

187–188 *"I am pleased to enclose":* Melania Trump (@FLOTUS), Twitter, September 14, 2016, 9:30 a.m., https://twitter.com/MELANIATRUMP/status/776050512772886529.

188 *"I thank Michael Wildes":* "In The News," Wildes & Weinberg P.C. Law Offices, https://www.wildeslaw.com/news-events/in-the-news/melania-trump-on-safe-haven-in-america.

188 *"Following a review":* Michael J. Wildes, public letter, September 14, 2016, embedded in tweet by Melania Trump, https://twitter.com/MELANIATRUMP/status/776050512772886529.

189 *"We called it the Einstein visa":* Mary Jordan, "Questions Linger About How Melania Trump, a Slovenian Model, Scored 'the Einstein Visa,'" *Washington Post*, March 1, 2018, https://www.washingtonpost.com/politics/questions-linger-about-how-melania-trump-a-slovenian-model-scored-the-einstein-visa/2018/02/28/d307ddb2-1b35-11e8-ae5a-16e60e4605f3_story.html.

190 *"There is no reason to adjudicate":* Ibid.

190 *"What did she submit?":* Ibid.

190 *Melania was paid more than $20,000*: Alicia A. Caldwell, "Melania

Trump Modeled in US Prior to Getting Work Visa," Associated Press, November 4, 2016, https://apnews.com/37dc7aef0ce4407793 0b7436be7bfd0d/Melania-Trump-modeled-in-US-prior-to-getting -work-visa.

191 *"He has a double standard"*: Bruce Morrison, phone interview with author, April 2020.

191 *"I came here for my career"*: Alex Kuczynski, "Melania Trump's American Dream," *Harper's Bazaar*, January 6, 2016, https://www. harpers bazaar.com/culture/features/a13529/melania-trump-interview-0216/.

191 *"the greatest privilege in the world"*: Julia Zorthian, "Read Melania Trump's Campaign Speech Addressing Cyberbullying," *Time*, November 3, 2016, https://time.com/4557033/transcript-melania-trump -campaign-speech/.

192 *"more doors in the world"*: Dušan Nograšek, "The Slovenian Language Is Like a Song," *Nedeljski Dnevnik* (*Sunday Daily* newspaper), September 20, 1998.

192 *"It is important to note"*: "Dual Nationality," United States Department of State, Bureau of Consular Affairs.

193 *her sister, who is Barron's godmother*: Ines Knauss (@inesknauss), Twitter, March 20, 2020. On Barron's birthday, Knauss tweeted, "my godson is 14 today."

193 *"What are the options"*: Eric Bland, interview with author, New York City, April 2019.

193 *"Your parents will be"*: Eric Bland interview.

195 *"And how about chain migration"*: Donald J. Trump, remarks at rally in Lewis Center, Ohio, August 4, 2018, transcript published by the website Factba.se, https://factba.se/transcript/donald-trump-speech -maga-lewis-center-oh-august-4-2018.

196 *"Thank you"*: Michael R. Sisak, "Meet the Newest US Citizens: Melania Trump's Parents," Associated Press, August 9, 2018, https:// apnews.com/e9ef38a1031744ae9e3a098c96f6a706/Melania-Trump's -parents-are-sworn-in-as-US-citizens.

196 *"This is an example of it going right":* Julia Reinstein, "Melania Trump's
Parents Became US Citizens Using the 'Chain Migration' Program
That Trump Has Repeatedly Attacked," *Buzzfeed News*, August 9,
2018, https://www.buzzfeednews.com/article/juliareinstein/melania
-trumps-parents-have-been-sworn-in-as-us-citizens.

196 *"are not part of the administration":* Sisak, "Meet the Newest US Citizens: Melania Trump's Parents."

196 *He called Trump's opposition:* Kristine Phillips, "Melania Trump's Immigration Lawyer Calls President's Attacks on 'Chain Migration'
'Unconscionable,'" *Washington Post*, August 11, 2018.

196–197 *"She said, 'Make it clear'":* Michael Wildes interview.

197 *Denials of new applications for H1-B visas:* National Foundation for
American Policy, "H-1B Denial Rates: Analysis of H1-B Data for
First Three Quarters of FY 2019," October 2019, https://nfap.com
/wp-content/uploads/2019/10/H-1B-Denial-Rates-Analysis-of-FY
-2019-Numbers.NFAP-Policy-Brief.October-2019.pdf.

197 *average processing time:* "AILA Policy Brief: USCIS Processing De-
lays Have Reached Crisis Levels Under the Trump Administration,"
American Immigration Lawyers Association, January 30, 2019.

197 *just 200,000 immigrants:* William H. Frey, "US Foreign-Born
Gains Are Smallest in a Decade, Except in Trump States," Brook-
ings Institution, October 2, 2019, https://www.brookings.edu/blog
/the-avenue/2019/10/01/us-foreign-born-gains-are-smallest-in-a
-decade-except-in-trump-states/.

197 *"reminds us of our past mistakes":* Michael Wildes, interviews with author between 2016 and 2020.

CHAPTER 9: JEWELRY AND CAVIAR

200 *"He called Melania":* Michael Streck, phone interview with author,
December 23, 2019.

200 *"I will never again":* Nancy Collins interview with Donald J. Trump

on " 'Baby Anna'—An Update on Baby Jessica," *Primetime Live*, ABC News, March 10, 1994.

201 *"Is he really running":* Joy Behar, interview with Melania Trump, *The Joy Behar Show*, CNN, April 20, 2011.

203 *"The whole thing was crazy":* Michelle Obama, *Becoming* (New York: Crown, 2018), 352–53.

204 *"Bill and Hillary Clinton":* Melania Trump, "5 things you don't know about me," *Glamour*, January 2006, 79.

204 *"After ten years of researching":* The Apprentice, Season 13, Episode 6, "How Do You Spell Melania?," NBC, aired April 7, 2013, https://www.imdb.com/title/tt2811688/.

205 *"intense collaboration with Melania's":* "Melania Beauty Caviar Complexe C6 Collection," MelaniaTrump.com, archived by the WayBack Machine, https://web.archive.org/web/20160102181847/http://www.melaniatrump.com/melania-beauty/.

205 *"from head to toe":* Lesley Messer, "Melania Trump: My Son, 7, Is 'Not a Sweatpants Child'," ABC News, April 11, 2013, https://abcnews.go.com/blogs/entertainment/2013/04/melania-trump-my-son-7-is-not-a-sweatpants-child/.

207 *In March 2013, Melania received notice:* Merchant Capital, LLC and New Sunshine, LLC vs. Melania Marks Skincare, LLC, No. 1:13-cv-00873-JMS-DML, United States District Court in the Southern District of Indiana, Document 105, Order, https://www.govinfo.gov/content/pkg/USCOURTS-insd-1_13-cv-00873/pdf/USCOURTS-insd-1_13-cv-00873-2.pdf.

207 *"grossly favorable":* Jeff Swiatek, "Melania Trump's company caught in Ind. contract dispute," *USA Today*, November 11, 2013, https://www.usatoday.com/story/money/business/2013/11/11/melania-trump-john-menard-contract-dispute/3502669/.

208 *"pretty much nothing other than Mrs. Donald Trump":* Merchant Capital, LLC and New Sunshine, LLC vs. Melania Marks Skincare, LLC, No.

1:13-cv-00873-JMS-DML, United States District Court in the Southern District of Indiana, transcript of bench trial, day 3, closing statement by plaintiff attorney Kevin C. Tyra, 91.

208 *"It's hard to find emotion"*: Peter Moskowitz, "What Happened to Melania Trump's Caviar Skincare Line?," *Racked*, August 22, 2016, https://www.racked.com/2016/8/22/12556786/melania-trump-caviar-skincare-lawsuit.

208 *"This is not how the business"*: *Merchant Capital, LLC and New Sunshine, LLC vs. Melania Marks Skincare, LLC*, transcript of bench trial, day 3, direct examination of Melania Trump by her attorney Norman T. Funk, 73.

209 *Tomisue Hilbert is listed:* Report of Donations Accepted for Inaugural Committee by the 58th Presidential Inaugural Committee, April 18, 2017, Federal Election Commission, 385, https://docquery.fec.gov/pdf/286/201704180300150286/201704180300150286.pdf.

209 *"This was a passion of Melania's"*: Stephen Hilbert, interview with author, 2016.

209 *"If the media reports"*: Moskowitz, "What Happened to Melania Trump's Caviar Skincare Line?"

210 *"Would you please explain to the judge"*: *Merchant Capital, LLC and New Sunshine, LLC vs. Melania Marks Skincare, LLC*, transcript of bench trial, day 3, direct examination of Melania Trump by Norman T. Funk, 50; quoted by Moskowitz.

211 *"He was sweet with her"*: Jose Gabriel Juarez, phone interview with author, November 2019.

212 *"I got it all ready"*: Victorina Morales, phone interview with author, November 2019.

213 *a site called Trump Golf Count:* Trump Golf Count, last updated March 8, 2020, page created and maintained by Sophie German, https://trumpgolfcount.com/.

214 *"Melania is always very apart"*: Sandra Diaz, interview with author, New York City, September 10, 2019.

216 *"They're the same size"*: Joshua Partlow and David A. Fahrenthold, "How two housekeepers took on the president—and revealed that his company employed undocumented immigrants," *Washington Post*, December 4, 2019, https://www.washingtonpost.com /politics/how-two-undocumented-housekeepers-took-on-the-pres ident-and-revealed-trumps-long-term-reliance-on-illegal-immigrant s/2019/12/04/3dff5b5c-0a15-11ea-bd9d-c628fd48b3a0_story.html.

216 *"Nobody could wear the red hat"*: Partlow and Fahrenthold, "How two housekeepers took on the president."

217 *"that fucking guy"*: Sandra Diaz interview.

217 *"I never saw them together"*: Jose Gabriel Juarez interview.

218 *"You're still here?"*: Partlow and Fahrenthold, "How two housekeepers took on the president."

218 *"I don't understand"*: Sandra Diaz interview.

CHAPTER 10: "WE GIVE A SPACE TO EACH OTHER"

222 *"Melania was a very, very successful person"*: Donald J. Trump, interview with author at Trump Tower, April 2016.

222 *"Not a lot of people know me"*: Melania Trump, phone interview with author, April 2016.

226 *"She knew Bannon was no good"*: Chris Christie, interview with author, April 8, 2019.

227 *"people misread her because she is quiet"*: Corey Lewandowski, interview with author, May 9, 2019.

228 *"many things—some language"*: Eric Bradner and Theodore Schleifer, "Melania Trump: I Don't Always Agree with Donald, and That's OK," CNN, February 29, 2016, https://www.cnn.com/2016/02/29 /politics/melania-trump-donald-trumps-language/index.html.

CHAPTER 11: BE BEST

232 *"will never show you her emotion"*: Stephanie Winston Wolkoff, interviews with author, 2019 and 2020.

233 *In January 2018:* Michael Rothfeld and Joe Palazzolo, "Trump Lawyer Arranged $130,000 Payment for Adult-Film Star's Silence," *Wall Street Journal*, January 12, 2018, https://www.wsj.com/articles /trump-lawyer-arranged-130-000-payment-for-adult-film-stars -silence-1515787678.

233 In Touch *magazine published: In Touch* Magazine Staff, interview conducted by Jordi Lippe-McGraw, "'In Touch' Explosive Interview with Stormy Daniels: Donald Trump Cheated on Melania with Me," *In Touch*, January 19, 2018, https://www.intouchweekly.com/posts /stormy-daniels-affair-donald-trump-151571/.

233 *"We got naked":* Ronan Farrow, "Donald Trump, a *Playboy* Model, and a System for Concealing Infidelity," *New Yorker*, February 16, 2018, https://www.newyorker.com/news/news-desk/donald-trump -a-playboy-model-and-a-system-for-concealing-infidelity-national -enquirer-karen-mcdougal.

234 *"It is not a concern and focus":* Tom Llamas interview with Melania Trump, "Being Melania," ABC News, October 13, 2018, https://abc news.go.com/Politics/show-care-melania-trump-reveals-details-life -white/story?id=58393164.

237 *"going straight to hell":* Lin-Manuel Miranda (@Lin_Manuel), Twitter, September 30, 2017, 8:21 a.m., https://twitter.com/Lin_Manuel /status/914102927744217088.

238 *"Honored to join":* Melania Trump (@FLOTUS), Twitter, September 6, 2019, 7:47 a.m., https://twitter.com/FLOTUS/status/1169940208357 392384.

238 *"Knauss would have little trouble":* K. C. Baker, "A Model First Lady for New Century?," New York *Daily News*, October 8, 1999.

238 *"How many languages":* Mika Brzezinski, "Melania Trump on Her Life, Marriage and 2016," *Morning Joe*, MSNBC, February 24, 2016, https://www.youtube.com/watch?v=XbvGxDmD3dY.

239 *"Thank you. Nice to meet you":* AP Video, "Pope to First Lady: What

Do You Feed Trump?," Associated Press, May 24, 2017, https://www
.youtube.com/watch?v=40NB3WtMoTw.

239 *"I'm going to visit a hospital, for bambinos":* Ruptly, "Holy See: Melania
and Ivanka Trump Wear Black Veils to Meet Pope Francis," May 24,
2017, https://www.youtube.com/watch?v=XCCEpZ1JzjU&t=33s.

239–240 *"We have our own Jackie O":* Steve Doocy, Jillian Mele, and Brian
Kilmeade, interview with Donald J. Trump, *Fox & Friends,* June 14,
2019.

240 *modeling agent Wolfgang Schwarz:* Wolfgang Schwarz interview.

241 *"Bonjour! Bonjour!":* AP video, "Melania Trump Visits Children's
Hospital in Paris," Associated Press, July 13, 2017, https://www.you
tube.com/watch?v=trR3GtAWe0M.

241 *"Wait. I thought Melania":* Keith Boykin (@keithboykin), Twitter,
August 26, 2019, 10:43 a.m., https://twitter.com/keithboykin/status
/1165998296508358661.

243 *"There are no leaks":* Corey Lewandowski, interview with author,
May 9, 2019.

243–244 *"She really relieved":* Anita McBride, phone interview with author, February 12, 2020.

244 *Melania Trump made eight speeches:* Lauren Wright, "Melania Trump
'Be Best' Platform Is a Lost Opportunity for White House," *The
Hill,* May 15, 2018, https://thehill.com/opinion/white-house/387738
-melania-trump-be-best-platform-is-a-lost-opportunity-for-white
-house.

244 *"stay in her lane":* Philip Bloch, interviews with author, January
–February 2019.

245 *"The most important and joyous":* Abby Hamblin, "Read Melania
Trump's U.N. Speech on Bullying, the Golden Rule," *Daily Press,*
September 20, 2017, https://www.dailypress.com/sd-melania-trump
-un-speech-20170920-htmlstory.html.

245 *"She's electric!":* Geoff Earle, Carly Stern, and Erica Tempesta, "She's

Electric! Melania Trump Dons an Eye-Catching $3,000 Neon Pink Coat to Speak About Anti-Bullying at United Nations Luncheon in New York," *Daily Mail*, September 20, 2017, https://www.dailymail .co.uk/femail/article-4903776/Melania-Trump-wears-3000-neon -pink-dress-UN.html.

246 *"As a mother and as First Lady"*: "Remarks by the First Lady at the Launch of the 'Be Best' Initiative," White House release, May 7, 2018, whitehouse.gov/briefings-statements/remarks-first-lady-launch -best-initiative/.

247 *they had considered other names:* Stephanie Winston Wolkoff interview.

248 *"I am well aware"*: Mary Jordan, Emily Heil, and Josh Dawsey, "Inside Melania Trump's Complicated White House Life: Separate Schedule, Different Priorities," *Washington Post*, May 6, 2018, https://www .washingtonpost.com/lifestyle/inside-melania-trumps-complicated -white-house-life-separate-schedules-different-priorities/2018/05/06 /60f6f07e-4703-11e8-9072-f6d4bc32f223_story.html.

248–249 *"It is my pleasure"*: "First Lady Melania Trump Remarks on Opioids," C-SPAN, November 26, 2019, https://www.c-span.org /video/?466768-1/lady-melania-trump-delivers-remarks-opioid -awareness.

249 *"We live in a democracy"*: Eugene Scott, "Boos Aimed at Melania Trump Show There's No Transcending Politics for This First Family," *Washington Post*, November 27, 2019, https://www.wash ingtonpost.com/politics/2019/11/27/boos-aimed-melania-trump -show-theres-no-transcending-politics-this-first-family/.

250 *"We profile women in the magazine"*: Interview of Anna Wintour by Christiane Amanpour, CNN, April 8, 2019, http://transcripts.cnn .com/TRANSCRIPTS/1904/08/ampr.01.html.

250 *"To be on the cover of* Vogue*"*: Sasha Savitsky, "Melania Trump's Rep Dismisses Anna Wintour *Vogue* Diss: 'She's Been There, Done That,'" Fox News, April 12, 2019, https://www.foxnews.com/enter tainment/melania-trump-anna-wintour-vogue-cnn-first-lady.

251 *"It's 1,000 percent false":* Jordan, Heil, and Dawsey, "Inside Melania Trump's Complicated White House Life: Separate Schedule, Different Priorities."

251 *"an urban legend":* Ibid.

251 *"Trump loves her cool":* Stephanie Winston Wolkoff interview.

CHAPTER 12: "THE PROTECTOR"

255 *"He was very knowledgeable":* Steven Goff, "Barron Trump Likes Soccer. And Arsenal. And D.C. United?," *Washington Post*, April 18, 2017, https://www.washingtonpost.com/news/soccer-insider/wp/2017/04/18/barron-trump-likes-soccer-and-arsenal-and-d-c-united/.

255 *"If it were me":* Lindsey Graham (@LindseyGrahamSC), Twitter, July 16, 2018, 12:13 p.m., https://twitter.com/LindseyGrahamSC/status/1018891400245600257.

256 *"She is her left hand":* Stephanie Winston Wolkoff interview.

258 *a childhood friend of Melania's was quoted:* Matej Klaric, "Melania Trump: From a Small White House in Slovenia to the Big One in DC," Australian Broadcasting Corporation News, November 16, 2016, https://www.abc.net.au/news/2016-11-17/melania-trumps-journey-from-slovenia-to-the-white-house/8028340.

258 *"What kind of nonsense":* Ines Knauss (@inesknauss), Twitter, June 16, 2019.

258 *"once or twice a month":* Richard Johnson, "Whom Melania Trump Turns to for Fashion Advice," *Page Six*, December 4, 2018, https://pagesix.com/2018/12/04/who-melania-trump-turns-to-for-fashion-advice/.

258–259 *"this zero-tolerance policy":* Laura Bush, "Separating Children from Their Parents at the Border 'Breaks My Heart,'" *Washington Post*, June 17, 2018.

259 *"Mrs. Trump hates to see children":* Kate Bennett, "Melania Trump 'Hates to See' Children Separated from Their Families at Borders," CNN, June 18, 2018, https://www.cnn.com/2018/06/17/politics/melania-trump-children-separated-immigration/index.html.

259 *"It was unacceptable for me":* Tom Llamas interview with Melania Trump, "Being Melania Trump—The First Lady," ABC News, October 13, 2018, https://abcnews.go.com/Politics/transcript-abc-news-chief-national-affairs-correspondent-tom/story?id=58469532.

259–260 *"Ivanka feels very strongly":* Jessica Taylor, "Melania Trump Pressured President Trump to Change Family Separation Policy," NPR, June 20, 2018, https://www.npr.org/2018/06/20/621930721/melania-trump-pressured-president-trump-to-change-family-separation-policy.

261 *"I REALLY DON'T CARE":* Donald J. Trump (@realDonaldTrump), Twitter, June 21, 2018, https://twitter.com/realDonaldTrump/status/1009916650622251009.

261 *"It's obvious I didn't wear":* Tom Llamas interview with Melania Trump, "Being Melania Trump—The First Lady."

262 *"I wish people would focus on what I do":* Drew Cornejo, "Melania Trump: 'I Wish People Would Focus on What I Do, Not What I Wear,'" *Washington Post*, October 8, 2018.

262 *"Thank you for educating them":* Emily Heil, Sudarsan Raghavan, and Mary Jordan, "Melania Trump Wraps First Solo International Trip in Egypt with Comments on Kavanaugh and Ford," *Washington Post*, October 6, 2018.

262 *"Many Ghanaians are saying":* Max Bearak, "'The Nicer of the Trumps': Melania's Africa Trip Scripted to Avoid Major Stumbles," *Washington Post*, October 5, 2018, https://www.washingtonpost.com/world/the-nicer-of-the-two-trumps-melanias-africa-trip-scripted-to-avoid-major-stumbles/2018/10/05/9a4a4c3c-c501-11e8-9c0f-2ffaf6d422aa_story.html.

263 *"I wanted to be here to see the successful programs":* Lauren Monsen, "Melania Trump Delivers Books, Balls and Hope in Malawi," Share America release, October 5, 2018, https://share.america.gov/melania-trump-delivers-books-balls-hope-malawi/.

263 *"I am so proud of the work":* "First Lady Melania Trump Announces

Planned Stops During Visit to Africa," White House release, September 26, 2018, https://www.whitehouse.gov/briefings-statements/first-lady -melania-trump-announces-planned-stops-visit-africa/.

264 *"It is the position of the Office"*: Felicia Sonmez and Josh Dawsey, "First Lady Melania Trump's Office Calls for Firing of White House National Security Official," *Washington Post*, November 13, 2018, https://www.washingtonpost.com/politics/first-lady-melania-trumps -office-calls-for-firing-of-white-house-national-security-official/2018 /11/13/1b4c3f28-e77d-11e8-bbdb-72fdbf9d4fed_story.html.

264 *not "just the striking-looking"*: Katherine Jellison, interview with author, November 26, 2019.

265 *The conflict between Ricardel and Melania's staff*: This account of the dismissal of Mira Ricardel is based on interviews with several former White House officials.

268 *"I thought it was outrageous"*: John Bolton, email to author, February 28, 2020.

269 *"I am deeply concerned"*: Melania Trump (@FLOTUS), Twitter, September 9, 2019, 12:19 p.m., .https://twitter.com/FLOTUS/status /1171095740510277632.

270 *"He didn't know much about the issue"*: Josh Dawsey and Laurie McGinley, "Trump Backs Off Flavored Vape Ban He Once Touted," *Washington Post*, November 17, 2019, https://www.washingtonpost .com/national/health-science/trump-pulls-back-from-flavored-vaping -ban/2019/11/17/30853ece-07ae-11ea-924a-28d87132c7ec_story.html.

271 *"The Constitution says"*: Pamela Karlan testifying at the House Judiciary Committee Hearing on Constitutional Grounds for Impeachment, December 4, 2019.

271 *"A minor child"*: Melania Trump (@FLOTUS), Twitter, December 4, 2019, 4:50 p.m., https://twitter.com/FLOTUS/status/120234444192457 1136.

271–272 *"So ridiculous"*: Donald J. Trump (@realDonaldTrump), Twitter,

December 12, 2019, 7:22 a.m., https://twitter.com/realDonaldTrump /status/1205100602025545730.

272 *"Be Best is the First Lady's"*: Stephanie Grisham statement, first tweeted by CNN reporter Kate Bennett, December 13, 2019, https:// twitter.com/KateBennett_DC/status/1205564997012770817.

273–274 *Trump personally leaked*: Philip Rucker and Carol Leonnig, *A Very Stable Genius: Donald J. Trump's Testing of America* (New York: Penguin Random House, 2020), 337–38.

274–275 *"Democrats and the opposition media"*: Dartunorro Clark, "Melania Trump Joins Husband's Attacks on Democrats, 'Fake News' in Fundraising Appeal," NBC News, November 3, 2018, https://www .nbcnews.com/politics/politics-news/melania-trump-joins-husband-s -attacks-democrats-fake-news-fundraising-n930821.

276 *"She is very happy"*: Paolo Zampolli interview.

277 *"Feminism was established"*: Oliver Willis, "Rush on Tour: AIDS, Misogyny and Suicide Used as Punch Lines," *Media Matters,* March 15, 2012, https://www.mediamatters.org/rush-limbaugh/rush-tour-aids -misogyny-and-suicide-used-punchlines.

278 *"decades of tireless devotion"*: Josh Dawsey and Philip Rucker, "Rush Limbaugh Awarded Presidential Medal of Freedom at State of the Union," *Washington Post*, February 4, 2020, https://www.washington post.com/politics/trump-says-he-plans-to-award-presidential-medal -of-freedom-to-rush-limbaugh/2020/02/04/2d8f6a76-47a7-11ea-ab15 -b5df3261b710_story.html.

278 *"top scum"*: "Remarks by President Trump to the Nation," White House release, February 6, 2020, https://www.whitehouse.gov/briefings -statements/remarks-president-trump-nation/.

279 *But for weeks U.S. intelligence officials had warned*: Shane Harris, Greg Miller, Josh Dawsey, and Ellen Nakashima, "U.S. intelligence reports from January and February warned about a likely pandemic," *Washington Post*, March 20, 2020, https://www.washingtonpost.com /national-security/us-intelligence-reports-from-january-and

-february-warned-about-a-likely-pandemic/2020/03/20/299d8cda
-6ad5-11ea-b5f1-a5a804158597_story.html.

279 *"I am excited to share"*: Melania Trump (@FLOTUS), Twitter, March
5, 2020, 12:20 p.m., https://twitter.com/FLOTUS/status/12356161748
99171328.

279 *"I encourage everyone who chooses to be negative"*: Melania Trump
(@FLOTUS), Twitter, March 7, 2020, 9:40 a.m., https://twitter.com
/FLOTUS/status/1236300725036158976.

279–280 *"Opened up and just raring to"*: Andrew O'Reilly, "Trump calls for
restarting economy by Easter: 'We have to get back to work'," Fox News,
March 24, 2020, https://www.foxnews.com/politics/trump-during
-fox-news-coronavirus-townhall-signals-desire-to-ease-guidelines
-we-have-to-get-back-to-work.

280 *"Stay safe and remember"*: Melania Trump (@FLOTUS), Twitter,
March 20, 2020, 9:00 a.m., "A Message for Parents from First Lady
Melania Trump," https://twitter.com/FLOTUS/status/12409864498
74309120.

280 *She thanked "doctors, nurses"*: Melania Trump (@FLOTUS), Twitter,
March 16, 2020, 12:13 p.m., https://twitter.com/FLOTUS/status/123
9585567509184518.

280 *"Our great country is fighting hard"*: Melania Trump (@FLOTUS),
Twitter, March 11, 2010, 10:10 p.m., https://twitter.com/FLOTUS
/status/1237923775619923970.

280 *"If we support one another"*: Melania Trump (@FLOTUS), Twitter,
March 18, 2020, 9:48 a.m., https://twitter.com/FLOTUS/status/12402
73768393703426.

280 *"I just don't want to be doing"*: "Remarks by President Trump, Vice
President Pence, and Members of the Coronavirus Task Force in
Press Briefing," White House release, April 3, 2020, https://www
.whitehouse.gov/briefings-statements/remarks-president-trump
-vice-president-pence-members-coronavirus-task-force-press
-briefing-18/.

281 *"Remember, this does NOT replace"*: Melania Trump (@FLOTUS), Twitter, April 9, 2020, 11:50 a.m., https://twitter.com/FLOTUS /status/1248277174072860672.

281 *"noted shared concern over"*: "Readout of First Lady Melania Trump's Call with Mrs. Elke Büdenbender of Germany," White House release, April 14, 2020, https://www.whitehouse.gov/briefings-statements /readout-first-lady-melania-trumps-call-mrs-elke-budenbender -germany/.

Photo Credits

16. Courtesy of Scott Woodward
17. Courtesy of Scott Woodward
18. Davidoff Studios/Getty Images
19. Davidoff Studios/Getty Images
20. Evan Vucci/AP
21. Toni L. Sandys/The Washington Post
22. Saul Loeb/AFP/Getty Images
23. Andrew Harnik/AP
24. Jabin Botsford/The Washington Post
25. Jabin Botsford/The Washington Post
26. MAURIX/Gamma-Rapho/Getty Images
27. Oliver Contreras/The Washington Post
28. Ricky Carioti/The Washington Post
29. No Credit

PHOTOS THROUGHOUT

Page 12   Mark Wilson/Getty Images

Page 24   Jabin Botsford/The Washington Post

Page 46   Getty Images

Page 46   Nino Mihalek, from *First Lady Melania Trump—As She Once Was*

Page 80   Matthew Atanian/Facebook

Page 98   Ron Galella/Getty Images

Page 126   Kevin Sullivan

Page 150   Rose Hartman/WireImage/Getty Images

Page 162   Alberto Rodriguez/Berliner Studio/Shutterstock

Page 198   Jim Spellman/Wireimage/Getty Images

Page 220   Jabin Botsford/The Washington Post

Page 220   Jabin Botsford/The Washington Post

Page 230   Jabin Botsford/The Washington Post

Page 252   Jabin Botsford/The Washington Post

Index

Page numbers in *italics* refer to photographs.

327